Branding the Migrant

Arguments of Rights, Welfare and Security

Branding the Migrant

Arguments of Rights, Welfare and Security

EDITED BY
Atig Ghosh

frontpage

frontpage
www.frontpagepublications.com

First published 2013

Frontpage Publications Limited
Level 2, 13 John Prince's Street, London W1G 0JR, United Kingdom

Frontpage
Level 6, Constantia
11 Dr U N Brahmachari Sarani, Kolkata 700017, India

British Library Cataloguing in Publishing Data
A catalogue record for this book is available from the British Library

ISBN: 978 93 810430 9 7

Printed in India
By Sadhana Press Private Limited
76 B B Ganguly Street, Kolkata 700012, India

Typeset by Compuset International
85 Park Street, Kolkata 700016, India

Contents

Acknowledgement

The history of this book is counterintuitive. When Ashish Rajadhyaksha and other colleagues at the Centre for the Study of Culture and Society (CSCS), Bangalore, approached the Calcutta Research Group (CRG) to organise a workshop on the theme of UID and the migrants, the idea of this book had not yet germinated. The outcome was an intense discussion in the form of a two-day workshop on digitisation of identity and its impact on the migrant masses. The workshop, titled 'Digital Deliberations', was held in Calcutta on 29 & 30 June 2012. We at the CRG owe them all a debt of gratitude. Appropriately, therefore, this book has been dedicated to Ashish Rajadhyaksha and other colleagues at the CSCS. It was their initiative which got the ball rolling.

The workshop raised knotty questions and dark concerns which were not laid to rest easily. As we debated and discussed the issue at the CRG in the days following the workshop, the remit of our concerns broadened. We started to ponder on the general question of identification and its impact on the migrants, though the core issue – the lynchpin, as it were – remained the UID/Aadhaar scheme. CRG was already working on various dimensions of migration. Against this background, it became apparent that another broad-based discussion in a workshop-format was necessary. Members of the CRG network of scholars, journalists, and activists from all over the country responded with heartening alacrity. A second two-day workshop was convened in Calcutta on 14 & 15 September 2012, which was, somewhat unimaginatively, titled 'Digital Deliberations-II'. This forms the kernel of the book. As such, I am deeply indebted to all the participants and discussants of the two workshops, who agreed to participate, contribute and hotly debate the now-expanded theme. Most of the essays in this book were presented in their earlier versions in these two workshops.

The assistance of the Ford Foundation in publication of the volume is gratefully acknowledged. The views expressed, however, are not necessarily those of the Foundation. The work has drawn also from the CRG's decade-long orientation programme on forced-migration studies continued with the support of the Finland Government.

Nikhil Roshan travelled dangerously in the strife-torn western districts of Assam, photographing the turmoil. When I asked him if I could use his photographs for the cover of this book, he agreed immediately. He is more than a friend.

All my colleagues at the CRG have been a great help – they have always been. But, it indeed takes a 'fast intent', to quote from *King Lear*, 'to shake all cares and business from our age; conferring them on younger strengths.' Ranabir Samaddar has demonstrated such remarkable confidence in his junior colleague by entrusting the compilation and editing of this volume to a greenhorn. Throughout, he has been a pillar of support – a constant source of counsel on academic *démarches*. I hope I have not failed him.

Abhijit Mazumder of Frontpage forbore from expressing his disappointment at my insipid style of working. I thank him for that.

I think of this book as it should have been, its shortcomings eliminated, its prolixities docked, and its dullness enlivened. Yet, the need to address the snowballing impact of the UID on the migrants had to be addressed without delay. On the crucial question of how migrants are branded, while much has been said, much remains. One hopes that this book even if in a small way will serve, as one of the contributors correctly points out, to challenge 'the industry and the establishment of the ruling elite' by forming 'an understanding of the political economy of the era'.

Kolkata
25 December 2012

ATIG GHOSH

Dedication

For Ashish Rajadhyaksha and other colleagues
at the Centre for the Study of Culture and Society,
Bangalore, for inspiring us to undertake collective research

The Contributors

RITAJYOTI BANDYOPADHYAY is with the State and Democracy Research Group, Centre for Modern Indian Studies, Georg-August-Universität Göttingen, Germany.

SAHANA BASAVAPATNA is an advocate based in New Delhi.

JAYANTA BHATTACHARYA is Bureau Chief of Press Trust of India, Agartala.

BHARAT BHUSHAN is a senior journalist based in New Delhi.

BYASDEB DASGUPTA is Associate Professor, Department of Economics, University of Kalyani, West Bengal. He works on aspects of labour and finance in the context of contemporary globalisation and financialisation.

ATIG GHOSH is associated with the Mahanirban Calcutta Research Group and is Assistant Editor, *The Bengal Post.*

MANISH K. JHA is Associate Professor and Chairperson, Centre for Community Organisation and Development Practice, Tata Institute of Social Sciences, Mumbai.

SAMIR KAR PURKAYASTHA is a freelance writer and journalist.

BADRI NARAYAN TIWARI is Professor, Social History/Cultural Anthropology at G.B. Pant, Social Science Institute, Allahabad.

DIPANKAR SINHA is Professor and Head, Department of Political Science, University of Calcutta.

Introduction

Atig Ghosh

The genie is well and truly out of the bottle. The Unique Identification (UID)/Aadhaar project, which was 'conceived by the Planning Commission as an initiative that would provide identification for each resident across the country and would be used primarily as the basis for efficient delivery of welfare services' and 'would also act as a tool for effective monitoring of various programmes and schemes of the government',[1] has been put to work. The government has proposed to roll out Aadhaar-enabled cash transfer for 29 schemes in 51 districts, spread over 16 states. It also plans to cover the entire nation by the end of December 2013. Later, the cash transfer would cover all the 42 welfare schemes. Union Finance Minister P Chidambaram has called the direct cash transfer (DCT) plan 'nothing less than magical' and a 'game-changer'.[2] It is expected that the DCT scheme will cut flab in the middle by eliminating predatory intermediaries and inept public distribution agents who divert, waste or sit on resources. It is also expected to prune hugely government spending, not to speak of facilitating the empowerment of the needy via greater financial inclusion and unique identification. The last bit, of course, is going to be achieved leveraging Aadhaar. Yet, it is far from clear if Aadhaar is such a benevolent initiative of the government, seeking to empower the needy and maximise the outreach of social-security schemes. Legal experts, scholars and activists have trenchantly criticised the Aadhaar and the governmental logic underlying it. To cite just one, very recent example, civic activist and former defence scientist Mathew Thomas thinks the UID scheme is a 'bundle of self-contradictions', a combination of impudence and imprudence.[3] He writes: 'A few, who have studied UID and similar schemes, realised that this is a sinister ploy of Government. We are among those who have understood that the gathering of people's data, in the manner in which it is done through private foreign and Indian firms poses dangers to the Nation and all of us. We questioned UIDAI and governments and failed to receive satisfactory answers. We have addressed [our] elected representatives, in Parliament and in the States. Our approach to Parliament was singularly successful. A Parliament Standing Committee to which, the National Identification Authority of India, Bill 2010 was referred trashed the Bill as well as the UID scheme.'[4]

The condemnation of the Parliament Standing Committee on Finance[5] and torrential commentary against the UID scheme notwithstanding, the Aadhaar juggernaut is surely forging ahead. And the middle-class intelligentsia has failed to pre-empt establishmentarian designs. As such, we decided to put in our bit by way of engaging with the issue. In doing so, however, we have at a time widened and narrowed our scope of concerns. On the one hand, we have gone beyond the specifics of the UID project to situate the issue in the broader context of identification technologies sponsored by the state and the market over time. On the other hand, we have narrowed our focus to engage specifically with the impact of the UID and like identification technologies on migrants, rather than on residents at large. The logic undergirding the latter strategy should be self-evident. The migrants, as individuals who remain mostly beyond the embrace of the state, represent a limit on its penetration; they mostly remain at the metaphorical margins of the state's will to encompass all. And as Mary Douglas had pointed out some time back, 'All margins are dangerous. ... [A]ny structure of ideas is vulnerable at its margins.'[6] This volume therefore aspires to test the idea and effect of the UID at its limits focussing on its impact on migrants – and interrogate if the *reach* of the state can after all exceed its *grasp*.[7] The thematic imperatives adumbrated here, of course, do not wholly subsume the concerns of the various articles – there are myriad productive transgressions. They merely serve as the anchor for the ongoing discussions in the various chapters.

ISSUES AT STAKE

States, certainly from the nineteenth century, have sought to reach out or penetrate societies. One reason for this would be the modern territorial state's need to keep track of all potential taxpayers, workers, soldiers and citizens. Another reason could be that to derive its legitimacy, to become a 'nation'-state, the state, especially multi-ethnic states like India, must of necessity render variety in terms of a solidary identitarian unity – to constitute Bengalis, Punjabis, Marathis, Tamils or what you will in terms of Indian-ness, of being Indians. There is the compulsion to identify 'one' people for 'one' nation. Hence, the need to penetrate, as has been argued by numberless scholars.[8] Jürgen Habermas has further expanded the argument to characterise statist penetration as the activity of both the modern bureaucratic state and the capitalist economy, a position many articles in this volume endorse. Habermas thus speaks of the 'colonisation of the life-world' by the 'steering media' of money and power.[9] Some theorists find the metaphor of 'penetration' too invasive, even sexual, which invokes the masculinised image of penetrating states surmounting societies. John Torpey, for instance, seeks to supplement 'penetration' with 'embrace', a concept-metaphor he draws from the German word *erfassen* (to 'grasp' or 'lay hold of' in the sense of 'register'). He believes that the 'metaphor of the states' embrace of societies directs our awareness to the ways in which states bind – and in certain senses even "nurture" – the societies they hold in their clutches'.[10] He argues that states must embrace societies in order to penetrate them effectively. To be sure, Torpey is not jettisoning the aggressive statist bid to map and organise population on legible registers but, in an enabling argument, providing us the means to understand how the language of care and welfare may accompany such an aggressive bid.

The question is: how does the state or the state-market complex go about penetrating/embracing societies? This brings us to the issue of identification. Michael Mann has correctly pointed out that the 'unusual strength of the modern state is infrastructural'.[11] In infrastructural power inheres the modern state's capacity to embrace their own subjects and to exclude unwanted others. In other words, infrastructural power is deployed to identify and categorise resident/citizen population and wean out, so to speak, the 'outsiders'. For Torpey, this the state seeks to do through expropriation of legitimate means of movement from individuals and private entities. That is, the state monopolises the legitimate means of movement. This monopoly does not work solely vis-à-vis 'movers' across international borders – the visa-holding, passport-bearing traveller obviously, but also, and more importantly for our purposes, refugees, asylum-seekers, stateless groups, and so on. It also impinges upon the life of migrant workers within the national territory. *Pace* Torpey, state controls of movements operating within a state today, especially when these are to the detriment of particular 'negatively privileged' status groups, are not necessarily a sign of authoritarian governments, technically speaking.[12] In the largest functioning democracy of the world, India, there have been state governments run by certain political parties which routinely regard as 'foreigners' those from another state every bit as much as those from other countries. However, to control movement and tie down populations to state-engendered identities, the state resorts to formalised, codified, objectified systems of categorisation developed by powerful, authoritative systems. In culturalist extensions of the Weberian sociology of the state, notably those influenced by Pierre Bourdieu and Michel Foucault, the state monopolises or seeks to monopolise, not only legitimate physical force but also legitimate symbolic force. This includes the power to name, to identify, to categorise, to state 'what is what' and 'who is who'. In this context, it is fruitful to look at identification quite literally: as the attachment of definitive markers to an individual via passport, fingerprint, photograph, and signature, and the amassing of such identifying documents in state repositories.[13] It is also worthwhile to emphasise the modern state's efforts to inscribe its subjects onto a classificatory grid: to identify and categorise people in relation to gender, religion, property ownership, ethnicity, literacy, criminality or sanity. Censuses apportion people across these categories, and institutions – from schools to prisons – sort out individuals in relation to them. These individualising and aggregating modes of identification and classification, one could argue *qua* Foucauldians, are at the core of what defines governmentality in a modern state.[14]

Needless to say, the state is not the only identifier that matters. As Charles Tilly has shown, categorisation does crucial organisational work in all kinds of social settings, including families, firms, schools, social movements, and bureaucracies of all kinds.[15] Even the most powerful state does not monopolise the production and diffusion of identifications and categories; and those that it does produce may be contested by actors on the ground, practices of everyday life and projects of social movements. The hard work and long struggles over identification, producing uncertain outcomes, are described in and exemplified by the chapters of this volume. However, the traction of the state as a very powerful identifier does not spring from its ability to generate hard, solidary identities – generally it cannot – but from the fact that it has, more than anybody or anything else, the material and symbolic resources to impose the categories, classificatory schemes, and modes of social counting and accounting with which bureaucrats, judges, police, doctors, teachers and so on must work and to which non-state actors must refer. So powerful can coercive external identification and categorisation become in certain cases that they may overwhelm and override self-understandings, the latter being the polar opposite of state-sponsored identification. The Croatian novelist Slavenka Draculic, for instance, poignantly writes about being 'overcome by nationhood' as a result of the war in former Yugoslavia.[16]

From the point of view of the state's interests, identification – keeping track of populations and their movements – renders people little more than stigmata, appropriately processed for administrative use.[17] The examination of individual stigmata becomes the essential form which lies at the heart of all modern systems of identification. It 'places individuals in a field of surveillance [as well as] situates them in a network of writing; it engages them in a whole mass of documents that capture and fix them. The procedures of examination [are] accompanied at the same time by a system of intense registration and of documentary accumulation. A "power of writing" [is] constituted as an essential part in the mechanisms of discipline.'[18] This documentary accumulation follows an attempt to 'read off the body', and 'reading off the body'[19] in its turn entails the deployment of technology. These technologies have become more and more sophisticated over time, shifting from unreliable subjective descriptions and anthropometric measurements to photographs (themselves sometimes considered unreliable by administrators, as my chapter in this volume shows), fingerprinting, electronically scanned palm-prints, DNA fingerprinting and retina scans, the most dramatic avatar of which has appeared before us recently as the Aadhaar. The Indian effort to introduce Aadhaar may be considered one in a long line of precedents, though – the driver's licence and/or social security card in the United States, the *carte d'identité* in France, the *Personalausweis* in Germany, and so on. And, interestingly, the persistent tinkering with these techniques, in an effort to make them *more* effective, shows that states have a powerful and enduring interest in identifying persons; yet, there is the constant anxiety that the technology-at-hand is failing to do its work.

The state fails – or perhaps deliberately refuses – to understand, and so does the market these days, that the 'question concerning technology' is not a technological question, that 'the essence of technology is by no means anything technological.'[20] To elaborate, the problem for Martin Heidegger is not so much the existence of technology or the forms it takes, but rather our *orientation* to technology. If we accept this formulation of the problem, then it becomes clear that our response to the various problems brought about by technology cannot be solved simply by making the technology better. It is also impossible to ignore these difficulties simply by 'opting out' of technology: 'Thus we shall never experience our relationship to the essence of technology so long as we merely conceive and push forward the technological, put up with it, or evade it. Everywhere we remain unfree and chained to technology, whether we passionately affirm or deny it.'[21] It would not do, as Dipankar Sinha in his essay in this volume argues, to be either techno-romantic or techno-phobic. Nor is there a middle-ground between the two poles. One will have to overcome this binary, supersede it, to understand the work of (identification) technology. If we stuck around with Heidegger a little longer, his point about technology allows us to move our discussion of technology out of the domain of technological 'experts.' This attempt to 'open up' the conversation is at once a democratic gesture *and* a strategy to shift the discussion farther afield. The state-market complex, however, would like to keep the discussion firmly harnessed to technological expertise; for it serves the obfuscatory and undemocratic end of removing from the domain of public debate the questions concerning technology, in our specific context those involved in Aadhaar assignment. Many of the essays in this volume push past this negatively 'enframing' imperative of the state, so to speak, and discuss the issue of Aadhaar-assignment technologies on different registers, radical fields.

This brings us to our final observation, before an attempt is made to outline the drift of the essays that follow. What is the impact of these technologies of identification on the migrants? Well, the jury is still out; but the chapters in this volume make some informed observations either on the basis of historical experience of the impact of identification technologies on migrants or on the strength of ethnographic work done at sites where the UID has already been introduced. Here, we may recall what Gérard Noiriel said a long time back, 'It is often overlooked that legal registration, identification documents, and laws are what, in the final analysis, determine the "identity" of immigrants.'[22] In its ambition to construct durable relation between themselves and their subjects/citizens to further its own aim, the state individualises populations, tearing out people from their communal contexts and fixing a solidary, singular identity onto each of them. This has gained greater momentum with the spread of neo-liberalism and the rise of finance capital, as both Byasdeb Dasgupta and Ritajyoti Bandyopadhyay argue in this volume. Bandyopadhyay goes a step further to argue that such disembedding is not merely social but political, as under Aadhaar identification the individual ceases to be a citizen with rights but becomes merely a targeted 'head', allegedly for state benefits. Be it as it may, what can be seen in this process is the growing role of surveillance in the development of 'direct rule' – Anthony Giddens draws our attention to this. In contrast to 'traditional states', Giddens notes that modern states presuppose a regularised administration and that much of the necessary administrative capacity of the modern states is rooted in *writing*. It is through written documents – such as identification papers – that much of the surveillance entailed by modern state administration is carried out: 'Administrative power can only become established if the coding of information is actually applied in a direct way to the supervision of human activities.'[23] Only, in the case of the UID, this coding of information is not held in Weberian 'files' as an important element of bureaucratisation but in databases. These databases then can be made interoperable between different agencies and systems and, more importantly, they can be accessed across the length and breadth of the country and perhaps also across international borders – anytime, anywhere. This is ideally suited to track the footloose labour population of the Indian subcontinent – an issue that had exercised the colonial administrators of South Asia as much as it now worries the post-colonial nation-state(s). The database can be viewed as a mobile society of control that moves with the moving population. The UID then is the latest phase of tracking precarious and flight-footed people.

It is not difficult to see how this is likely to complicate matters for the migrants – the refugees, asylum-seekers, stateless groups surely, but also migrant labourers and internally-displaced people who may not be able to establish residential claims consistently and permanently in one location. They face the possibility of being identified and pushed back into situations out of which they have been forced to begin with. The UID could also become the stick in the hands of interested groups to beat weaker opponents with, to label the latter as foreigners and hound them. This is a point Samir Kar Purakayastha explores in his essay on Assam. Also, the confident borders which run jauntily through standard maps are on the ground sometimes fictitious. People transgress them routinely in search of livelihood options or simply better life. If the state succeeds in appending an Aadhaar to each and every identified 'citizen', then these networks of survival would be torn asunder and at the receiving end will be exclusively the poorest of the poor. But then such anxieties are perhaps overstated. While critical engagement with the UID project is necessary, it should also be noted in the same breath that such technologies of identification have from time to time been introduced by frenetic states. People – migrants in particular – have always found a way to sabotage them, or at least circumvent them. Each time an identification technology is introduced, it is claimed to be *the* identification technology which will supplant all previous modes. Yet, soon enough loopholes appear, lapses are detected and anxiety of illegibility again rears its head among administrators. The UID too may not be an exception. Consider the following statement of Sunil Abraham, Head, Centre for Internet and Society: 'UIDAI's latest 23-page biometrics report is supposed to dispel the home ministry's security anxieties. It says "biometric data is collected by software provided by the UIDAI, which immediately encrypts and applies a digital signature." Surely, what works for UIDAI, that is digital signatures, should work for citizens too. The report does not cover even the most basic attack – for example, the registrar could pretend that UIDAI software is faulty and harvest biometrics again using a parallel set-up. *If biometrics are infallible, as the report proclaims, then sections in the draft UID Bill that criminalise attempts to defraud the system should be deleted.*' He adds immediately, 'The compromise between UIDAI and the home ministry appears to be a turf battle for states where security concerns trump developmental aspirations.'[24]

THE LIE OF THE LAND

As has been said in so many words, the chapters in this book are not uniform in their focus, although they share a common concern. They shed light on the issue of identification technology – particularly the UID/Aadhaar scheme – and its impact on migrant groups. Some authors are openly critical of the project, refusing to grant any benevolent valence. Yet others are more ambiguous, although they mostly finally emerge on the side of critical scepticism. But there is at least one contributor who is ready to see the UID in kinder light. In the course of my heretofore short engagement with the issues that are at stake in this volume, ineluctably I have referred to certain contributors, engaged with their arguments. The act of writing the introduction, somewhat paradoxically, comes after the reading of the chapters. As such, it is not unnatural that their thoughts will cross my mind as I write on the subject. Even so, a brief and formal engagement with the chapters is perhaps necessary, if for nothing else then to demonstrate the rich variety and range of scholarship and experience that has been amassed in this volume.

Dipankar Sinha's essay, which opens the book, sets out the theme – the *parte medular* – of this book. He situates the UID project in the broader context of the process of digitisation in order to trace the possible ramifications of the project in the life of the migrants. His essay provides us a picture of the politics of digitisation and the dialectics of the corporal and the technological. There is perhaps no need for overreaction, he contends; no need to descry an 'evil motive' behind the project. However, he cautions the readers that aggressive promotion of such digital intervention runs the risk of exclusion of the under-privileged, of which migrants invariably constitute a sizeable section. For such projects to be viable what is needed is a technologically-inclusive society; and for a technologically-inclusive society to thrive, it needs to be solidly backed by the construction of an information-inclusive order. Further, he contends that we need to cultivate a 'cultural understanding' of technology based on decentralised inter-subjectivity, which in turn would go beyond mechanistic and technocratic notions of governance. At another level, Sinha seems to be posing the question whether identity can be digital at all. If one were to do a study of the political economy of information, then it will become clear that digitisation is in tune with technologies of control; claims of unfailing precision; and the end of trial-and-error method. Now, migrants, given their unanchored and mobile nature, provide the irritant to these claims. However, the IT boom has made the state insecure. It must map all forms of mobility and turn them into legible data. As such, migrants are subjected to multitudinous exclusionary strategies, some in the form of digitisation. Is this a new form of post-human techno-authoritarianism, Sinha seems to ask.

The two essays that follow are on the history of identificatory technologies in South Asia. Atig Ghosh contends that identificatory technologies (where technology is understood in the broader sense of being the aggregate of governmental practices designed to produce docile bodies) have, through colonial history, claimed to be unique, universal, ubiquitous. The 'tangible' nature of the technology may have changed depending on context or time – it has been fine-tuned over time, its penetrability and scope deepened and broadened – but the undergirding logic has remained the same: to encompass all in the power-knowledge complex of governmentality. Be it penal tattooing in early nineteenth century, photography, *Bertillonage*, dactyloscopy, anthropometrics, or the introduction of passports, technological identification has served the abovementioned end faithfully. The dual language of welfare and securitisation, too, is not unique to the postcolonial dispensation, the paper argues. In the case of criminals and migrant labour, that is marginal groups or groups considered comparatively untameable, however, Ghosh argues, security concerns have always outweighed the welfare rhetoric – the impact of such identity-fixing techniques on these groups have been relentlessly oppressive. The sane and sanitised self-image of such identificatory technologies, of colonial and postcolonial provenance alike, cannot stand up to historical re-interrogation.

The paper by Badri Narayan Tiwari focuses on indentured-labour migration to Suriname. Basing itself on the study of colonial photo-archives, the paper makes use of two kinds of photographs – one captured by the colonial lenses as part of the documentation of indentured migrants; the other captured by the Danish Protestant Mission. This results in an analysis of the politics of special photo-sessions organised by recruiters at depots, ports and in plantations. The politics of recruiters appears to represent labourers in plantations as happy human beings to counter the nationalist propaganda of ill-treatment. Women wearing attractive jewelleries and well-dressed men were advertised by recruiters and planters. This gave birth to a visual archetype in almost all photo-documentation by colonial masters. Another kind of ID documentation was certificates provided by the colonial recruiters to the indentured labourer. In them, detailed descriptions of the village of the recruited labourer, *thana, pargana,* depot of recruitment, ports of departure and destination, plantation, name of the planters, height of the labourer and other specificities of the body were mentioned. Apart from these, all the details of the labourer's physical examinations and her/his health were also documented in the recruitment register maintained by the recruitment depot at the country of departure as well as in the country of arrival. From time to time commissions and enquiry committees formed by British government to investigate conditions of the migrants also documented the health and physical details of the investigated indentured labourer. This was done to counter the allegations of nationalists in India who were not in favour of the continuation of the indenture system. The bio-politics and image-politics of colonial masters are observable in such processes of documentation. Also, within the scope of a detailed case study, Tiwari's presentation demonstrates the general point Atig Ghosh has made previously: in case of marginal groups, identity documentation inevitably meant surveillance, securitisation and the desire to produce docile bodies; welfare, or in this case 'well being' of the subject thus identified, was either an eyewash to silence critics, or simply a rhetorical justification.

In bringing together the UID project of the government and the precarious state of asylum-seekers, Sahana Basavapatna pitches her concerns on a broader plane that interrogates the security-welfare complex of a modern state. How does the Indian state propose to strengthen 'authorised' migration and prevent/disrupt 'unauthorised' or 'irregular' migration at the same time? On the basis of rigorous legal research and rich ethnographic fieldwork, Basavapatna engages with the issue of the migrant population that seeks asylum in India with specific reference to the purposes for which they are counted and/or documented. This theme, she argues, remains largely unexplored in the Indian context. The Aadhaar is the newest form of such population-counting projects that aims to cover the entire resident population so that welfare schemes and service delivery reach the beneficiary. As such, she discusses Aadhaar conjointly with other population-counting projects. She concludes that little public discussion preceded the implementation of the Aadhaar project and in any case little or no discussion is visible on the possible impact of Aadhaar or other surveillance mechanisms on refugees and asylum seekers. Independent of how these projects seek to implicate the non-citizen into the state mechanism of surveillance, the projected goals of the Aadhaar project have not been proven satisfactorily, leading one to ask what the real aim of creating such large databases without considering their potential misuse is. As people on the margins, asylum seekers and refugees are reluctant to part with information which they would have no control of. What has also not been proven beyond doubt, Basavapatna submits, is whether the availability of exhaustive information, in the Indian context, has led to a better and more efficient system of delivery of services, both in case of refugees and citizens.

Bharat Bhushan gives us a detailed account of Hindu migrants from Pakistan to India. Curiously, these are migrants who are by and large not averse to getting the Aadhaar. Their community leaders believe that

Pak migrants should be given UID cards. They feel that there is no negativity attached to covering the Pak migrants under UID. They think that once the migrants have Aadhaar cards, they can do all those things which they cannot otherwise do for want of an ID proof. For the West Pakistani migrants to Jammu & Kashmir – who have been given Indian citizenship rights and voting rights in national elections, but not voting rights in the state assembly — getting a UID card would mean little as they already have some kind of a local address proof because they have a Voter's ID card for voting in parliamentary elections. Additionally, the West Pakistan Refugee Action Committee has issued its own official ID-cards to the refugees and their children. Apparently, these are a great help in proving the domicile of the children while seeking admission in schools. However, not all Hindu migrants from Pakistan to India comprise an undifferentiated group. There are still the illegal migrants who have stayed on in India once they had somehow arrived. For them, getting the Aadhaar card may not be such a good idea, as it may increase state surveillance over their activities.

Jayanta Bhattacharya's essay, in certain ways, stands out from the rest. It is the only essay in the volume that tries to judge the UID by the good work it has done in Tripura. He begins by outlining the porosity of the border of Tripura with Bangladesh in the northeast. He elaborates how movement of people across the border continues almost unhindered. Yet, in the same breath he points out that Aadhaar enrolment work has been extremely successful in Tripura. Aadhaar enrolment work commenced in Tripura on 18 November 2010, and by 15 January 2012, about 90 per cent of the total population (3,277,109 residents to be precise) had been enrolled. He also points out that Tripura occupied the first position in India in terms of the implementation of the UIDAI project and received the Aadhaar Excellence Award on 29 September 2011, at New Delhi. He explains that the credit for this astounding success of Tripura in Aadhaar enrolment goes to the 'political will' and efficiency of the state government (at the time of writing, India's only Left Front government). However, Bhattacharya does not explain how one could fit together the two parts of his presentation: porosity of border and mixed and massive flows across it, on the one hand, and the success of the UIDAI project on the other, political will or not. That is to say, uncontrolled flows across border imply demographic flux; and how can precise figures (such as the meticulous 3,277,109) be computed on the basis of such unstable demographics?

Samir Kar Purakayastha begins his essay by arguing that the word 'identity' in Assam has a divisive character, fraught with inherent contradictions. 'Any attempt to profile identity – digital or otherwise – is, therefore, a tricky proposition,' he says, adding, 'More so since enumeration processes have in the past triggered many a mutiny in the state.' He tracks this mutinous history at length before he takes up the issue of the UID. However, he does not take an entirely critical view of the UID and its possible impact on Assam. He is sceptical alright, but he is ready to concede that the UID may facilitate some peace-building processes. He hopes that the government, armed with biometric information of its residents, will easily track down any stranger. Even those provided with resident status will find it difficult to fake their citizenship status once their biometric and demographic information is recorded. The information collected for the NPR- UID can also be accessed in the central database from anywhere in the country. He is not entirely convinced that the NRC alone is enough to deal with the problem. The citizenship register, no doubt, itself is adequate to settle the issue of who an illegal migrant is, he says. But an NPR-UID will empower the relevant agencies with vital biometric and demographic digital backups to prevent further intrusion and faking of identity by detected illegal immigrants. The benefits of these projects, therefore, lie in their integration and not isolation. Stressing the advantages of interoperability among various systems and databases, Kar Purakayastha is trying to argue that the UID might actually help in solving Assam's vexed problem of illegal migration. What would actually happen once the UID is in place, of course, is still an open question.

Three locations in Mumbai were chosen by Manish K. Jha to study the impact of UID on migrants. The first location was Rafiq Nagar, known as an 'illegal settlement' which borders the Deonar dumping ground in the M-East ward of Mumbai. The second location was the Juhu line area which is a regularised area and home predominantly to the minority population. The third area selected was that of migrants who have been in the city for so long that some of them are not even migrants in the real sense of the word: i.e. Jai Ambe Nagar, which is home to the Pardhi community who are a de-notified tribe of Maharashtra. Though the nature of insecurity and access vis-à-vis Aadhaar vary across these locations, Jha found a prevalent distrust for the UID among his respondents. And this, he argues, is unsurprising, given that the state in Maharashtra has consistently employed languages of exclusion and discrimination against the migrants. The logic that the data would be used to facilitate welfare and development for the dispossessed and the deprived is hard to believe, going by the mindset of the governing class. Jha's ethnography found respondents echoing his apprehensions. Going by the history of similar processes in other parts of the globe, Jha concludes, it is only natural for such apprehension and scepticism to persist.

With Byasdeb Dasgupta and Ritajyoti Bandyopadhyay we come to the last two chapters of the volume. Though differing in emphases, the two chapters somewhat mimic each other's key argumentative movements. Both locate the UID within the expanding state-market nexus of neo-liberal economics. Talking specifically about financial inclusion and its link with UID, Dasgupta asserts that achieving cent per cent financial inclusion for the poor migrant workers through digitisation of their identity may not be feasible in the present neo-liberal scenario. Aadhaar is necessarily a national security project. The larger question of identity is posed in the context of national security. As a nice-sounding justification, the scheme is tagged with the rhetoric of delivery of welfare schemes and services like the formal financial services. It is presumed that delivery of welfare schemes and services, which are public goods in nature (like financial services), have failed so far miserably owing to the lack of identity of the targeted population. So, Aadhaar project will fill that gap. However, the big question remains whether the lack of proper identification of the poor and migrant workers is the principal reason behind the benefits not accruing to them. Dasgupta believes both Aadhaar and financial inclusion are neo-liberal projects. And like any neo-liberal developmental agenda, they lack any holistic approach and do not take into account the fact that exclusion, be it financial or otherwise, is systemic in nature.

The fiery Parthian shot comes from Ritajyoti Bandyopadhyay. His finely-crafted paper is an intervention in the ongoing public debate on 'India's super-ambitious UID project', to use his words. The UID moment is important for observing the changes in dominant class coalitions in post-liberalisation India. The paper makes three major arguments: a) it argues that the UID project is part of a series of processes that reify the individual as the unit of the economy and governance, bridging the gap between finance capital and commercial capital; b) it shows how the Indian state is shifting its basic functions from governing production and redistribution to managing consumption; c) it proposes that the anti-UID movement hitherto restricted to the metropolitan middle class quarters has to combine the concerns of civil liberties with an understanding of the political economy of the entire edifice of digital governance to break its existing class content. In his own words, 'the first step to challenge the industry and the establishment of the ruling elite is to form an understanding of the political economy of the era.'

THE WAY AHEAD

This volume is not a comprehensive commentary on identification technologies, not even on the UID. But then that was never the intention either. Perfectionism, like its twin procrastination, is the thief of time, and the timely production of a collection of engaged commentary on the UID/Aadhaar project was the need of the hour. While the state and the market is busy clamping the Aadhaar on to its 'residents', it was necessary that a body of work reflected on the possible implication it carries for the 'non-residents', the migrants. They may not be a majority, but in states like West Bengal or in the whole of the north-east they comprise a sizeable section of the population. This population, the state has always tried to de-legitimise and jettison from national territory. With the UID, such statist imperatives could acquire teeth. This volume has tried to delve into that possibility, working its way through complementary comments and contradictory contestations.

Even as I write, the body of literature on the UID project continues to grow, with more and more people making their opinion known on the issue. This is perhaps one way of building what Dipankar Sinha has called an information-inclusive order. It is hoped that this volume would meaningfully contribute in that direction. There is no need to consider this book as a novel *manqué* of which the conclusion is over the tired novelist's horizon. Rather, it should be looked at as a *roman-feuilleton*: here's our instalment, there have been valuable others before us, *et la suite au prochain numéro.*

NOTES

1. UIDAI, "Background," Unique Identification Authority of India, Planning Commission, Government of India; http://uidai.gov.in/index.php?option=com_content&view=article&id=141&Itemid=164 [last accessed 4 December 2012]
2. "Chidambaram calls Direct Cash Transfer a magical step," *The Hindu*, 1 December 2012; http://www.thehindu.com/news/national/chidambaram-calls-direct-cash-transfer-a-magical-step/article4154155.ece [last accessed 4 December 2012]; Smita Gupta, "Cash Transfer Scheme is a game-changer: Chidambaram," *The Hindu*, 27 November 2012; http://www.thehindu.com/news/national/cash-transfer-to-cover-29-schemes-in-first-phase/article4140318.ece [last accessed 4 December 2012]
3. Thomas, Mathew *et al*, *UID is Not Yours: Your ID under Government/Political/Bureaucratic/Private Company Control!* November, 2012, p.10, 31; http://kractivist.files.wordpress.com/2012/12/uid-is-not-yours.pdf [last accessed 4 December 2012]
4. Ibid, p. viii
5. Rajshekhar, M., "Reasons why the Standing Committee on Finance rejected the UIDAI Bill," *The Economic Times*, 16 December 2011; http://articles.economictimes.indiatimes.com/2011-12-16/news/30525319_1_aadhaar-uid-scheme-data-protection [last accessed 15 November 2012]
6. Douglas, Mary, *Purity and Danger: An Analysis of Concepts of Pollution and Taboo*, Routledge & Kegan Paul: London, 1996, p.121
7. John Torpey is of the opinion that it cannot, an argument most of the essays in this volume seem to bear out. See, John Torpey, "Coming and Going: On the State Monopolisation of the Legitimate 'Means of Movement'," *Sociological Theory*, 16:3, November 1998, p.244
8. See, for example, Michael Mann, *The Sources of Social Power*, vol. 2: *The Rise of Classes and Nation-States, 1760-1914*, Cambridge University Press: New York, 1993; Charles Tilly, *Coercion, Capital and European States, AD 990-1992*,

Blackwell: Cambridge Mass., 1990; Theda Skocpol, *States and Social Revolutions: A Comparative Analysis of France, Russia and China*, Cambridge University Press: New York, 1978

9. Habermas, Jürgen, *The Theory of Communicative Action* vol. 2: *Lifeworld and System: A Critique of Functionalist Reason*, translated by Thomas McCarthy, Beacon Press: Boston, 1987
10. Torpey, "Coming and Going," p.245
11. Mann, *The Sources of Social Power*, p.60
12. Torpey, "Coming and Going," p.243
13. Noiriel, Gérard, *The French Melting Pot: Immigration, Citizenship, and National Identity*, translated by Geoffrey de Laforcade, University of Minnesota Press: Minneapolis, 1996 [1988]; Jane Caplan and John Torpey eds., *Documenting Individual Identity: The Development of State Practices in the Modern World*, Princeton University Press: Princeton NJ, 2001
14. Foucault, Michel, "Governmentality," in Burchell, Graham, Colin Gordon and Peter Miller eds., *The Foucault Effect: Studies in Governmentality, with two lectures by and an interview with Michel Foucault, Harvester, Wheatsheaf:* Hemel Hempstead, Hertfordshire, 1991, pp.87-401; also see, for example, Bernard Cohn, *Colonialism and Its Forms of Knowledge: The British in India*, Princeton University Press: Princeton NJ, 1996
15. Tilly, Charles, *Durable Inequality*, University of California Press: Berkeley CA, 1998
16. Draculic, Slavenka, *The Balkan Express: Fragments from the Other Side of the War*, translated by Maja Šoljan, W.W. Norton: New York, 1993, pp.50-52
17. Here the idea of the operation of and responses to stigmata in informal interaction, as analysed by Erving Goffman, is being expanded to the ambit of bureaucratic institutions such as the state. Erving Goffman, *Stigma: Notes on the Management of Spoiled Identity*, Simon & Schuster: New York, 1963
18. Foucault, Michel, *Discipline and Punish: The Birth of the Prison*, Penguin: India, 1991 [1978], p.189
19. Caplan and Torpey, 'Introduction,' in Jane Caplan and John Torpey eds., *Documenting Individual Identity*, p.8
20. Heidegger, Martin, "The Question Concerning Technology," in Martin Heidegger, *Philosophical and Political Writings*, edited by Manfred Stassen, Continuum (German Library series): London, 2003, p.279
21. Ibid, p.278
22. Noiriel, *The French Melting Pot*, p.45
23. Giddens, Anthony, *The Nation-State and Violence*, University of California Press: Berkeley, 1987, p.47
24. Abraham, Sunil, "Do we need the Aadhaar Scheme?" *Business Standard*, 1 February 2012, emphasis added; http://www.business-standard.com/india/news/do-we-needaadhar-scheme/463324/ [last accessed 15 November 2012]

1

Politics of Digitisation
UID as Governmental Technique

Dipankar Sinha

INTRODUCTION

The essay has the primary objective of situating the Unique Identification (UID) project, also known as the Aadhaar project, in the broader context of the process of digitisation in order to trace the possible ramifications of the project in the life of the migrants. Its purpose is not to provide an empirical brick-by-brick account of the project vis-à-vis the migrants as such, but to understand and visualise the possible ways in which the migrants may negotiate with the project which needs some more time to produce clearer manifestations. In identifying the contours and mechanisms, on the one hand, and the constraints and/or 'missing links', on the other hand, of the process of digitisation and its outcome, the digital database, the essay has some underlying premises. First, that it is important to relate the construction of UID project to the advent of new technologies in general and the process of digitisation in particular, rather than treating it in a compartmentalised fashion. Second, that beyond its immediate and apparent technological form, the project is political in the sense that it strategises a control-mechanism on the part of the policymakers, in which the people are supposed to be 'benefited'.

Third, while the project has minimal reference to 'migrants' it does have huge implications for them. It is also to be noted that in not having adopted a dismissive and contemptuous view of the project, the essay has a bottom-line of sorts: howsoever technologically fine-tuned and ambitious the project is, it is bound to remain 'imperfect' in its constitution and 'incomplete' in its mission.

It is often asserted that we live in a world propelled and sustained by the 'Information Revolution'. The main attribute of the revolutionary effect emerges from a scenario in which we continue to witness newer and newer inventions and the steep ascendance of new technologies. As the argument goes, the new technologies have firmly co-opted the twenty-first century in their fold. In this scenario, digitisation, somewhat paradoxically, is both the new buzzword and a supposedly 'inescapable' process in administration and governance. But there is more to the Information Revolution than information technologies. After all, the question of technology is not simply a technological question. Technology – no matter how powerful a tool of the interventionist claim of government promising to usher in revolutionary change in the life of the people – has to be contextualised in specific time, space and objective conditions. The locale in which technology is to be introduced is a product of the complex dynamics of economic, social, cultural and not the least, political factors, which have to be surely and constantly negotiated by it. This is *particularly* true in the case of new technologies: *particularly* because this genre is often invented and 'deployed' beforehand, with the futuristic claim that the benefits would gradually trickle down and contribute to the welfare of the people 'in the years to come'. This is at variance with the general trend of the 'old' technologies which would mostly be produced out of the felt needs of the people; conversely, people as 'potential users' are now expected to change their mindset and behavioural mode in order to adopt, and adapt to, the new technologies.

Then again there is the inevitable issue of access, or the lack of it. The power and reach of the 'old' technologies might have been much restricted in comparison with their new counterpart but the fact remains that the problem of access was there, but not to the extent it is so in the case of new technologies. This is not to argue that the old technologies were marked by highly democratic access. The issue of differential access has been a perennial problem in the technology scenario, in constant need of being addressed, but it was not as threatening as it is in the context of the Digital Divide – a phenomenon primarily associated with new technologies. Such a divide, resting on the division between the 'digital have-nots' and the 'digital haves', has complicated the access issue to an overwhelming degree, and as we shall mention subsequently, with far-reaching implications. Judging by the trends in different parts of the world one might wonder whether the increasing use of the new technologies as 'control technologies' would let the promise of democratisation be anything more than a rhetoric. The problem is more complex, because discarding the new technology lock, stock and barrel is not a viable way of addressing the problem. While one should guard against the uncritical celebration of the power of (new) technology by the techno-romantic, at the same time any foundational and fundamental opposition to new technology, as is displayed by the techno-phobic, perhaps, provides a wrong solution to the problem at hand. Being in the denial mode and negating the power of new technologies and the utility of their various forms do not necessarily make the world a better place to live in. We would submit that the process of digitisation has to be approached and problematised, maintaining equidistance from the two extreme poles.

TECHNIQUE BENEATH TECHNOLOGY

Digitisation, technologically speaking, is the process of converting information into digital format. But, when it is linked to and manipulated by the business of governance, it is instantly enmeshed in the web of power relations, thereby becoming too multilayered in both depth and spread to warrant simplistic generalisations and technological reductionism. Invoking it in the name of welfare, administrative efficiency and effectiveness, the powers that be ensure a gradual but steady transformation of digitisation into a political project. In its ever-increasing urge to manage 'human affairs', now through the 'fusion' of new technologies and bio-physiological features (of which the increasing dependence on biometrics-based rhizomatic surveillance in recent times, especially post-9/11, is an instance), digitisation, despite its late emergence, seems to have become a good reference point for the Frankfurt School's idea of the *totally administered society* and of the classical Foucauldian concepts of *governmentality* and *biopolitics*. While there is a need to update Foucault's contentions regarding (panoptic) surveillance with the passing of time, the fact remains that he provided a much-needed boost to studies such as this by relating acts and practices of self-disciplining behaviour to the system of power. The concept of governmentality 'presupposes, on the one hand, rational forms, technical procedures, instrumentations through which to operate and, on the other hand, strategic games which subject the power relations they are supposed to guarantee to instability and reversal,'[1] with various forms and mechanisms, including discursive practices, ensures that scientific categories like 'population' rather than juridical ones, become the object of systematic, sustained political attention and intervention. No less important in the case of biopolitics; the disciplinary technologies approach the body not directly in its biological dimension, but as an object to be manipulated and controlled – 'subjected, used, transformed and improved'. Against this background in which both 'governmentality' and 'biopolitics' are intertwined with the expansion and intensification of information networks, in addressing the complex assemblage and dynamics of digitisation and in relating the UID to the state and fate of the migrants, one has to go beyond the usual parameters, boundaries of analyses and methodological thumb rules. The complexities abound because even if apparently digitisation seems to be a 'concrete', 'rational' and 'transparent' process, with the explicit purpose of creating 'reliable database', when one goes deeper into it one finds an inevitable interplay of the material and the immaterial, especially in the cultural context of self, personhood and (in)dividuality. Thus, drawing attention to the 'central tension of digital technology' beyond the concrete issues Paul Taylor and Jan Ll. Harris explain, '. . . technology is often assumed to involve a process of abstraction, an escape from the matter/matrix within which the human has been fashioned and reproduced. But the effects of this immaterial form are frequently felt within society at a material level, either by individuals using digital technologies or, more subtly, by the alterations it produces on the whole cultural environment

. . . The paradox of this *im/materiality* . . . manifests itself in numerous ways. For instance, we might note that much of contemporary capitalism is simultaneously abstract in appearance yet powerful in its material effects for those on its receiving end . . . In this context, the matrix describes both the physical technological infrastructure of advanced capitalism and the abstract forces that, although difficult to pin down, constitute the very real vectors of influence within digital matters.'[2] Within the scope of this essay it would not be possible to analyse the issue in great detail but it needs to be noted that later when we refer to the possible ways of negotiating the UID project by the migrants this dialectics is bound to operate at the foundational level of strategies and actions.

Let us turn to the political economy side of it. The power of the state, on the one hand, and the rights and freedoms of the citizens, on the other hand, – notwithstanding the endeavour of the social and political thinkers – have remained set in a binary relation. While serious and sincere attempts are being made for centuries to arrive at some kind of reconciliation between the two domains, for all practical purposes the two have been involved in a zero-sum game. In this game one is supposed to thrive at the cost of the other. The state has for a long time in history remained much too powerful and, as a result, there is a long tradition of the rights and freedoms of the citizens being under threat. However, in the contemporary era an interesting development has taken place. While the state has been a key player in the management and control of technologies, the market too, since the late twentieth century in particular, has overwhelmingly been in control. Yet there is a catch. On the one hand, the market, which is now on the centre-stage of information capitalism, is reorienting and restructuring itself with the advent of new technologies which assure it both profit and power. On the other hand, despite its continuing reservations about the power of the state, and the consequent effort to make the state less powerful, the market relies on the state to 'popularise' new technologies. Thus, when it comes to the dissemination of the symbolic power, messages and items of new technologies we find a very interesting 'convergence' between the state and the market. Strange though it may seem, this is not something unnatural because new technologies serve the interests of both the state and the market. While this collaboration in which the state adopts the new technologies ensures greater profit for the market it also supposedly imparts greater credibility to the state in matters of development and welfare in general and of public policy in particular. No wonder in the contemporary discourse of the state 'governance' is often prefixed by the vowel 'e', with the underlying belief that 'electronification', of which digitisation is a strategy-cum-tool, provides much greater legitimacy to governance. How is digitisation rationalised and defended by the government as part of its promotion of 'e-governance' in particular and good governance in general? The main planks in this context are efficiency, accountability, responsiveness and transparency. Ideally, transparency enables the citizens to see and understand what is going on in the policy arena; accountability results in a sense of responsibility on the part of rulers (that they are answerable to the citizens out there); and responsiveness enhances the credibility and effectiveness of governance in the mind of the people. A closer scrutiny of the related discourse would, however, reveal a not-so-subtle privileging of efficiency over the other attributes. The design and the discourse of the new technologies, constructed by their proponents, thereby imbibe a fundamental claim – of the 'end of trial-and-error method' and its 'unfailing precision' in making us sub-divisible and documenting 'who we are'. All such attributes are supposed to minimise, if not eliminate, 'endemic problems' like delay, uncertainty, corruption and nepotism, excessive expenditure and so forth. There is hardly any reason to contest such a scheme, especially in the light of the everyday experience of the ordinary people, who in one way or other are compelled to come face-to-face with the administration.

The interplay of the material and the immaterial, mentioned earlier, comes to the fore in publicising e-governance. On the one hand, it promotes certain specific and concrete 'e' strategies and tools for pure administrative convenience. On the other hand, in a related, but less overt, manner it seeks to penetrate the psyche of the people and the socio-spatial domain by suggesting that with the adoption of digital orientation life can be a lot better with relatively greater transparency and accountability and better access to goods and services. But every point is supposed have a counter-point, at least when it concerns democratic governance. Thus, there is already a strong argument that in this whole process there is a subtle strategy of establishing a surveillance society in the name of information society. The logic in this case is that the new technologies, especially the marriage of digitisation and biometrics, are often used to constrain the privacy of the citizens. Arthur Kroker, gives a vivid description of the 'biometric state' and its control of subjects in these words: 'In the new biometric state, your history is embedded in a card; your future is scanned; and your life is imprinted. Biology is security. Framed by a dialectic of security and terrorism, set in motion by a technological alliance between biology . . . and digitality . . . and circulating through the body in the form of bio-power, the new biometric state is the decisive product of the war on terrorism. Sweeping aside traditional protections of privacy and civil rights in the name of combating terrorism, the new biometric state takes full advantage of the spectre of terrorism to install a fundamental regime change in the future of political culture. Populated by biometric subjects, tracked by electronic scanning, and invaded by the sign of biogen, from food to surveillance, the new biometric state represents that epochal moment when the language of biology, fleeing its previous association with the history of epistemological struggles, allies itself with a form of power which speaks in the name of absolute security in a dangerous world.'[3] Kroker contextualises the biometric state in the US context and he is pegging it on the 'spectre of terrorism'. But in the context of states like India, and the UID project is a prime instance, the biometric indicators are rationalised in a welfarist vein, in terms of people's impending benefits.

While thinking of the UID project and its direct and indirect promotion of the 'beneficial effects' one can well keep in mind the fate of India's pioneering digitisation programme – Bhoomi. The programme introduced the computerisation of land titles in the state of Karnataka with the promise of transparent, accountable and responsive governance. But the outcome did not match the expectations. Research findings reveal that the programme was plagued with severe constraints and problems. First, it has made life much more expensive for the farmer, especially of the smaller category. Second, corruption has increased on many counts with bribe levels increasing many times over. Third, the time to access records for land transactions have also increased manifold. In terms of its long-term implications, the programme also made life more insecure for smaller land occupiers who now face a threat from very powerful agents and land developers. Significantly for our discussion here, the findings also reveal that the 'digitally mastered' titles allow larger corporate interests to consolidate land. The following point is indeed significant: 'Many of . . . land value enhancing infrastructure investment are publicly funded and argued on grounds of public purpose often requiring public acquisition of land under eminent domain. Thus what is being created is huge private value at public costs – allowing big business to compete globally not on their intrinsic efficiency but rather public subsidy!'[4] Drawing attention to the broader power dimensions of a 'promising' technological process the researchers assert, '. . . Bhoomi is but a small aspect of a larger process that is shaped by an intensive power dynamic, driven by high-level administrative and political players in some locations. It is naïve to assume that computers and well-designed software, or the rigorous training of support staff driven by a well-meaning project champion can address such structural political issues.'[5]

Politics – as the process of management of conflicts – in the domain of governance is supposed to be entwined with formulation and implementation of public policies. But paradoxically the precinct of public policy is being overwhelmingly marked by 'colonisation of politics', which implies 'almost unconditional surrender of politics – at least in all visible, publicly accessible aspects of communication.'[6] Such trend is often promoted in the name of 'transparent, accountable and responsive' governance but in effect it only serves the interests of the rulers who often decide to adopt public policies unilaterally, without subjecting them to sustained and systematic public scrutiny. This is particularly so, as in the UID project, in the case of technology-centred policies. As Judy Wajcman warns[7], the view of technology as an external and autonomous force exerting an influence on society narrows the possibility for democratic engagement – through debates and dissent – with the order of technology. The citizens remain 'silent onlookers', having little scope for deliberating and critiquing the vital issues that are associated with the policies concerned in varying degree. In this way, the 'inputs' of the public policies concerned become extremely limited. Critical engagement with public policies becomes a victim when in the mechanistic, bureaucratic and technocratic mind-set of the powers that be the content of public policies is considered to be 'too sophisticated', 'too complicated' and 'too specialised' to be understood by the ordinary people, setting a 'sort of boundary-line preventing the ordinary citizens from crossing over to the specialised domain', by robbing them of the much-needed public character.[8] (We shall take this point up again in the section entitled 'Ways Out'.) The outcome often is a huge gap between the promise and the performance. Here one might also find Ulrich Beck's concept of *subpolitics* (*of welfare*) of much relevance despite the fact that it was developed in the context of the late modern western societies.[9] He explains, as part of the broader thesis on reflexive modernisation, how the ascent and dominance of certain specific techno-scientific rationalities, having their roots in expert knowledge tend to marginalise lay knowledge, reduce *polis* into sub-*polis*. Subpolitics, which according to Beck is neither political nor non-political, is marked by a trend of avoiding legitimisation of domination, power and interest by undermining democratic procedures and bypassing formal politics and representative institutions. It does not escape one's sight that increasingly under the cloak of normality the 'digital revolution' is sought to be justified and enforced in the shrinking public domain without much deliberations and debates. The UID project has to be situated against this background.

SCANNING THE UID: DATAVEILLANCE AND BEYOND

The UID project, initiated in the year 2009, is the flagship project of India today. Conducted by the Unique Identification Authority of India (UIDAI), attached to the Planning Commission, it has the eminent tech-guru Nandan Nilekani, co-founder and former chief executive officer of the Infosys Technologies Limited, as the chairperson. No less important is the fact that the legal foundation of the UID project is somewhat flimsy. Having been set up as an attached office of the Planning Commission (through a notification dated 28.01.09) the UIDAI is being run mainly on the basis of a series of memoranda of understanding. The UIDAI and the Planning Commission have already been served legal notices questioning its legal authority.

UIDAI has a mandate to ensure a 'unique' number to 'each resident across the country', based on an individual's demographic and biometric information (ten finger prints, scanned iris of eyes, photo of the face). In the words of Nilekani, 'The name Aadhaar communicates the fundamental role of the number issued by the UIDAI the number as a universal identity infrastructure, a foundation over which public and private agencies can build services and applications that benefit residents across India.'[10] It is also stated, in an ambitious manner, that being a foundation for 'effective enforcement of individual rights', it would 'act as a tool for effective monitoring of various programmes and schemes of the Government'. As part of its promise of 'inclusive' enrolment the project also claims that it will empower poor and underprivileged 'residents' in accessing services 'anytime, anywhere', such as the formal banking system, and give them the opportunity to easily avail various other services provided by the government and the private sector. Neither is it clear, considering the fact that the 'residents' are supposed to be those who stay in a particular place for at least six months and a day, how the project perceives and places the 'highly problematic' non-citizen residents like refugees, asylum seekers and stateless persons.

The concept of a unique identification was first mooted and worked upon since 2006 in the context of the 'below poverty line' families. Later it was expanded in scope. *The UIDAI Strategy Overview* reflects an overwhelming concern for the subaltern segment of the Indian society. As it states, 'In India, an inability to prove identity is one of the biggest barriers preventing the poor from accessing benefits and subsidies. . . . [T]ill date, there remains no nationally accepted, verified identity number that both residents and agencies can use with ease and confidence. As a result, every time an individual tries to access a benefit or service, they must undergo a full cycle of identity verification . . . . Such duplication of effort and "identity silos" increase overall costs of identification, and cause extreme inconvenience to the individual. This approach is especially unfair to India's poor and underprivileged residents, who usually lack identity documentation, and find it difficult to meet the costs of multiple verification processes. There are clearly, immense benefits from a mechanism that uniquely identifies a person, and ensures instant identity verification. The need to prove identity only once will bring down transaction costs for the poor. A clear identity number would also transform the delivery of social welfare programmes by making them more inclusive of communities now cut off from such benefits due to their lack of identification. It would enable the government to shift from indirect to direct benefits, and help verify whether the intended beneficiaries actually receive funds/subsidies. A single, universal identity number will also be transformational in eliminating fraud and duplicate identities. . . .'[11] There is also the related claim that the centralised technological infrastructure is to 'enable "anytime, anywhere, anyhow" authentication'. It is only in this context that the project refers to the 'migrants', with the claim that it would give them 'mobility of identity'.[12] There is sufficient reason to believe that 'mobility' is not an innocuous concept; nor is 'identity'. As Evelyn Ruppert reminds us, the logic of the state and its view of population objects lead to detection through transactions with commercial and government authorities such that citizens (and we may add, residents) can then be segmented into different 'classes' of conduct.[13] Interestingly, in the UID project the very use of the 'migrants' as an umbrella term is problematic as it does not accord any attention to their diversity and fragmented character. Migrants are supposed to include women, elderly, children and so forth whose conditions and responses cannot be the same. Nor does it take into account the fact that there are huge numbers of migrants, most of whom are engaged in the informal sector, who are under too vulnerable conditions – occupational, economic, social and political – to get enrolled and enjoy the 'mobility of identity'. It could also be viewed as an instance of 'lip service' to the migrants, without taking the trouble of qualifying the category further and leaving enormous scope for manoeuvring.

The UID project is a landmark in the Indian context of governmentality. It involves the use of technical, administrative and social knowledge to manage population groups; it rests on identification, categorisation (in terms of inclusion and exclusion); it unleashes a monitoring process to create a disciplinary, hegemonic regime based on self-normalisation. But the moot question is: can it be perfect? True, in terms of its apparent attributes, objectives and functions the project provides the impression of a kind of 'awakening' of the rulers who have come to realise the importance of entitlements of the ruled. In a way it also reveals a tacit admission by the state that regarding the delivery of services and ensuring inclusive governance much remains to be done. However, beyond its apparent form, at a deeper level, the project is also to be viewed as part of the Indian state's ongoing negotiation with its own identity, which is subject to severe challenge, and is under the process of great churning. The realisation by the state of the power and potential of new technologies has also made it somewhat anxiety-prone and insecure for several reasons. It is primarily because the Information Revolution is essentially a corporate-sponsored, private capital-sourced phenomenon, having the highest priority in agenda of market-driven information capitalism, in which the state is not exactly in overall control. One can make a provocative point that the UID project, though introduced by the Indian state, is not necessarily its brainchild but an imperative propelled by the movers and shakers of new technologies in constant search for the market. Apart from the fact that Nandan Nilekani is in its charge, it is also noteworthy that during the design phase and programme management phase of the Pilot UIDAI project a report on the *Strategic Vision on the UIDAI Project* was prepared by the IT corporate giant Wipro Ltd – its consultant.

At the same time the project might be an imperative that the Indian state has found convenient at this juncture of governance. In the post-liberalisation era, the state – having lost a lot of leverage in governance and decision-making to the market forces, that too on the ground of (lack of) efficiency – needs some sort of 'aggressive show of efficiency' in welfarist governance to assert its effectiveness and legitimacy among the people. Second, the migrants are an important 'item' in state agenda because the less technologically-sophisticated modes hitherto adopted have been ineffective in locating, profiling and enumerating them. The UID project supposedly fits the bill as an 'authentic' identification process to leave out the illegal and unwanted migrants out of the database and to also subject them to various exclusionary strategies and actions. The Indian state in this context seems to have been inspired by the claims of grand success of surveillance technologies elsewhere in the world. Thus, for instance, the European borders are now digital biometric borders – thanks to the Schengen Information System, the EU Visa Information System and the Eurodac System – in which the control of the flow of (irregular) migrants and in the latter case, of asylum-seekers, is one of the most important 'stated' goals. As Broeders observes, '. . . from the perspective of irregular migrants the panopticon Europe can indeed be considered a "factory of exclusion", as it ultimately aims to facilitate expulsion. . . . The panoptic focus on territory has shifted to a focus on population, and in the case of surveillance on (irregular) migrants. . . . New technologies of computerisation and the construction of digital databases have further favoured the strategy of tracing the movement of people. . . . This new surveillance of motilities also mobilises and digitalises the border itself. . . .'[14] It is gradually becoming evident that the convergence of demographic data and the standardised and 'crystal-clear' biometric data is also gaining popularity the world over, as part of the zero-tolerance policy, both to encounter the 'big threat' of unidentifiable and inestimable flow of 'undocumented migrants' and to ensure their exclusion from various public services like public education, health and other welfare benefits. However, such digital determinism underlines the point that the migrants, particularly those without any legal status, continue to bother the governments across Europe.

This is not to argue in a simplistic fashion and provide the impression that the UID project is an outcome of a series of international and national conspiratorial designs; the matter is much more nuanced. Having been devised within the set parameters of the politics of digitisation, explained earlier, the UID by its very constitutive logic cannot but be a governmental technique with extremely vast, highly diffused but much less visible networks of power and subtle threads of control. The control-mechanism has so much depth that one can go even to the extent of arguing that in introducing the twelve digit-number for the benefit of the 'residents', an exceptionally broad term, the sponsors of the UID project might be administering a kind of development on which they neither have any conscious planning nor any decisive control, but it is something which they nevertheless have to justify somehow.

One can substantiate the argument being made here by referring to certain points – all of which have great implications for the migrants – however small a space they are accorded in the mission statement of the project.

First and foremost, amidst the self-promotional claims of 'unfailing precision' of the new technologies the UID project picks it up in claiming 'authentic' identification and verification. The claim is backed by the logic that it is 'robust enough to eliminate duplicate and fake identities'. But is such a process, along with such claims, necessarily final and faultless? The project provides a long list of 'introducers' – elected local body members, members of local administrative bodies, postmen, teachers, health workers, doctors, Aanganwadi/ASHA workers, representatives of local NGOs and so forth. What if an illegal migrant manages to procure an 'introducer' from among his informal network of acquaintances or from fly-by-night organisations thriving on illegal migration and get the coveted number to possess a false identity or even a 'stolen identity' of a resident/ citizen? Even technologists acknowledge that the digitisation of 'coded' identity in binary (0 and 1) format and even the 'most precise' biometric attributes of individuals are not necessarily perfect, raising doubts about its claim of de-duplication. When it comes to the biometric forms of identification there are quite a few possibilities of 'mistakes' or 'slips' committed by biometric technologies, and no less important, the almost nonexistent mechanisms for finding out and correcting them. As Aas points out, biometrics 'tend(s) to be presented as "silver bullet" solutions to pressing problems. However, the implementation of these technologies, as any other, is not unproblematic as they are open to inaccuracy, misuse and privacy violations. . . .'[15] Interestingly, the claims of 'authenticity' is weakened by the warning of 'strict action' against the collusion of introducer with the candidate for enrolment – which reveals scope for manipulation. The Indian rulers, it can be pointed out, have not yet gone as far as their counterparts in Europe in which the Eurodac database is also supposed to identify 'stereotypical narratives' of asylum-seekers and thereby look for any 'external help' in filing false declaration.

Second, on a more abstract and complex question, the UID, which is essentially an identification exercise, claims that it would 'guarantee identity', with the implicit assumption and implication that without the number we are 'identity-less'. Here one can explain, following Aas's observation, that the very assumption behind the notion of identity loss has a subtle but strong materialist dimension that identity is something detached from one's self, having an objective and thing-like quality, like money. Describing asylum-seekers as 'identity-less' therefore presupposes that they do not have the kind of identity required by state bureaucracy: a stable, objective, unambiguous and thing-like identity.[16] But apart from the fact that the project does not differentiate between 'identity' and 'identification', in this very claim it brings to the fore a fundamental question: can identity as a whole be digitalised, or at best can certain segments be? Even while acknowledging the fact that digitisation till date is the most sophisticated mode in the long historical trajectory of technological mediation of human agency and in the even longer tradition of recording of data, it is not yet powerful enough to reduce all of us to digitally mediated signifiers – something which the UID project, at least by implication, aspires to.

Third, the UID project in celebrating the power of the number reminds us of Armand Mattelart's compelling analysis of the 'politics of number fixation'. In the specific context of the project the Indian state provides us with a *voluntary-in-proclamation but not-so-voluntary-in-practice* opportunity to lead life with a number. The contradiction is inscribed in the following manner. While it states that 'enrolment will not be mandated,' it observes that 'benefits and services that are linked to the UID will ensure demand for the number.' It also adds that nothing precludes governments or Registrars 'from mandating enrolment.' It also proclaims, '[t]here is tremendous value to be gained from widespread adoption of the UID for authentication, especially for residents. While enrolment in the UID database will ensure that residents are not denied access to fundamental services and rights because they cannot present positive proof of identity, adoption in authentication could go one step further, and ensure that residents consistently receive these services. This can include a wide range of benefits such as education, health coverage, old-age pensions and subsidised food grains, thereby fulfilling the UIDAI's pro-poor agenda.'[17] Thus, while possessing the number has not been made mandatory by it, simultaneously it makes adequate arrangements by forging linkage and coordination among various governmental, public sector, non-governmental and private organisations in a manner that one may develop the feeling of being severely constrained in day-to-day dealings by not having the number. Thus, by generating a sense of insecurity among its people the insecure state seeks to 'secure' itself.

Lastly, its welfarist claims of 'efficient delivery of welfare services', of 'effective monitoring of various programmes and schemes' of the government and of financial inclusion notwithstanding, the project betrays huge security obsession. While the security issue has not been made explicit, by implication it assumes great proportions, beginning with its linkage with National Intelligence Grid (NATGRID) and associated linkage with various security and intelligence agencies, including the Intelligence Bureau, Research and Analysis Wing, Central Bureau of Investigation, Directorate of Revenue Intelligence, central boards of excise and customs and of direct taxes, Narcotics Control Bureau and so forth. The organisational coordination also reiterates our claim of the anxiety-prone 'insecure' state. The nature of organisations mentioned here reveals that the state, rather than being assisted by relevant organisational network for efficient and effective delivery of services and welfare schemes is more guided by 'threat perception' from within, which makes such organisational 'convergence inevitable.'[18] From yet another vantage point, this is in tune with the status of the UID as governmentality-driven technique because in operating through the regime of living governmentality requires to be distributed throughout the society through various institutions and organisations.

All the aforementioned points reinstate our claim that the project is 'imperfect' and 'incomplete'. In this context one can cite the observation of the Standing Committee on Finance (2011-2012) of the Parliament on the project: 'The UID scheme has been conceptualised with no clarity of purpose and leaving many things to be sorted out during the course of its implementation; and is being implemented in a directionless way with a lot of confusion.'[19] No doubt the migrants (at least those with some legal recognition), many of whom are forced to be so out of compulsion, are in dire need of access to various forms of social security, food entitlement, education, health and so forth. It is also apparently an attractive proposition that they would have all these entitlements by carrying a number. But even if for a moment one accepts the concern of the government for the migrants to be genuine, the fact remains that with the existing distributional system with all its shortcomings remaining intact and the prevalent power relations unchanged, there can at best be cosmetic change in their entitlements.

WAYS OUT: SUBVERSION AND 'VOICE'

In the specific context of the UID project, it is worth remembering that giant strides are being taken without much public debate. We have already mentioned that technology-related debates show a marked tendency to be relegated to the zone of silence. Elia Zureik depicts a bleak, if not dreadful, picture of the future, which is attributed to the scant attention being paid to unsubstantiated claims of the technology and its unintended consequences.[20] Zureik refers to three main convergent forces: first, there is little willingness to question the reliability of the technology lest one is accused of being a Luddite and against progress; second, the formidable lobbying campaign, mounted by corporate stakeholders since 9/11, to adopt biometric technology has found more than willing partners in the corridors of power; and third, the use of biometrics for surveillance purposes will contribute to widening the surveillance net and gathering of personal information that goes beyond security concerns to include aspects of day-to-day governance and administration.[21] In the foregoing discussion we have dealt with all the three in some detail. Yet, we would continue to reinforce the adage that control begets resistance and agency. It is no less true in the case of the UID project and the migrants' negotiation with it. While technology boasts of precision and exactness human agency remains elusive even to best modes of control. All over the world, migrants, especially the 'unwanted' variety, are showing remarkable skill in escaping monitoring and surveillance, when sought to be captured as 'disembodied avatars' in digital realm. Even the most efficiently administered states of the west are not immune to the subversive counter-strategies of the migrants who continue to violate, transgress and overturn the strategies of monitoring and surveillance.

As already mentioned, there are various 'nodes' – from informal networks to organisational networks – to take up the cases of the migrants favourably by minimising their risks.

We may contextualise the UID project, in the light of the experience of the illegal migrants' subversive negotiations with passports and ration cards – the traditional tools of documentation – in India. It is an open secret that in different parts of India a vast number of illegal migrants have efficiently and effectively procured both, and thereby acquired legal status. Border states, like Assam and West Bengal, can be cited here as leading instances. In the specific context of the UID, it is worth exploring the case of Tripura which has been 'most successful' in terms of enrolment among the states – reinstating its earlier success in cent per cent enrolment in voter's identity cards. Does it emerge from a government seeking to refurbish its image in governance, or does it come out of a hidden concern of a state which has seen some of the worst cases of violence on the migration issue, or is the obsessive zeal[22] for enrolment an outcome of both? In contrasting cases, the strategy of the migrants – of both the legal and illegal variety – can be to escape the radar and simply not get enrolled, not even by fraudulent means. Remaining undocumented, and un-digitised in the case of the UID project, can prove to be a great advantage because it not only makes them 'unmanageable' but also protects them from any kind of offensive measures and retaliation by the state to which the immigrants, to borrow Aas's term, are more of 'crimmigrants'.[23] On some other occasions the urge can be to get enrolled, by fair (in the case of legal migrants) or foul means (in the case of unwanted migrants) to procure the promised benefits. Even in a single migrant family, and the probability is much more in terms of the broader migrant community, the response might vary not only among men, but also in cases of women, children and the elderly.

In both the contrasting strategies – urge for enrolment and the rationale of non-enrolment – the migrants might be acting reflexively and meaningfully to engage/ disengage with the project. Antje Ellerman relates this to the liberal state by observing that even in the space of greatest powerlessness migrants (particularly those without legal standing) by rendering themselves unclassifiable often succeed in tying the hands of the liberal state, which not only is forced to operate within the constraints of the international legal order – making repatriation contingent on the possession of identity documents – but is also constitutionally and normatively limited in its exercise of coercion against the individual.[24] There is a marked tendency among the leading scholars analysing the subversive techniques as 'everyday forms of resistance' of the migrants to bring back James Scott's well-known phrase 'weapons of the weak' and include acts of passive non-compliance, sabotage, subtle evasion, and deception in it.[25] The reference is also made to 'everyday politics of mystification' to further explain that the counterstrategies can be captured under the notion of 'foggy social structures', social structures that emerge from efforts by individuals and organisations to avoid the production of knowledge about their activities by making them either unobservable or indeterminable – the practical production of fog.[26] One can even argue that there is a strong possibility that the migrants, being in the objective conditions that they are in, would more carefully weigh the pros and cons of engagement and disengagement with projects like the UID more than their much more secure counterparts who may become 'highly active' in enrolling themselves in hordes and thereby lose the capacity to critically engage with and mediate these kinds of projects.

Yet, subversive strategies though widespread do not comprise the only counterpoint to –the only way of resisting or protesting against – the modes of monitoring and surveillance and the use of new technologies as technique of governance. The act of resistance or protest does not only concern the migrants, within the broader horizons of politics of digitisation; it concerns others as well. While for the migrants, who are at a particularly disadvantageous position, subversion, resting on a kind of cat-and-mouse game, may have its immediate attraction, for the 'population' (the referent object of the techniques of governmentality and biopolitics) it is important to initiate and intensify resistance or protest 'from within', especially in their struggle for rights and claims making. Following Hirschman's well-known formulation, we would argue that 'voice', rather than 'exit', perhaps provides the way out. Interestingly, because of a dominant trend set by the economists, Hirschman's framework, despite the inclusion of the 'states' in the title of the book, has been mostly restricted to firms and organisation. In our view, we can reinstate, through the idea of 'voice', its scope in the context of the state's negotiations with citizens, residents and migrants. Let us quote Hirschman to substantiate our claim: 'Exit is . . . neat – one exists or one does not, it is impersonal – any face-to-face confrontation . . . is imponderable and unpredictable elements is (*sic*) avoided and success and failure of the organisation are communicated . . . by statistics, and it is indirect . . . . In all respects voice is just the opposite of exit. It is a far more "messy" concept because it can be graduated, all the way from faint grumbling to violent protest; it implies articulation of one's critical opinions rather than a private, 'secret' vote in the anonymity of a supermarket, and finally, it is direct and straightforward rather than roundabout. Voice is political action par excellence.'[27] 'Voice', Hirschman adds, is also '. . . any attempt at all to change, rather than to escape from, an objectionable state of affairs, whether through individual or collective petition to the management directly in charge, through appeal to a higher authority with intention of forcing a change in management, or through various types of actions or protests, including those that are meant to mobilise public opinion.'[28]

'Voice' thus is an active-constructive behavioural mode while 'exit' is inherently detached and destructive. To reiterate Hirschman's argument, 'voice' is dynamic and constantly evolving in new directions while 'exit' rests on an either/or logic. 'Voice', as distinct from the economistic action of 'exit', results in the validation of adopted positions and policies of the rulers – including the emergence of appropriate institutions and mechanisms – through the interplay of varying and contending opinions, ideas and perspectives. It thus prevents the possibility of remaining inactive, often induced by passive modes like 'loyalty' (in Hirschman's phrases, 'waiting and hoping that things will improve', 'giving things some time', 'praying for improvement' – which may only on certain occasions give rise to 'voice'), or 'neglect' ('refusing to discuss problems' or 'just letting things fall apart') vis-à-vis the policies. 'Voice' also significantly reduces the blind conformity to the policies adopted and implemented in the name of the people.

In this context, India can learn a thing or two from another developing country, Brazil. I have elaborated elsewhere the process of democratisation of the information technology policies of Brazil.[29] Suffice it to mention here, in terms of 'domestic' efforts at constructing an IT-friendly inclusive society, Brazil has devised a National Information Society Plan (NISP), which is intimately connected to the ambitious Avanca Brasil (Advance Brazil) Development Plan. The major goal of the NISP is to integrate, coordinate and foster actions for utilisation of IT and, in turn, to contribute to 'the social inclusion of all Brazilians in the new society'. The idea is to ensure that the technical leap forward has results in terms of human, ethical and economic development. More important in our context, the NISP calls for the creation of: i) a more just society based on preservation of cultural identity and wealth of diversity; ii) a sustainable development path that respects differences and promotes regional equality; iii) effective participation of the society in the process as the prime requirement of political democracy. *Information Society in Brazil: Green Book* (2000) is the main reference point for the construction of an IT-inclusive society in Brazil. In his 'Presentation' in the book, the then Minister of State for Science and Technology, Ronaldo Mota Sardenberg, notes that the report has been created with a conscious effort to 'fuel a debate' among the political leaders, bureaucrats, business community and other concerned segments of the Brazilians.[30] The minister implores civil society to come forward and involve itself in debates and deliberations 'to establish clear political lines of action to be followed' and 'to develop strategic activities'. It mentions that the government and civil society 'must work together' in order to assure the prospect that positive aspects of such a society 'effectively benefit all Brazilians'. One can also cite the case of Israel in this context. 'Voice' has also achieved success there amidst an intense debate in which the civil society organisations played a pro-active role. On 23 July 2012, Israel's High Court of Justice held a hearing on a petition filed by civil rights advocates who sought to strike down a law establishing a governmental biometric database and an associated two-year pilot programme.[31] The law approving the database, enacted in 2009, met with public resistance until the government backed down and agreed to begin with only the pilot programme. The pilot was supposed to be a test for determining whether it was actually necessary to move forward with building the biometric database, but an Interior Ministry decree that sanctioned the programme did not actually contain any criteria to measure whether the programme succeeded or failed. While the judgment does not abandon the project it determined that the pilot-programme description has to present clear criteria for success and failure. The ruling requires the Interior Ministry to examine the very necessity of a central database, and to seriously weigh possible alternatives. The court also called for an independent review of the programme. One can see a positive trend in India in which the 'voice', scrutinising the UID project, is increasingly becoming shriller though it has to acquire much more momentum. Politics of technology has never been an issue in the otherwise impressive array of social movements and civil-society activism in India but the UID project has given a fillip to explore this hitherto underrated dimension.

This brings us back again to the question of governance. In the specific contexts of e-governance and digitisation there is no doubt that a systematic process of awareness generation, prompted by adequate publicity, is of great importance. But the problem occurs when the publicity blitz reaches such an extent that governance itself becomes a 'victim' of e-governance. As a result, the impression gains ground that human interactions are replaceable by electronic connectivity, and more dangerously, it has to be so in the name of better governance. As part of the process, the whole discourse of e-governance-induced development is constructed in terms of *interactivity* and *connectivity*, and much less on the basis of *interactions* and *connections*. But governance is supposed to be a process that slowly but steadily builds itself up on the basis of trial-and-error method, which involves a search for the 'best alternative' by scrutinising past and future course of actions and policies. When e-governance is presented as too 'smooth' and too 'smart' a process it misses the rigour of governance. Simply put, digitisation should add to such rigour, rather than eliminating it in the name of efficiency, mostly measured in economistic and technical terms. This in turn results in underdeveloped and half-formed institutions, low level of citizen participation in issues of common concern and lack of normative dimension of development and governance.

CONCLUSION

The preceding discussion, keeping the UID project and the migrants' issue at the forefront, provides certain clues to the politics of digitisation and the dialectics of the corporal and the technological. One need not go as far as to trace an 'evil design' in the digitisation process, and in not doing so one might even find some 'good intentions' at work to ensure better governance. But at the same time one needs to reiterate that aggressive promotion of such digital intervention runs the risk of exclusion of the underprivileged, of which migrants invariably constitute a sizeable section. The argument here is not that since the digitisation process, or for that matter any kind of introduction of new technologies, is an expensive venture, it should not be undertaken in a developing society. It is more important to emphasise that any effort to adopt a 'fast track' approach in this regard without adequate information generation might be counterproductive. The whole process involves multi-layered communication, which in a major way includes various intersections arising out of ground-level, face-to-face, *organic* interactions among policymakers, community members/leaders/ opinion-makers at local levels, and the potential and/or actual users/ stakeholders. While we are supposed to be in the midst of an Information Revolution of some sort, 'information drought' lies at the base of an extraordinary variety of social exclusion and marginalisation of ordinary citizens in developing countries like India. A technologically-inclusive society, however promising, cannot take effective shape unless it is solidly backed by the construction of an information-inclusive order. To take advantage of the power of Information Revolution and to utilise the benefits of digitisation for creating enabling environment, we need to have a *cultural understanding* of technology based on decentralised inter-subjectivity, which in turn would go beyond the black box of mechanistic and technocratic notions of governance and the dreadful vision of panoptican India bent on translating human identity into information bytes.

NOTES

1. Rabinow, Paul, ed., *The Foucault Reader*, Pantheon Books: New York, 1984, p.338; for further discussion on the emergence of the concept of governmentality, G. Burchell, C. Gordon and P. Miller, eds., "Governmentality", *The Foucault Effect: Studies in Governmentality, with two lectures by and an interview with Michel Foucault, Harvester, Wheatsheaf*: Hemel Hempstead, Hertfordshire, 1991, pp.87-104. For the concept of biopolitics see, Michel Foucault, "The Birth of Biopolitics" in Michel Foucault, *Ethics, Subjectivity and Truth*, ed. by Paul Rabinow, the New Press, New York, 1997, pp.73-79
2. Harris, Jan Ll., and Paul A. Taylor, *Digital Matters: Theory and Culture of the Matrix*, Routledge: London and New York, 2005, p.x.
3. Kroker, Arthur, "The New Biometric State", *Born Again Ideology: Religion, Technology, and Terrorism*, http://www.ctheory.net/articles.aspx?id=549 [Accessed on 15 November 2012].
4. Benjamin, Solomon, R. Bhuvaneswari, P. Rajan and Manjunatha, "Bhoomi: 'E-Governance', Or, An Anti-Politics Machine Necessary to Globalise Bangalore?" *a CASUM-m Working Paper*, January 2007, p.26
5. Ibid
6. Meyer, Thomas (with Lew Hinchman), *Media Democracy: How the Media Colonise Politics*, Polity Press: Cambridge, 2002, p.57.
7. Wajcman, Judy, "Addressing Technological Change: The Challenge to Social Theory", *Current Sociology* 50(3), 2002, pp.347-63
8. Sinha, Dipankar, "On Forgetting History: Information and Communication Technology and the Colonisation of Politics in Post-Colonial India", in Amiya K. Bagchi, Dipankar Sinha and Barnita Bagchi (eds.), *Webs of History: Information, Communication and Technology from the Early to Post-Colonial India*, Manohar, Delhi, 2005, pp.135-61.
9. Beck, Ulrich, "Subpolitics: Ecology and the Disintegration of Institutional Power", in *World Risk Society*, Polity: Cambridge, 1999, pp.91-108.
10. http://uidai.gov.in/index.php?option=com_content&view=article&id=145&Itemid=2 [Accessed on 15 November 2012]
11. "UIDAI Strategy Overview: Creating a Unique Identity Number for Every Resident in India", Unique Identification Authority of India, Planning Commission, Government of India, April, 2010, p.1, http://uidai.gov.in/UID_PDF/Front_Page_Articles/Documents/Strategy_Overveiw-001.pdf [Accessed on 15 November 2012]
12. Ibid, p.4
13. Ruppert, Evelyn, "Population Objects: Interpassive Subjects", *Sociology* 45(2), 2011, p.228

14. Broeders, Dennis, "The New Digital Borders of Europe: EU Databases and the Surveillance of Irregular Migrants', *International Sociology*, January 2007, Vol.22(1), p.89.
15. Aas, Katja Franko, "'The Body Does Not Lie': Identity, Risk and Trust in Technoculture", *Crime, Media, Culture*, 2 (2), 2006, p.151
16. Ibid, p.147.
17. "UIDAI Strategy Overview," p.26
18. Ramanathan, Usha, "A Unique Identity Bill", *Economic and Political Weekly*, 45: 30, 2010, pp.10-14
19. *Forty Second Report; Standing Committee on Finance (2011-2012)*, Lok Sabha Secretariat, New Delhi, 2011.
20. Zureik, Elia, "Governance, Security and Technology: The Case of Biometrics", *Studies in Political Economy 73*, Spring/Summer, 2004, pp.113-37
21. Ibid, p.133
22. Incidentally, in the UID enrolment form the Government of Tripura has added an extra section requiring more information than what is required under the project.
23. Aas, Katja Franko, "'Crimmigrant' Bodies and Bona Fide Travellers: Surveillance, Citizenship and Global Governance", *Theoretical Criminology* 15:3, 2011, pp.331-46
24. Ellermann, Antje, "Undocumented Migrants and Resistance in the Liberal State", *Politics & Society*, 38:3, p.409
25. Ibid; Also, Dennis Broeders and Godfried Engbersen, "'The Fight Against Illegal Migration': Identification Policies and Immigrants' Counterstrategies", *American Behavioural Scientist* 50:12, 2007, pp.1592-609
26. Broeders and Engbersen, "The Fight Against Illegal Migration", p.1594.
27. Hirschman, A. O., *Exit, Voice, and Loyalty: Responses to Decline in Firms, Organisations, and States*, Harvard University Press: Cambridge, Mass, 1970, pp.15-16
28. Ibid, p.30
29. Sinha, Dipankar, "(De)Politicising Information Technology: Towards an Inclusionary Framework", Working Paper 19, Department of Media and Communications, London School of Economics, 2010, www2.lse.ac.uk/media@lse/research/mediaWorkingPapers/pdf/EWPP19.pdf [Accessed 15 November 2012]
30. *Information Society in Brazil: Green Book*, Ministry of Science and Technology, Brasilia, 2000
31. Bowe, Rebecca, "Israel's Biometric Database Deemed 'Harmful' by High Court Justices", *Electronic Frontier Foundation*, 27 July 2012, www.eff.org/deeplinks/2012/07/israels-biometric-database-deemed-harmful-high-court-justices [Accessed on 15 November 2012]

II

The Long and Short History of Identification Technologies

Atig Ghosh

Members of the small pastoral community of the Toda people, who live on the isolated Nilgiri plateau of Southern India, dislike uttering their own names. The taboo is so powerful among some that, if they are asked for their name, they will ask someone else to give it.[1] The Todas are, of course, not unique in their passion to preserve onomastic secrecy. In a custom that is almost extinct today, Bengali wives fought shy of naming their husbands in public – or even in private. In situations of public interaction that made the naming of one's husband obligatory, therefore, women of an anterior generation would resort to elaborate riddles that gave away their spouses' names. This way they did not have to name names, so to speak. World over, too, such instances are legion. The Sakalavas of Madagaskar do not communicate their own name or the name of their village to strangers in case mischievous use is made of it. In fairytales and folklore, there are many examples of forbidden names which, when revealed, break the evil power of their owners – Dancing Vargaluska, Joaidane, Daiku to Oniroku, Ruidoquedito, or most famously for Anglophone readers, Rumpelstiltskin. In New Zealand and Australia, people of some tribes are given two names – a 'public' name, for general use, and a 'secret' name, which is known only to God, or to the closest members of their group; for to get to know a secret name is to have total power over its owner.[2] To many, such practices may seem quaint. Yet, for the members of such groups these practices have powerful emotional traction and their violation may cause, at the least, extreme mental duress.

Prefacing a paper on the historical logic and trajectory of technologies of identification with an inventory of cautious onomastic-identitary socio-cultural practices serves two purposes. It identifies the conundrum that is central to all-encompassing strategies of identification – specifically, in the context of this book's principal concern, the Aadhaar scheme (a unique identification project under the aegis of the Unique Identification Authority of India, or UIDAI, established in February 2009). Even in the case of recording something that would seem as accessible in the public domain as the proper name, identities may be destabilised and imperilled. It also raises questions about the effectuality of all-encompassing identificatory projects *per se* (and *mutatis mutandis*) trans-historically for South Asia. And, following on the idea that to know a secret name is to have total power over its owner, the paper begs the question whether such a power-knowledge nexus is not at work among the officials and proponents of Aadhaar. The Aadhaar scheme, of course, far exceeds the onomastic brief that is being propaedeutically set out here. It encompasses, or proposes to encompass, all axes of an individual's identity and, in doing so, stokes a number of knotty questions and angry debates. As this paper hopes to demonstrate, much of the technological drive to identify and slot people totally and permanently has over the last two centuries remained mired in the same sort of controversy.

Also, relevant to the theme of this book is the argument that the introductory discussion on proper names shows how groups (societies?) assume an interlocutory Other – the stranger. Without this shadowy figure's lurking presence, such secretive practices would be pointless. Now, the stranger is not a person who belongs to another world – a world which is beyond far and near. 'The stranger, like the poor and like sundry "inner enemies", is an element of the group itself. His position as a full-fledged member involves both being outside it and confronting it,' says Georg Simmel. The figure of the stranger represents a 'unity of nearness and remoteness', since strangeness means that 'he, who . . . is far, is actually near.'[3] The figure of the stranger presents the unity between the two *conceptional* poles of wandering – understood as the liberation from every given point in space – and fixation at such a point. The stranger is thus not a wanderer who comes today and goes tomorrow, but rather the person who comes today and stays tomorrow. 'He is . . . the *potential* wanderer: although he has not moved on, he has not quite overcome the freedom of coming and going. . . . [H]is position in th[e] group is determined, essentially by the fact that he has not belonged to it from the beginning, that he imports qualities into it, which do not and cannot stem from the group itself.'[4] The figure of the stranger then simultaneously challenges, and inflects, what may be loosely termed the Weberian *Zusammengehörigkeitsgefühl* – the feeling of belonging together, the sense of 'groupness'.[5]

The Simmelian 'stranger', of course, stands in as a hypocorism for a range of figures who challenge and inflect the homogenising, boundary-drawing imperatives of groups, which, as has been argued above, by their very ontological compulsions have to be somewhat xenophobic. On statist registers, the 'stranger' is rendered as the quasi- or non-citizen – the refugee, the asylum seeker, the stateless person, even the IDP, and so on – who represents the imminent irruption of the Heimlich pleasures of the hearth, who shakes up the smug and secure self-image of the state.

An account of colonial constitutionalism indicates that the rights discourse started with the right to conquest and colonise – a classic case is of the attempts made by the colonial stranger to map the 'strangers' among the 'natives', as we shall see. Legitimising conquest and violence became the concern of political theories and laws, in South Asia and beyond. The question that has to be asked today is: Have these foundational features of colonial politics dwindled with the advent of a democratic post-colonial system? In answering this question, one agrees with Ranabir Samaddar's observation: 'in the light of the daily skirmishes, and the massive conflagrations, which occur in the wake of the conflicts around immigrations into a settled society of a nation-state, and show that while political theorists were predicting that by and large large-scale violence was over, conquest was no more a feature of politics, and all it needed was to study the cultural chronicles of life to understand politics, immigration brings out the deep insecurity that a nation lives with and therefore gets busy with making laws, promulgating measures, and forging weapons to prevent an invading army of aliens.'[6]

This apocalyptic vision is not overstated. That the state is 'making laws, promulgating measures, and forging weapons to prevent an invading army of aliens', to my mind, is not in doubt. The UID project itself is an example. In an official site dedicated exclusively to the subject, the UIDAI claims that '[t]he UIDAI's mandate is to issue every resident a unique identification number linked to the resident's demographic and biometric information, which they can use to identify themselves anywhere in India, and to access a host of benefits and services.'[7] Governmental expatiation on the subject is couched in the language of welfare. It speaks in terms of the benefits and advantages that would accrue to the people once they enrol themselves. It seeks to reconstitute, in a more solid, unambiguous incarnation, the figure of the citizen. However, in proposing to do so, it inevitably invokes the spectre of the non-citizen – she who is beyond the ambit of citizenship. The non-citizen residents make up, though a minority in terms of numbers, a significant cross-section of the resident population in India; they find themselves in a polity (and society) that displays unique features in terms of how it regulates the presence and exit of foreigners in its territory, which is often configured and visualised in terms of circles. Thus one may be a migrant in one part of the territory, in another part not. One may be allowed to visit or settle in one area, in another part not. And the state-sponsored 'benefits and services', surely, would not accrue to them. The language of welfare therefore masks an anxiety for securitisation. It is also important to note that the UID project proposes to gather demographic and biometric information on the individual citizen to produce a single-window identificatory device. It would be the identification to end and supersede all other identification – be it the ration card, the Permanent Account Number (PAN), the Electoral Photo Identity Card (Epic), or what you will. It would be the state's master marker of identity.

This paper will build upon the logic of this statist digital-identification project to contend that identificatory technologies (where 'technologies' are understood as strategies of power implicated in the ordering, classification and control of individual bodies, as governmental practices designed to produce docile bodies[8]) have, through colonial history, claimed to be unique, universal, ubiquitous.[9] The 'tangible' nature of the technology may have changed depending on context or time – it has been fine-tuned over time, its penetrability and scope deepened and broadened – but the undergirding logic has remained the same: to encompass all in the power-knowledge complex of governmentality. Be it penal tattooing in early nineteenth century, descriptive rolls, convict photography, *Bertillonage*, anthropometrics, dactyloscopy, or the introduction of passports, technological identification has served the abovementioned end faithfully. The dual language of welfare and securitisation, too, is not unique to the postcolonial dispensation – this paper will try to argue. Further, in the case of criminals and migrant labour, that is marginal groups or groups considered comparatively untameable, it seems security concerns have always outweighed the welfare rhetoric – the impact of such identity-fixing techniques on these groups have been relentlessly oppressive. The sane and sanitised self-image of such identificatory technologies, of colonial and postcolonial provenance alike, cannot stand up to historical re-interrogation.

From the incunabula of the nineteenth century at least, in the metropolis as well as its colonial peripheries, attempts to technologise, and therefore render foolproof, identification have been legion. Identificatory techniques aimed to mark the body in some way and render it visible was necessary in Britain because the massive social and economic changes of the nineteenth century – notably industrialisation and migration – disrupted the community networks and personal connections on which identification had formerly relied. The effort to establish a broader, more stable relationship between sedentarisation, statecraft and social legibility, as witnessed signally in the introduction of the first census in 1801, has been surveyed by James C. Scott, among others.[10]

In South Asia, the colonial government could act with a far greater degree of impunity, and therefore arbitrariness, than at 'home', but that does not mean it could act completely without at least a cover of welfarist rhetoric. This is not to overemphasise, as perhaps Anil Seal does, the importance of British imperial initiatives in achieving modernisation, neglecting the role played by South Asian initiatives,[11] but to emphasise that perhaps it is in the very nature and logic of liberal governance that it cannot wholly shed its welfarist self-image. To put it baldly, the colonial government did not hang all its criminals, not even the recidivist ones; it tried, conversely, to track them, document them, control them, render them productive for the purposes of the colonial state, as in, say, the use of criminal labour in road gangs.[12]

And, indeed, much of the identificatory technologies were directed at mapping and harnessing labour in general. The 'up-stick' nature of villages – labour villages – to use colonial administrator M.C. MacAlpin's words, unsettled the sedentarising, and thereby the stabilising, imperatives of the colonial state. But, how did the colonial government try to achieve this fit between the inherently mobile nature of labour and the need to garrison them at sites of production? To achieve this, the elusive figure of the labourer had to be rendered fixed, permanent and visible through identificatory technology and made amenable to colonial deployment. What was generated in the process was a state of mobile knowledge for a mobile population – a knowledge pool, that is, which was available at all centres of productive application across the empire. Here, already, and much before Gilles Deleuze would have us believe, we see that the 'walls' of the Foucauldian disciplinary society breaking down in the colony and making way for a mobile society of control – at least partially.[13] A *complete* passage from the striated space of disciplinary society to the smooth space of the society of control may still have to wait till the world wars of the next century, but the coexistence of the two societal modes – coexistent in a co-constitutive tension, if I may add – can hardly be contested: an argument we shall return to later. This 'total' identificatory project, of course, remained, in Antoinette Burton's telling phrase, yet another 'unfinished business' of colonial modernity.[14] And it may not be rash to suggest that this imperative to garrison inherently footloose labour at the site of production continues to animate at least a part of the initiative behind the postcolonial state's identificatory projects.

As I have been trying to argue, the colonial state invariably found technological solutions to identificatory conundrums. At the heart of all such supervisory strategies lies the desire to establish stable identities. To the statist optic, this can be done by linking individual identity firmly and finally to the body of an individual, which is taken to be a stable entity across space and time. If the body could be rendered legible, then it could be easily controlled and managed. Knowledge of the body constitutes power relations, and those power relations also constitute a field of knowledge.[15] For the colonial state (as for its post-colonial heir), this will to power-knowledge was sought to be realised through typically technological solutions.

Perhaps one of the best documented sites for the workings of such colonial technological desires directed at identity fixing was a marginal body – that of the criminal, say. The choice of criminal bodies is appropriate. Criminals of colonial South Asia (especially those described as belonging to the criminal tribes after the promulgation of the notorious Criminal Tribes Acts from 1871) were often itinerants, resisting the sedentarising and identity-fixing imperatives of colonial rule. In this sense, they were the original migrants, the standard bearers of what Christopher A. Bayly has described as the other India – that of the itinerants, the migrants, the peripatetic groups[16] – which the British sought to tame and the post-colonial state continues to seek to tame. By the year of independence, the Acts classified 13 million people as criminal types, and imposed disciplinary measures to control them. Criminal tribes, once classified, were made subject to registration and a pass system, and forced into reformatory and agricultural settlements, which like prisons and penal settlements tried to restrict their mobility. This was an attempt to transform groups into settled communities and reclaim them as what Sanjay Nigam calls 'the moral subjects of the Raj.'[17] What the post-colonial state does to the migrants, IDPs, refugees, stateless people and sundry other non-citizen groups is not much unalike; only one is tempted to say, speaking in the name of the 'people', the contemporary state can sometimes be harsher, yet retain its moral legitimacy. This state, like its colonial predecessor, must also overproduce 'moral subjects' who conform.

Further, to look at how the colonial state tried to tame and micro-manage certain obstreperous groups is not merely to track the continuum of the colonial and post-colonial state's attitude towards migrants but also to approximate the idea as to how identificatory technologies tested on marginal groups, to begin with, could then be seamlessly mapped on to the society at large. As David Arnold has persuasively demonstrated in a slightly different but germane context, prisons were metaphors for broader social practices in the construction of colonial knowledge.[18] And to extend the point, we may quote Deleuze, who writes, 'It's the prison which serves as the analogical model.' He cites the example of Roberto Rossellini's neorealist film *Europa '51* (1952) in which the heroine, on seeing some labourers, could exclaim: 'I thought I was seeing convicts.'[19] Approaching the issue from the opposite end, Clare Anderson, looking at three photographs of South Asian male convicts taken in 1875, remarks: 'Though it was clear that they were not typical ethnographic shots, at least at first glance they could have been photographs of South Asian labourers.'[20] So compellingly pervasive can be the carceral analogical model – even to the tutored eye.

Attempts at technological inscription of identity on to errant bodies had started in the late eighteenth and early nineteenth century, when the colonial government resorted to penal tattooing or *godna*, the permanent marking of name, crime and date of the sentence on the forehead of the convicted offenders. One comes across this permanent mark of criminality in convict descriptive rolls, detailed records of physical appearances that accompanied Indian convicts into transportation to penal settlements in South East Asia and the Indian Ocean during the first half of the nineteenth century. Like transportation convicts, life prisoners incarcerated in mainland gaols were also subject to *godna*, which can be looked at as the inscription of colonial power on the body. However, *godna* was abolished in 1849. British opinion deemed it too inhuman to permanently scar a body with penal marks.

It could also be that the British found *godna* to be an ineffective measure, from the punitive point of view as well as the identificatory. Clare Anderson, drawing on Ashis Nandy's idea of the colonial ordering of gender identities, though, believes that *godna* was perhaps punitively effective: it emasculated men who thought of tattoos as feminine embellishment.[21] This could be true, but for an unsettling caveat. Tattoo could also be a mark of military status in South Asia. The *chehra-o-dagh* system – keeping detailed description of each soldier and each horse, the latter accompanied by branding – of Alauddin Khalji (reigning from 1296 to 1316), once introduced, had become the standard procedure of (military) administration for all the Sultans and the Mughals later.[22] That is to say, for the South Asian male population, 'tattoo' was not something that exclusively adorned female bodies, but could as well be associated with military identification. Underlying the humane concern of the colonial government, then, was the concern about its doubtful punitive efficacy. But greater perhaps was the anxiety that penal tattooing could not effectively render the body legible. Textualisation of the body – the 'conquest of [individual] illegibility'[23], so central to the process of centralised state-building – proved to be an intractable process. There is of course the valuable argument that identities and bodies are mutually constitutive. Shifting identities render the body intractable. But even at a more prosaic level, bodies do actually, physically change: people go bald, blind, grow old, teeth fall off, beards grow, moustaches disappear, scars fill out, congenital marks and tattoos fade: thus rendering hopelessly ambiguous the jaunty circulation of power-knowledge. And then there is ample evidence to suggest convicts sometimes wilfully tried to spoil or erase their tattoos. The gaol clerk describing Nubba, who was transported to Mauritius in 1815, for instance, wrote 'the Bengally characters written with the Godena on his forehead is [*sic*] nearly effaced.'[24]

Did Nubba deliberately try to erase the penal tattoo, or was it the natural mutation of the body that had 'nearly effaced' it? One can never be sure. The British, however, not unlike the postcolonial state, approached the problem not as one of the body's social and physical mutability but as a glitch in technological sophistication. That is, better-conceived technology would more effectively textualise the elusive body; render it transparent to the state's Sauron-like all-seeing gaze. They refused to understand, as Martin Heidegger would insist much later in 1949, that the question concerning technology is not a technological question, that 'the essence of technology is by no means anything technological.'[25] To elaborate, it is not so much the existence of technology or the forms it takes, but rather our *orientation* to technology that is crucial. This formulation of the problem makes it clear that our response to the various problems brought about by technology cannot be solved simply by making the technology better. But the colonial administrators could not have read Heidegger (nor clearly have their postcolonial heirs). As such, they persisted in chasing the elusive goal of finding a solution to the identificatory challenge through technological improvement.

Since technologies of marking the body permanently were proving to be ineffective, colonial administrators resorted to documenting the body in detail in order to, at a later stage, to be able to relate the 'exhaustively documented' description to the potentially criminal body. That is, 'writing on the body gave way to reading off it,' as Jane Caplan and John Torpey put it in their analysis of the development of identificatory techniques in Europe.[26] This generated numberless descriptive rolls in the colony (curiously reminiscent of the earlier *chehra-o-dagh* system) with details of height and stature, together with marks, scars and other physical peculiarities. The purpose was, clearly, the verification of identity. That is to say, when convict identities were in question – for instance if an individual was suspected of being an escaped prisoner or an absconder from one of the penal settlement, but had no *godna* mark – all that the authorities had to do, or so they thought, was carefully inspect the body of the suspect and compare the observations with the descriptive rolls. Here too the older problem of the instability of bodily appearances played spoiler. Add to this the subjectivity of clerks' descriptions and the lack of an effective and uniform system of indexing prisoners' rolls, and one sees how offenders – habitual ones especially – could slip away easily. If a newly arrested individual used an alias, it was almost impossible to access their prior records.

The next stage of technological solution, as such, was found in convict photography, which was now added to the descriptive rolls. However, with the generation of the voluminous descriptive rolls, even as photographs were added to them, a somewhat new problem confronted the colonial authorities: recording information was one thing, but ordering and processing such vast information banks another. In the words of Simon A. Cole, 'the most acute problem facing the nineteenth-century police and penal bureaucracies was not *recording* information, but *ordering* it.'[27] Badri Narayan Tiwari's paper in this volume deals with the subject of photography as identificatory technology. So I will limit myself to emphasising two points. In the first place I wish to indicate that, though separated by time and employing different technologies (the needle against the camera), penal tattooing and convict photography are not so different. Both attempted to make a permanent record of individual criminality. The second, more important point has to do with the logic of governmentality that does not brook multiplicity of identificatory strategies. It is obsessed, it would seem, with establishing the best technology of identification which would subsume, supersede and supplant all previous ones. In this, the neoliberal state too does not seem to have changed much, what with the UID's proposed all-encompassing embrace. Paradoxically, however, all attempts at trying to harness – conflate – multiple technologies of identification to produce a single-window meta-identificatory method have foundered. Firstly, various pre-existing technological solutions could compete to undermine such total claims. Though it had been banned in 1849, for instance, penal tattooing found many supporters. In 1858, Superintendent James Walker of the Andaman Islands lobbied for its reintroduction;[28] then again in 1870, Superintendent H. Mann suggested that life prisoners be branded.[29] Secondly, the messy change from one overarching identificatory technology to another (or in the case of contemporary India, from several identificatory devices to one meta-device) is certain to dislocate several previously established identities, leave out a wide range of people and allow a great deal of slippage, so to speak, thus relentlessly adding to governmental anxiety.

In any case, what Reverend Joseph Mullins had referred to at the Photographic Society of Bengal as the 'stern fidelity' of photography[30] also proved relatively short-lived. Photos could be taken and filed away with voluminous notations accompanying them, yet reading them and, more importantly, linking them later to the person of the criminal proved an insurmountable hurdle. Generating copious identificatory information and data is one thing, and processing them efficaciously, another. By the end of the nineteenth-century, the limitations of photography for the identification of old offenders and convicts were apparent. In 1891, ER Henry was appointed Inspector-General of Police, Bengal, who immediately discarded photography as a useful identificatory technology and recommended that the Bengal authorities adopt a new method of criminal identification that had been trialled in Paris: Alphonse Bertillon's system of anthropometry, or Bertillonage. In an uncannily similar rehearsal of previous confidence it was said, anthropometry promised a valuable means of verifying the identity of old offenders. It has to be borne in mind that by the last decades of the nineteenth century the urgency to ensure the reconviction of old offenders, or the recapture of dangerous ones in the event of escape, had attained a feverish pitch. As the previous Inspector-General of Gaols, Bengal, F.J. Mouat, writes in 1891, commenting on 'M. Bertillon's Discourse on the Anthropometric Measurement of Criminals', 'nothing impressed me more strongly [at the time of his service] than the need of some unerring test of the identity of habitual criminals.'[31] By this time, of course, Bertillonage, was emerging as that 'unerring test' of habitual criminal identity. If individuals were arrested for crimes that carried additional penalties for a second offence, trained police officers would take six measurements of them. The measurements were: length of the head, width of the head, length of the middle finger of the left hand, length of the forearm, length of the left foot, and height. The combinations were said to be almost unique, and to remain stable over time. These measurements would be supplemented with photos of the face, one frontal and one in profile. Bertillonage, then, was the new total technology that subsumed within its scope photography. Allan Sekula argues that the Bertillon system successfully transformed bodily signs into a text.[32]

But this master-technology, too, soon lost its purchase and was challenged and eventually replaced in the twentieth century by dactyloscopy or, as we know it today, fingerprinting. What happened to the massive photographic and anthropometric archives that Bertillonage had generated? They did not go waste but fed into the burgeoning race ethnography of the twentieth century, pioneered arguably by Herbert Hope Risley. Race sciences bloomed with the inclusion of phrenology, anthropometric photography and retinology and continued, across the so-called great divide of 1947, to inform the work of the anthropologists of the government-commissioned All India Anthropological Survey of 1989.[33] But this long and complex story will have to wait for another occasion.

To return to our present concerns, fingerprinting was not new to the colony towards the end of the nineteenth century. As is well-known, in 1858, William Herschel, the Magistrate of Hooghly, used a handprint to secure a public works contract, and later claimed to have introduced finger-printing shortly afterwards.[34] The 'invention' of finger-printing, however, has been a bitterly contested theme.[35] 'Indians' never tire of pointing out that the history of finger-printing was rewritten with the principal Indian actors removed. The crucial role played by two South Asian sub-inspectors of police – Aziz ul Haq and H.C. Bose – in the development of the system of fingerprint classification was never acknowledged by Henry. As one British police officer, T.G. Holman, put it in his memoirs, 'They invented the system of classification by whorl, but the British got most of the credit.'[36] In a way, this is unsurprising, for the history of taking fingerprints betrays a racist bias. Fingerprints were taken selectively. Registering officers in the North West Provinces, for instance, were told to 'relax the rule' of taking fingerprints for Europeans and 'other persons of position' whose identity was not in question.[37] Long before fingerprints were adopted as the 'new' master-technology of identification, impression of digits were taken as receipts for government pensions, land transfer deeds, debt bonds and in gaol admission registers. However, until the 1890s, the permanence of fingerprints was not established though Herschel made some tentative suggestions to this effect earlier on.[38] In fact, as late as 1893, Henry – noting that during the process of anthropometric measurement, thumb impressions were also taken – opined, 'I must admit that I do not see my way to utilising them.'[39] The inspector-general would soon have to eat his words, for, within a year, thumbprints were an important part of the operation of the Bertillon system. In the mean time, scientist Francis Galton had argued in favour of the fingerprints' permanence, as Henry himself faithfully records later in his *Classification and Uses of Finger Prints* (1900). The scientist wrote, 'there appear to be no bodily characteristics other than deep scars and tattoo marks comparable in their persistence to these markings.'[40]

From this point onward there was no looking back. This was indeed the moment when fingerprints were acknowledged as what Shreenivas and Saradindu Narayan Sinha have described as a 'physiological and natal autograph.'[41] If fingerprints were unique, then they could be used to unequivocally fix identities on to protean bodies. Dactyloscopy, therefore, offered afresh the hope of being able to settle the 'one body-one identity' principle once and for all. Fingerprints now became indexical traces of presence that anchored identities to permanent bodily signs. Also, it was way easier to take fingerprints than to perform the elaborate calculations and measurements of the Bertillon system. The former did not involve individuals having to touch each other, thereby eliminating the problem of a higher-caste person having to touch, say, the feet of a lower-caste individual; it did away with the need to undress an individual for detailed scrutiny and this greatly facilitated the documentation of women; fingerprints were easy to take and all that was required by way of training was half an hour's practice and by way of equipment a tin slab, printing ink, a roller and some turpentine; and, finally, the 'digital-imprint' archive, so to speak, thus generated was definitely less unwieldy than the elaborate data of the Bertillon system. As a consequence, from 1897 fingerprinting of all ten digits superseded the Bertillon system altogether.[42] This was then the new meta-technology of identification. It may be of some academic interest to note that fingerprinting was first developed in South Asia and only later used in Britain. It was not introduced in Britain until Henry was appointed Assistant Commissioner of Police at London's Scotland Yard and he set up the Fingerprint Branch in 1901.[43] This has led to the conceptualisation of the subcontinent as a 'colonial laboratory.'[44]

In any case, fingerprinting spread rapidly all over South Asia as the newest and best technology of identification, supplanting most previous modes. It was extended to members of the designated criminal tribes as well as to all prisoners. After 1905, adults registered under the Criminal Tribes Acts were fingerprinted as a matter of course.[45] By the 1930s, there was a fingerprint bureau in every province, and in the larger provinces there were up to 200,000 fingerprints on record. Every person who was arrested was fingerprinted, and the prints compared to those already taken. The earlier anxiety about not being able to apprehend recidivist offenders, fugitives and members of the criminal tribes was addressed, as fingerprinting allowed a greater, easier scope for what we call today interoperability. Indeed, the bureaux also received the fingerprints of arrested persons from neighbouring states[46] – a mobile database, so to speak, for a mobile population, accessible all over the empire.

With the coming of dactyloscopy, what we have is the terrible trio of identificatory technology: photography, anthropometry (later 'improved' into biometry) and fingerprinting. This triad, once established, rapidly became the standard basis of identification, in the colony as well as the post-colony. Any identification document that we come across even today has as its fundament a combination of these three, supplemented with 'descriptive details' – be it the passport or the Epic, the PAN card or, most recently, the UID.

Needless to say, this is by no means an exhaustive account – nothing of the sort was, in any case, attempted. This essay is intended to serve as a fleeting overview of shifting identificatory technologies in the nineteenth century to show the gradual, stage-ist intensification of the effort to stabilise the body-identity complex before the governmental eye. This process may have gone from strength to strength in the twentieth century and beyond; but the elusive goal is not in sight. Had it been, the Indian state would not have been so persuasively arguing for the merits of the UID project. The logic of governmentality remains unaltered: neat-fit identities have to be mapped on to monolithic, perfectly legible bodies; and technology has to be deployed to achieve this end – which could take the form of anthropometry and identifying bio-criminal subgroups in the nineteenth century or gathering 'demographic and biometric information' in the politically-correct twenty-first century. The welfare angle in the neoliberal state's propaganda of the UID project, too, should not be overemphasised, and not simply because 'neoliberal welfare' is an oxymoron. Even for the colonial régime, when identificatory technologies worked on marginal groups – as in the case of 'criminals' in colonial South Asia – a camouflage of welfare could be discerned in the arbitrary colonial state's effort to manage and productively deploy criminal bodies rather than eliminating them.

Admittedly, technology, understood in a mechanistic, functional way, have become more sophisticated with the passage of time; but, the technologies of governing, as it has been described here in the

Foucauldian sense of being strategies of power implicated in the ordering, classification and control of individual bodies, have not changed radically. It may be argued that, with globalisation, an interesting shift has taken place. The market has emerged as a key player in the control and management of technologies – as an authority parallel to the state. However, in the context of deployment of technology, the market-state dichotomy would seem a little overdrawn. It may be that the market, which is now on the centre-stage of information capitalism, is reorienting and restructuring itself with the advent of new technologies which assure it both profit and power. However, despite its continuing reservations about the power of the state, and the consequent effort to make the state less powerful, the market relies on the state to 'popularise' new technologies. Thus, as Dipankar Sinha argues in his essay in this volume, 'when it comes to the dissemination of the symbolic power, messages and items of new technologies we find a very interesting "convergence" between the state and the market.'[47] If this is true, then the logic of governmentality remains fundamentally intact. Also, viewed from another perspective, the colonial rule started as a commercial enterprise, which, only with considerable reluctance, assumed the mantle of governance, once its economic interests were threatened from within by political developments. Nonetheless, the colonial state remained till the end one which was overwhelmingly interested and invested in its economic gains. Under colonialism, the market and state remained practically indiscerptible. Therefore, the so-called transition from 'uniformly' state-driven technologies of identification to the 'dichotomous' market-and-state-driven technologies of identification – which may be neatly mapped onto the passage from imperialism, which was perfected primarily by the European nation-states in the quest for global domination, to Empire, today's world order[48] – leaves the underlying logic of feverishly trying to fix identities, particularly of marginal, migrant groups, intact.

Another line of argument could be that the 'change' has been one from disciplinary societies of the nineteenth and early twentieth century to present societies of control *à la Deleuze*. In Deleuze's evocative image, the structured tunnels of mole have been replaced by the infinite undulations of the snake. Whereas disciplinary society forged fluid, distinct castings, the society of control functions through flexible, modulating networks, 'like a self-deforming cast that changes continually, from one instant to the next, or like a sieve whose pattern changes from one point to the next.'[49] This distinction could hold in a general sense; but one would have to remember that the colonial state, confronted with the unmanageable, if not incomprehensible, motility of the colonial peoples, did evolve highly adaptable and mobile technologies of rule. This we have already seen. People were fleeing, masquerading, slipping away, hiding from the all-seeing eye. And the colonial state was relentlessly trying to create mobile knowledge pools for these people, accessible at any given point and moment of apprehension and application: mobile modes of control in the track of a footloose population. These technological trackings became what Rachel J. Tolen describes as 'tokens' of a criminality resistant to wage labour and changing modes of production.[50] A commercial-imperial enterprise could not have brooked such resistance and hence it had to innovate beyond familiar disciplinary-societal formats. As such, the Deleuzian distinction, if posed too rigidly, will not wash in the context of the South Asian colony. In the interstices of disciplinary society, modes akin to societies of control were already burgeoning.

As the late Roman scholar Frank Bourne would tell his class of Roman History at Princeton: *De nobis fabula narrator* – 'their story is our story.' Only, in this case, our story is our story all over again.

NOTES

1. Crystal, David, *The Cambridge Encyclopaedia of Language*, Cambridge University Press: Cambridge, 2007 (second edition), p.9.
2. Ibid.
3. Simmel, Georg, "The Stranger," in Kurt H. Wolf, ed. and trans. *The Sociology of Georg Simmel*, Free Press: New York, 1950, p.402.
4. Ibid.
5. See Frederick Cooper's discussion of the Weberian concept in 'Identity' (with Roger Brubaker) in Cooper, *Colonialism in Question: Theory, Knowledge, History*, University of California Press: Berkeley, Los Angeles, London, 2005, p.76
6. Samaddar, Ranabir, *The Materiality of Politics, Vol I: Technologies of Rule*, Anthem: Delhi, 2007, pp.243-44.

7. UIDAI, Planning Commission, Government of India http://uidai.gov.in/index.php/aadhaar.html [Accessed on 9 April 2012]
8. This is an insight borrowed from Michel Foucault, *Discipline and Punish: The Birth of the Prison*, Penguin: India, 1991 (1977); Foucault has famously conceptualised the relationship between scientific disciplines and social practices in the modern age which, he argued, are important 'technologies'
9. Usha Ramanathan coined this alliterative phrase in the course of a discussion at 'Digital Deliberations', a workshop held in Kolkata on 29-30 June 2012 (organised jointly by Mahanirban Calcutta Research Group and Centre for the Study of Culture and Society, Bangalore); also see Usha Ramanathan, "Foreword," to Jijeesh P.B., "AADHAAR; How a Nation is Deceived," Greenpeople: 2011; http://aadhararticles.blogspot.in/2011/11/1770-aadhaar-how-n-t-i-o-n-i-s-deceived.html [Accessed on 15 November 2012]
10. Scott, James C., *Seeing Like a State: How Certain Schemes to Improve the Human Condition Have Failed*, Yale University Press: New Haven, CT, 1998
11. Seal, Anil, *The Emergence of Indian Nationalism: Competition and Collaboration in the Later Nineteenth Century* Cambridge University Press: Cambridge, 1971
12. Second and Concluding Report of the Committee of Convict Labour, 28 January 1837; India Office Records P/141/9 (4 March 1837)
13. Deleuze, Gilles, "Postscript on the Societies of Control," *October* 59:Winter, 1991, pp.3-7; an engaging analysis of this essay is provided by Michael Hardt, "The Withering of Civil Society," *Social Text*, 45, 1995, pp.27-44
14. Burton, Antoinette, "Introduction: The Unfinished Business of Colonial Modernities," in Antoinette Burton, ed., *Gender, Sexuality and Colonial Modernities*, Routledge: London, 1999, p.1
15. Foucault, *Discipline and Punish*
16. The 'two-India' thesis, so to speak, – one settled and the other itinerant – of Bayly is a running theme in his work; for an elaboration, one could look at Christopher A. Bayly, *Indian Society and the Making of the British Empire* (the New Cambridge History of India series, Vol.2.1), Cambridge University Press, Cambridge, 1988.
17. Nigam, Sanjay, "Disciplining and Policing the 'Criminals by Birth', Part 2: The Development of a Disciplinary System, 1871-1900," *Indian Economic and Social History Review*, 27:3, 1990, p.287
18. Arnold, David, "The Colonial Prison: Power, Knowledge and Penology in Nineteenth-Century India," in David Arnold and David Hardiman eds., *Subaltern Studies VIII: Essays in Honour of Ranajit Guha*, Oxford University Press: New Delhi, 1994, pp.158-59
19. Deleuze, "Postscript", p.3
20. Anderson, Claire, *Legible Bodies: Race, Criminality and Colonialism in South Asia*, Berg: Oxford, New York, 2004, p.1
21. Ibid, p.39; also see, Ashis Nandy, *The Intimate Enemy: Loss and Recovery of Self under Colonialism*, Oxford University Press: Delhi, 1983, pp.52-53

22. All the horses presented for inspection by a particular noble were branded with a specific pattern to distinguish these from those of other nobles through a seal (*dagh*). The physical description of troops (*chehra*) was also recorded. The Tughluqs continued the tradition. In an attempt to reduce the gap between the number of horsemen on paper and those actually employed by a mansabdar, the Mughal emperor Akbar (1542-1605) re-introduced the branding or *dagh* system in the eighteenth year of his reign (1573-74). The system, in its new avatar, however, continued to imply 'that the descriptive roll of every soldier entertained by the mansabdar was noted, and the number and quality of the horses were periodically inspected.' According to the historian, Badayuni, who was himself a mansabdar of 20, '[w]hen he had presented those twenty horsemen through the brand (*dagh*) according to regulations, he could be given a mansab of 100.' Satish Chandra, *Medieval India: From the Sultanat to the Mughals, Part II: Mughal Empire (1526-1748)*, Har-Anand Publications: Delhi, 2006 (Second Reprint), p.158
23. Scott, James C., John Tehranian and Jeremy Mathias, "The Production of Legal Identities Proper to States: The Case of the Permanent Family Surname", *Comparative Studies in Society and History*, 44:1, 2002, p.7
24. List of Forty Convicts to Mauritius *per Lady Sophia*, 28 October 1815 (no. 20); India Office Records P/132/12, 31 October 1815
25. Heidegger, Martin, "The Question Concerning Technology," in Martin Heidegger, *Philosophical and Political Writings*, edited by Manfred Stassen, Continuum (German Library series): London, 2003, p.279
26. Caplan, Jane and John Torpey, 'Introduction,' in Jane Caplan and John Torpey eds., *Documenting Individual Identity: The Development of State Practices in the Modern World*, Princeton University Press: Princeton, NJ, 2001, p.8
27. Cole, Simon A., *Suspect Identities: A History of Fingerprinting and Criminal Identification*, Harvard University Press: London, 2001, p.29
28. National Archives of India (NAI) Home (Judicial), 3 September 1858, 1-2: Superintendent J.P. Walker to C. Beadon, Secretary to Government of India, 8 July 1858
29. NAI Home (Judicial A), 10 December 1870, 20-21: Superintendent H. Mann to E.C. Bayley, Secretary to Government of India, 3 November 1870
30. Reverend Joseph Mullins, cited in Christopher Pinney, *Camera Indica: The Social Life of Indian Photographs*, Reaktion: London, 1997, p.20
31. Mouat, F.J., "Notes on M. Bertillon's Discourse on the anthropometric Measurement of Criminals," *Journal of the Royal Anthropological Institute of Great Britain and Ireland*, 20, 1891, p.185
32. Sekula, Allan, "The Body and the Archive," *October* 39, 1980, p.33
33. See Crispin Bates, "Race, Caste and Tribe in Central India: The Early Origins of Indian Anthropometry," in Peter Robb ed., *The Concept of Race in South Asia*, Oxford University Press: New Delhi, 1997, p.219

34. Herschel, William J., *The Origin of Finger-Printing*, Oxford University Press: London, 1916, pp.7-31
35. Cole, *Suspect Identities*; also see, Chandak Sengoopta, *Imprint of the Raj: How Fingerprinting was Born in Colonial India*, Macmillan: London, 2000.
36. Cited in Martin Wynne ed., *On Honourable Terms: The Memoirs of Some Indian Police Officers, 1915-1948*, British Association for Cemeteries in South Asia: London, 1985, p.87.
37. NAI Home (Public A), June 1898, 589-611: Fingerprints
38. Radhika Singha, "Settle, Mobilise, Verify: Identification Practices in Colonial India," *Studies in History*, 16:2, 2000, p.177
39. NAI Home (Police A), June 1893, 129-45, Henry to H.J.S. Cotton, Chief Secretary to Government, Bengal, 25 February 1893
40. Cited in E.R. Henry, *Classification and Uses of Finger Prints*, George Routledge and Sons: London, 1900, pp.4-5
41. Shreenivas and Saradindu Narayan Sinha, "Personal Identification by the Dermatoglyphics and the E-V Methods," *Patna Journal of Medicine*, 31:3, 1957, p.100
42. NAI Home (Police A), December 1896, 88-9: Henry to Hewett, 3 December 1896
43. Finger Printing: India Office Records MSS Eur F161/185
44. Cole, *Suspect Identities*, p.90
45. NAI Home (Police A), August 1905, 86: Fingerprinting Prisoners
46. J.C. Curry, *The Indian Police*, Faber and Faber: London, 1932, pp.280-81.
47. See Dipankar Sinha's article in this volume; also see the Ritajyoti Bandyopadhyay's article in this volume which grapples with this theme in detail.
48. See Michael Hardt and Antonio Negri, *Empire*, Harvard University Press: 2001 (New Edition)
49. Deleuze, "Postscript", p.4
50. Tolen, Rachel J., "Colonising and Transforming the Criminal Tribesmen: The Salvation Army in British India," *American Ethnologist*, 18:1, 1991, p.112

III

Photos and Colonial Governance of Migrants' Identities

Case of Indentured Migrants from Bhojpur to Suriname

Badri Narayan Tiwari

After slavery was outlawed by the European powers in the first decades of the nineteenth century, the demand for cheap agricultural labour in colonial plantation economies was met by the development of a system of indentured labour. This involved transporting, under indenture agreements, large populations of poor agricultural labourers from population-rich areas such as India and China, to areas where they needed to service plantations. The practices of slavery and indenture thus resulted in world-wide colonial diasporas. India was one country which served as a source of this cheap labour and during the colonial period large-scale migration took place from the Bhojpuri-speaking region of India by way of which Indians were sent to various sugar-producing colonies. Over one million people went to Mauritius, Trinidad, Fiji, Guyana, Suriname, and other colonies. Of them 34,304 migrants went to the Dutch colony of Suriname between 1873 and 1916 to work on the Caribbean country's sugar, coffee, cotton and cocoa plantations.[1] The first group of Hindustani indentured labourers recruited from the

United Provinces of British India and Bengal arrived in Suriname in 1873 via Calcutta.[2] The Dutch authorities were helped by the English to recruit indentured labourers from this English colony. This illustrates how European colonialism – though highly competitive – was all the while a joint enterprise. This recruitment took place because the abolition of slavery in Suriname in 1863 left the Dutch planters in dire need of labourers to work in the sugar cane, coffee, cotton and cacao plantations.[3]

Most Hindustani migrants were from the Bhojpuri-speaking region of India (Uttar Pradesh and Bihar) – all of them, men and women, had signed a five-year contract to work on the Surinamese plantations. Calcutta was their port of departure. Upon expiry of their contracts, provided they were not in debt to the planter or other moneylenders, they were free to either return to India or stay in Suriname. If the latter was the case, a migrant received 100 guilders and had the choice of signing a new contract or settling as a free small farmer with some allocated land. Of the some 34,000 Hindustanis who arrived in Suriname between 26 February 1873 and 24 May 1916 roughly 11,000 returned to India after five years or more. A Surinamese Hindustani culture developed among those who settled in Suriname with accompanying Hindu, Islamic and Christian religious institutions and cultural practices, and a common language called Sarnami.[4]

The indentured migration was well-planned and well-documented on the part of the colonial government and governance of the migration was done at various levels. These included registrations at sub-depots, depots and ports in the country of origin, as also at the ports of the country of destination, at indenture offices and at plantations. ID numbers were allotted; various levels of health check-up and certifications were done and special photo-sessions on the ships, at the ports and in the plantations were organised as the part of governance. This documentation resulted in fixed kinds of images which suited the colonial masters. In addition to the documentation by the colonial masters, the process of migration was also documented by some European missionaries who were interested in carrying out proselytising work among the new immigrants. As a part of this effort, several missionaries visited India and Suriname to observe and document at first hand the migration process that was underway during that period. This documentation was done with the help of photographs and journals which were compiled by them during their visit to India and to the destination countries like Suriname, Mauritius etc.

The story of the journey of migrants from the Bhojpuri-speaking region of India who were sent to work as coolies in the sugarcane plantations of various European colonies including Suriname can be understood from the autobiography of Munshi Rahman Khan (1874-1972), an educated Muslim youth who fell prey to the diabolical plans of two men who worked as recruiters or agents of the British government. As a young lad in his mid-20s, he was tricked by them as they promised him a lucrative 'government job' overseas. However, Munshi Rahman Khan's hopes were dashed when he signed the indentureship contract before leaving India, which converted him into a coolie. After the end of his five-year indentureship period in Suriname, Khan remained there to become an independent agriculturist and lived in the country until his death. He kept a diary which provides a glimpse into the life and times of migrant coolies. He subsequently became a prolific writer and his autobiography, *Jeevan Prakash* (Life's Light), gives us a unique insight into the history of the indentured labourers in the Caribbean.[5]

While there is an assumption that the indentured labourers were of the lowest castes and lacked any education, the many individual biographies that have been unearthed in various receiving colonies show that there were a fair number of semi-educated and reasonably well-off individuals. Perhaps they hoped to obtain, or were promised, positions in the civil service in the colonies. It must have come as a huge shock when they discovered that they were destined to work as 'coolies' on the sugarcane plantations where they faced harsh living conditions and were forced to perform hard manual labour by their overseers. The various Coolie Ordinances passed after 1840, and consolidated in the late 1890s as Immigration Ordinance of British Guiana (1893) and Trinidad (1899), regulated every aspect of the working and, to a large extent, non-working lives of the immigrants (such as marriages, festivals, sickness, housing, and return to India). The technicians and managers who ran the plantations modelled them on the slave plantation with its rigid labour discipline and their belief in European racial superiority. Thus, a complete system of subjugation of the indentured population was put in place, the basis of which was the system of identification which fixed the identities of each migrant into that of coolies.

Photographs are an important source for analysing the colonial governance of the migration process that took place during the colonial period. According to Elizabeth Edwards, historical photographs work as 'a site of intersecting histories, . . . because they share experiences and yet have their own trajectories, encompassing sameness and difference.'[6] Photographs provide glimpses of a prior reality, the indexical traces of which were chemically inscribed on to a sensibilised film or plate. They transfer to view 'a fragment of time and space.' As fragments of the past, they may come to stand for the whole, reifying culturally formed images as observed realities.[7] Thus, by studying the photographs that were taken of the migration process from India during the colonial period, we can understand the nature of making of colonial identity of indentured migrants and the forms and media of colonial governance.

Another source for studying the colonial governance of the migration is letters that were written by migrants and their families. Many of these letters went missing since the officials who registered the addresses of the migrants at the ports often wrote wrong addresses of the migrants as they were unable to understand their pronunciation. These letters, which eventually returned to the post offices from where they had been posted, have been preserved in archives and they function as an important source for studying the governance of colonial masters. While official colonial narratives, based on the conclusions of the Sanderson Commission of 1912 which was appointed by the Colonial Office to consider ways of improving the system, claimed that the migration was in the economic interest of Indian labourers who were being provided the opportunity to acquire land in the European colonies the letters that were written by the migrants show that they had to cope with the grief of separation from loved ones. This sorrow was also pervasive in the homeland where family members of migrants had to cope with the trauma of the virtual 'disappearance' of loved ones.

In this paper, in the first part we will look at how photographs were used by colonial masters to fix the identity of migrants and how photographs are a medium to understand reality, while in the second part we will study a few letters written by the migrants and their families which went missing and are now preserved in the colonial archives.

VISUAL DOCUMENTATION THROUGH PHOTOGRAPHS

To study photographs as a source for understanding colonial governance in the case of Bhojpuri migrants to Suriname, I am using three kinds of photographs. The first kind was taken by the cameras of the colonial government as part of documentation work. These were not taken to cater to personal interest. The second kind consisted of the photos taken by Danish protestant missionaries in 1913. The third kind comprised the ID documentation certificates provided by the colonial masters in which details of the bodies of the migrants were mentioned.

When the migrants reached their destinations, special photo-sessions were organised by recruiters in the plantations. In these photographs, in which the colonial planters were also included, women were shown wearing attractive jewellery and dresses while men were shown wearing the traditional costumes worn by the Bhojpuris during that period. These

Both Indian and 'Negro' Indentured labourers in their traditional dresses

dresses distinguished them from the other ethnic communities already a part of Surinamese population at that time. Men usually wore *dhoti*, which was a long, white cotton cloth, wrapped first around the loins, then pulled between the legs and tied up in the back. It covered the thighs and gave enough space to walk freely. The upper part of the body was covered with a *kurta,* a cotton shirt without collar (sometimes short, descending just up to the hips, and sometimes long, going down to the knees). Several men also wore *pagris* on their heads, which were made of a long cotton cloth wrapped turban-like around the head leaving the upper part of the head free.

The women wore *sarees*, which were long cotton cloths wrapped around their bodies. Often women wore *lahangas*, which were long

Migrated Indian women in traditional ornaments in Suriname

cotton skirts, and blouses. *Orhnis*, or shawls covered their heads and hung down alongside their ears. Alongside the group photographs, separate photographs of women were also taken in which they were shown wearing heavy jewellery like head bands, earrings, necklaces, armlets, bangles, waist bands, anklets and so on.[8]

These photographs were advertised by the colonial masters extensively and hard-sold as a visual archetype. The politics of recruiters in the *camera lucida* appears both to represent labourers in plantation as happy human beings to counter nationalist concern over ill-treatment of the indentured population, and to fix the identities of the migrants as Bhojpuri migrants. The migrants and their women folk were depicted as eagerly awaiting a happy and pleasant future in the plantations after reaching the foreign ports.

The second set of photographs was taken by Peter Martin Legêne, a Protestant missionary who travelled to India in 1913 at the age of 28 in order to prepare himself to work among Hindustani migrants in Suriname. While in India, he compiled two albums of photographs – namely, album nos. 1866a and 1866b – which have been preserved in KIT, Amsterdam, and used later by Susan Legêne, the granddaughter of Peter Martin Legêne, in her excellent study.[9] Album 1866a records the trip to India and is a travelogue on India intended for insiders.[10] Album 1866b reconstructs the same trip from a greater distance in time and includes what happened 'afterwards'. It is a travelogue that pushes the story further, by visualising the transatlantic arrival as well and showing the promise of the better future to come.

In both the albums, the colonial authority of England and the Netherlands is barely visible and in India the photographer seems to have focussed on the daily life of the Indian people with a social background comparable to that of the people he would be meeting in Suriname as migrants. The photographs taken in India depict people in various parts of India, such as in Varanasi, Mathura etc. They mostly show poverty-stricken people who are leading deprived and unhappy lives. In contrast, the photographs taken in Suriname show the people to be happier and more civilised after the missionary intervention. The shift from photographs of people in India to Indian migrants in Suriname reflects the direction of the intervention and refers to the photographer's mission to care for the people, improve their living conditions and get them to know Christianity.

A closer study of the photographs reveals that although the authority of the colonial masters is not visible in them, the underlying colonial influence persists, since the photographs show the residents of India to be very poor and miserable and living in abject conditions while the photographs taken in Suriname show the migrants to be leading happy and contented lives and living in better conditions. According to Susan Legêne, her grandparents – both missionaries who lived and worked in Suriname – worked with the full support of colonial authorities, such as the Dutch Agent General (Protector of Immigrants) of the Hindustanis. The photographs taken by her grandfather in India provided visual backing of these activities. His albums were visual memory sites of the Indian context of migration to Suriname and what happened there, helping to shape his views and stories about the individual and collective background of the migrants.[11]

The third kind of ID documentation was certificates provided by the colonial recruiters to the indentured labourers. In these certificates, detailed description of the villages of the recruited labourers, *thana, pargana,* depot of the recruitment, port of embarking and port of destination, plantation, name of the planters, height of the labourers and other detail of the body were mentioned. Apart from these, every detail of their physical examinations and their health were also documented in the recruitment register maintained by the recruitment depots at home as well as the colonial offices at the destination. From time to time commissions and enquiry committees were formed by the British government to investigate into the conditions of the migrants. They too documented the health and body details of the indentured labourers in order to be able to counter the allegations of the Indian nationalists who were not in favour of continuing the indenture system. Here, the bio-politics and image-politics of colonial masters may be observed in the process of documentation.

Missionary documentation of the homeland of the migrants was for the purpose of understanding migrants better which may help missionary proselytisers in establishing better communication with the migrants. As such, this paper has offered as much a photo-narrative as a written one.

3. Encounters, probably near Varanasi, 1914.
Page 2 and 12 of the Album made in1920s, photographs printed on silver gelatine developing-out paper.
Col. numbers 00043473/4 and 0004 8486-8

Photos from the KIT collection

5. A visual story of Hindustani woman in Suriname. Page 47 from left to right clockwise: Wedding ceremony of two pupils of the children's home in Suriname; two children of the children's home in Suriname, two widows (in India or in Suriname); a smoking woman with a huqqa (in India). Page 48, from left to right: Esther Sriman twice, teaching children in Suriname; men and women working in the fields in Suriname
Page 47 and 48 of the Album made in the 1920s, photographs printed on silver gelatine developing-out paper. Col. numbers 0004-8545-51

Photos from the KIT collection

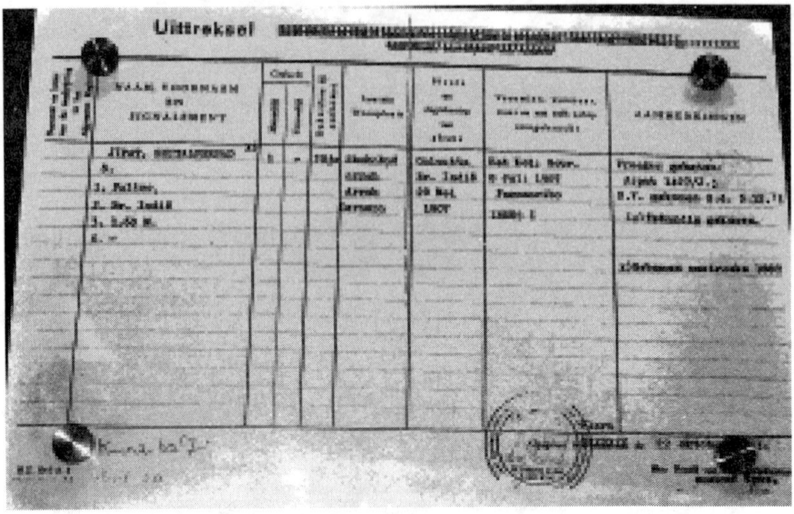
Uittreksel

Certificate given by the Colonial Officer to the migrants

MULTIPLE MOBILITY: MISSING AND SEARCHING

Official colonial narratives of the period claimed that the migration was in the economic interests of Indian labourers who were providing 'the greatest assistance' in increasing the prosperity of recipient colonies, and that the indenture was the only practical form of emigration to distant colonies on any considerable scale. These commissions highlighted such things as the opportunities available to Indians in the colonies to acquire land and called for the system to be judged purely on its economic results, ignoring a host of social and psychological problems attendant on the migrant. The historiography of this migration consisted mainly of official records created by the government or the colonial elite, including Christian churches and missionaries. It was only after scholars from the Indian diaspora began pursuing their own research agenda that a historiographical change occurred, with an attempt to reinterpret this history from the point of view of the labourers themselves. Many present-day historians observe that some of the indentured migrants migrated to one country but after sometime due to various reasons changed their documented destination in the colonial papers and records.

For example, Daulatia who migrated from Bhagalpur of Bihar for Fiji, as mentioned in the document preserved in her family in Paramaribo in Suriname, changed her destination and after a certain time arrived in Suriname. This engendered many cases of disappearances, in the teeth of colonial documentary and identificatory obsession and rigidity.

This phenomenon is also reflected in various letters written by family members of migrants from India. Many of the letters which did not reach the person for whom they were intended have been preserved in the Suriname National Archive, Paramaribo, and a study of these letters reveal the depth of emotional pain. While all the letters bring out the desperation of the writers to see and meet the addressees from whom they have been separated, there is a cold official note on them either saying 'so-and-so person of so-and-so village in India was not found', or 'so-and-so person was not found on so-and-so plantation in Suriname.' Many of the letters, written by family members left behind in India, urged the migrants to return to India and emphasised that the money sent by them as remittance was no compensation for their absence.

A letter written by Shiv Mangal of Asauli village in district Rae Bareli of Uttar Pradesh to his brother Bajrangbali, who was working in Sarmacca plantation in Suriname, strikingly brings out the emotional pain due to the separation.

> Greetings to Siddh Sri Sarvoprasayog Bajrangbali from Shivmangal Ram, Suryaram, Bhavani, Gayadin, Gangaprasad and your five nephews and Sevakram, Ramsahai, Bihari, Kairati, Benchu, Chhedi, Mandas, Chandi, Seetal and Bhikhari. May all their 'Ram Ram' [a form of greeting used in rural areas of UP] reach you. We are well and we are happy to hear that you are also well. Further news is that please know that we have received Rs48 in the month of *Kartik*. And your mother and sister-in-law and your woman [wife] and your five nephews are all well. You asked about the cultivation so please know that we have a farming of two oxen. By God's grace everything is going well. It is the desire of all of us in the house that you return home. Your mother thinks about you day and night, which you should come and see. And we have received the letter which you had sent and have

> informed about the reply of each person. I do not know whether you will receive it or not.[12]

It is noteworthy that the letter did not reach Bajrangbali. It carried a note from the emigration office in Paramaribo that they did not find any person of that name in Sarmacca plantation. The emotions hidden in the letter seem to have been waylaid during the journey and are still waiting to reach the person for whom they were intended.

The colonial archives in several countries that were the destinations of the Bhojpuri migrants also contain letters written by the officers of the Immigration Department searching for migrants working in plantations in different countries since many of the migrants were untraceable. An example of such a letter is the one written by the Immigration Department, British Guiana, to the Immigration Agent General, Suriname, on 22 September 1902. The letter was sent in response to a letter written to the Immigration Office in Suriname by a family member of a migrant called Jokhan, searching for him. The letter reads as follows:[13]

> Sir,
>
> In reply to your letter No. 1244, dated 25th last month, I have the honour to inform you that Jokhan, male, No. 55506, ex "Jura", 1892, arrived in this Colony on the 26th October 1892, and was allotted to Plantation "Farm", Demerara River.
>
> He has since left the estate, and his present residence is unknown, but the Manager of the "Farm" estate has promised to inform me, should anything be heard of him.
> I have the honour to be,
>
> Sir,
> Your Obedient Servant,
> (Signed)
> Ag: Immigration Agent General
> The Immigration Agent General,
> Surinam

These and other such letters which are lying in the colonial archive show that the entire story of migration from the Bhojpuri region was one of disappearance and searching and they document the depth of emotions generated in this process.

CONCLUSION

The above study shows how in the process of making of indentured identity, photographs played an important role. The photographs were taken in different places and at different times and with various intentions. Most of the photographs taken in the beginning of the migration process were facilitated by planters, colonial agents involved in the migration process, missionaries and other agents of the colonial authorities. Two kinds of politics are evident from these photographs. The first was to show the Indians living in the Bhojpuri-speaking region to be poor, deprived and poverty-stricken while those who had migrated led a happier and contented life with better hopes for the future. The second was that the certificates issued to the migrants by the colonial authorities contained all the information about the migrants from their roots to their destinations, which was a mode of governmentality to fix the identity of the migrants. However, the migrants tried to escape from these fixed identities by moving to other destinations and plantations. This need of multiple migrations of the indentured migrants must have produced a situation of escaping from given identification by colonial masters, as can be observed through the missing letters which did not reach the destinations provided in the colonial certificates. Thus the colonial authorities tried to fix the identities of the migrants through photographs and certificates but in many cases the migrants subverted these identities by moving away from them.

NOTES

1. Klerk, Cornelis Johannes Maria de, Boek-I: *Cultus en Ritueel van het Orthodoxe Hindoeïsme in Suriname*, Amsterdam 1951, and Boek-II: *Immigratie der Hindostanen in Suriname*, Amsterdam; Amrit: Den Haag, 1998 reprint.

2. Throughout this paper, the term 'Hindustani' or 'Hindustanis' is used for the indentured labourers who migrated to Suriname and their descendents. In colonial society, these migrants were either called British Indians, or coolies. In the course of the twentieth century, they raised strong objections against these names (that were also used in terms like: coolie school, coolie evangelist . . .), and chose 'Hindustani' as a common name
3. Legêne, Susan, *From India to Suriname: A journey into the future narrated by two photograph albums (1913-1930)*, Manav Vikas Sangrahalaya-GB Pant Institute, Bidesia Occasional papers Series no. 2: Allahabad, 2007, p.7
4. Klerk, Boek-II: *Immigratie*, pp.45-53
5. See, Kathinka Sinha-Kerkhoff, Ellen Bal and Alok Deo Singh (Translators), *Autobiography of An Indian Indentured Labourer: Munshi Rahman Khan (1874-1972): Jeevan Prakash*, Shipra Publications: Delhi, 2005
6. Edwards, Elizabeth, *Raw Histories. Photographs, Anthropology and Museums*, Berg: Oxford/New York, 2001, p.83
7. Ibid; also see, James R. Ryan, *Picturing Empire: Photography and the Visualization of the British Empire*, Reakton: London, 1997, p.19
8. *Kahe Gaile Bides, why did you go overseas? On Bhojpuri migration since the 1870s and contemporary culture in Uttar pradesh and Bihar, Suriname and the Netherlands*, Compiled & edited by Mousumi Majumdar, Mango Books/Spot Creative Services, 2010, p.49
9. Legêne, *From India to Suriname*, p.15. The project has been envisaged as an international exhibition and cultural exchange venture aimed at articulating aspects of Hindustani religion, culture and identity both in Suriname and the Netherlands that relate to their Bhojpuri Indian origins. The project has been executed by three institutes in the three countries concerned, namely, G.B. Pant Social Science Institute, Allahabad, India, the KIT Tropenmuseum-Royal Tropical Institute, Amsterdam, and the IMWO, (Research Institute of the Anton de Kom University of Suriname) in Paramaribo
10. Ibid, p.24
11. Ibid, p.13
12. A letter written by Shiv Mangal of Asauli village, district Ahmadpur in district Rae Barelli of Uttar Pradesh to his brother Bajrangbali who was working in Sarmacca plantation in Suriname. National Archive, Paramaribo.
13. Letter written by Immigration Department, British Guiana to the Immigration Agent General, Suriname on 22 September 1902. National Archive, Paramaribo. Letter no. 1889

IV

Protection, Welfare or Surveillance? Tracking Asylum Seekers and Refugees in India

Sahana Basavapatna

INTRODUCTION

The study of the migrant population that seeks asylum in India with specific reference to the purposes for which they are counted and/or documented remains largely unexplored in the Indian context. The Aadhaar is the newest form of such population-counting projects that aims to cover the entire resident population so that welfare schemes and service delivery reach the beneficiary; however, the census remains the oldest of such tools, on which is based the National Population Register as per Section 14A of the Citizenship Act, 1957. The broader idea appears to be to link the National Population Register with the Aadhaar project along with other relevant population counting and tracking exercises under the Mission Mode Projects[1] of the Government of India. Migrants, and in particular asylum seekers and refugees – who constitute the focus of this paper – are an important constituent of the population-mapping exercise underscored by the rationale of the Foreigners Act, 1946, which in its Statement of Objects and Reasons spells out the responsibility of the state to regulate the entry, residence and exit of the foreigner. The Foreigner's Act, 1946, in turn owed its rationale to the state-building project in the nineteenth century which involved harnessing the mobility of the 'bad' foreigner.[2]

Of particular relevance for the purposes of this paper are three projects that have the potential to impact the lives of refugees and asylum seekers – the Aadhaar, the National Population Register (under the Citizenship Act) and the Immigration Visa and Foreigners Registration and Tracking (IVFRT). These projects, in addition to the already existing legal framework (discussed in the succeeding sections of the paper), provide a complex scenario where tracking, sorting and supervising the migrant (which covers, in the Indian context, an asylum seeker, a refugee, a stateless person or a migrant for work) is legitimised. These projects are based, among others, on the idea that it is possible and even necessary to freeze identity of residents. Contrary to what historical experience would teach us, this imperative to freeze identities remains a compelling exercise. With the ability of asylum seekers and refugees to erase borders, as it were, the question of identifying, let alone tracking a migrant, assumes significance for the questions such an exercise raises – can identity be frozen, reduced to mere biometrics and, in South Asia, whether freezing of identity is even desirable. Against the backdrop of these underlying concerns, this paper attempts to understand the potential implications of the Aadhaar and other population-tracking and -mapping projects of the government of India. In particular, it tries to demonstrate the tricky terrain that the state is stepping into, in its quest to authoritatively identify the migrant for the purposes of its security and ostensible welfare concerns.

IDENTIFYING, COUNTING AND TRACKING FORCED MIGRANTS

The legal scenario and the identity conundrum form the core of this essay. At the outset, it is important to note that the law applicable to foreigners is also applicable to those seeking asylum in India. It is therefore pertinent to look at the Foreigners Act, 1946, and allied pieces of legislation for any insight it may offer for the present discussion. In addition, practices that profile Tibetan and the Sri Lankan Tamil refugees provide a picture of what one might expect for other refugee groups. Lastly, UNHCR's functioning in India and the registration procedures it employs in carrying out its 'protection' functions towards 'persons of concern' are also relevant.

Refugees or foreigners? The law

The Foreigners Act, 1946, and related pieces of legislation, regulates the entry, movement and exit of refugees and forms one of the several laws[3] that apply to refugees, in the absence of a refugee law. While courts in India have made a distinction between refugees and other foreigners and created a body of law that protects rights of refugees as a special category[4], for all other purposes they are subject to the requirements under these pieces of legislation on the same terms as a foreigner. While this is the broad context in which the legal status of refugees may be understood, one can also notice exceptions.

Three instances may be noted. First, like a foreigner, asylum seekers/ refugees run the risk of arrest and detention under Section 3(g), Foreigners Act, 1946, in the event that they do not register with UNHCR on the grounds of entering India without a valid visa. If convicted by a court of law, either for illegal entry or travel without valid documents, refugees are liable to be deported under Section 3(cc) of the Foreigners Act, 1946, unless it is brought to the notice of the concerned authority or court that the person seeks asylum in India.[5] For instance, Burmese asylum seekers in Mizoram have faced threats or actual deportation by the Young Mizo Association for illegal entry.[6] In a more recent case, a Rohingya faces trial for violation of the Foreigners Act, 1946, and Passport (Entry into India) Act, 1920, even though he seeks asylum in India. Second, in view of recent announcement by the Ministry of Home Affairs, Government of India recognised that refugees are entitled to a Residence Permit under Rule 7, Foreigners Order, 1948. An instance that provided sufficient evidence that refugees were treated as foreigners is the imposition of fine on Burmese refugees by the Foreigners Regional Registration Office, New Delhi (FRRO). In around December 2008, Burmese refugees, whose Residence Permits came up for renewal, were asked by the FRRO to pay a visa fee and a penalty fee in order to extend the validity of the permits. The fee was calculated on the basis of the date of arrival of the refugee in India and the date on which the application for Residence Permit was made. Prior to this period, refugees were exempted from paying a fine or a fee while applying for the Residence Permit.[7] The last aspect concerns biometrics. While the collection of biometric information has been questioned by critics of the Aadhaar project on the ground, among others, that a law allowing such collection and protecting the information is absent in India, biometric information including photograph, finger impressions, hand-writing impression and signature may be collected from foreigners under Section 3(e)(iv), Foreigners Act, 1946. Although biometric information has so far not been collected for a refugee, except in case of Aadhaar (a large number of Tibetan refugees have enrolled), such a move can be justified under the law.

Similarly, the recent policy decision of the government of India to grant 'long-term visas'[8] to all mandate refugees, on the one hand, may be said to amount to a tacit recognition of their refugee status while, on the other hand, this also functions as documentation and check on the individual. An announcement to this effect was first made in relation to Rohingya refugees. Rohingyas, living in various parts of the country for several years, protested before UNHCR in May 2012 seeking refugee status and access to protection. They also claimed that Rohingyas should be given 'refugee certificates' like other mandate refugees and not 'asylum cards' as is the practice. UNHCR announced that '. . . following discussions with the Government of India, UNHCR has been informed that the Government will give them long stay visas that will allow them to legally remain in India, based on their UNHCR asylum-seeker cards. For this purpose, they need to return to their places of residence in India and approach the local Foreigner's Registration Officers (FRO).'[9] For its part, the Ministry of Home Affairs (MHA) has stated that once registered with the FRRO or the concerned FRO, 'the superintendent of police in their city, who serves as the foreign registration officer, will conduct a thorough verification based on the internal guidelines of the government of India.' He adds, 'Only after such a verification, a case-by-case assessment will be made whether the person has a well-founded fear of persecution or it is purely for economic reasons they want to seek the refugee status, . . . After that, a decision will be made on whether or not they will be granted a long-term visa.'[10]

According to information available from the MHA and the FRRO, this process involves an application to the FRRO, a letter from the UNHCR confirming that the applicant is a recognised refugee, utility documents as proof of residence and a letter from the house owner confirming the same. The MHA claims that on the basis of the verification conducted by the FRRO or FRO (as the case may be), the Ministry will further verify whether the refugee is an economic migrant or a refugee fleeing persecution and issue a 'long-term visa' only to the latter.[11] The long-term visa will legally allow refugees to access education and employment in the private sector.

Existing identification projects applied to Tibetans and Sri Lankan Tamils refugees

Identification and tracking of refugees in India is not a new project; Tibetans and Sri Lankan Tamils, under the care of the government, are subject to procedures that include verification of identity, issuance of identity documents and once identity is established, provision of essential services. While it may be argued that the newer projects of identity have both welfare and security as its aims, the surveillance mechanism in place in case of Tibetans and Sri Lankan Tamil refugees more than hint that the central concerns of the government of India is not welfare, but surveillance. In the name of providing welfare, the process of identifying Tibetans and Sri Lankans not only primarily seek to watch over these foreigners but also indicate that welfare, if at all obtainable, is incidental.

Tibetans seeking refuge in India

In order to 'keep track of new arrivals, the Indian government, with the cooperation of the CTA [Central Tibetan Administration], issued Registration Certificates (RCs) to the majority of Tibetans' arriving in the 1960s through the 1970s.[12] These RCs are not proof of their legal status but only allow them to live in certain parts of the country. The MHA designates all Tibetans who arrived up to 1959 and to children born to them until 1987 as 'temporary refugees'. Those arriving after 1959 until 2003 are classified under the category of 'long term stay'.[13]

Tibetans arriving in the 1980s and 1990s through Nepal were allowed to come to India but none were granted legal status. According to the Tibet Justice Centre, the government reportedly turned a blind eye to the rampant practice by which new arrivals were able to obtain RCs fraudulently.[14] Only those arriving through the Sino-Indian borders were repatriated. While a large number of Tibetans were able to acquire RCs even if they were not legally entitled to, the fact that the government was unable to check this practice indicates its incapacity to track each Tibetan. Instances where individuals have been able to acquire official documents on the sly are not unknown. In the 1990s, owing, among other factors, to the increase in the number of Tibetans in India, the government began to curtail the practice of distributing RCs and many were also asked to return to Tibet.[15] In the mid-1990s, the Government's priorities appeared to change further. Voluntary repatriation appeared to overshadow all considerations, including the adherence to the principle of non-*refoulement*, recognised as a principle of customary international law. This policy, which was agreed upon between the Government of India and the CTA, led to denial of RCs for the new arrivals. Threats of deportation and detention of Tibetans were reportedly common during this time. Since 2000, India's position on Tibetan refugees have reflected on their legal status in India. The Tibet Justice Centre states that refugees have been stopped from entering India irrespective of whether they hold valid RCs. It is also reported that since 2003, the CTA and the Government of India started issuing Special Entry Permits (SEPs) to those arriving in India through Nepal. The Tibet Justice Centre argues, 'Some seven years later, at the time of this writing, the actual extent to which India has been issuing SEPs and implementing this new policy remains unclear. What is clear is that SEPs do not provide their bearers with a right to either citizenship or permanent residence in India. TJC's [Tibet Justice Centre] research suggests that India and the CTA have been trying to establish a better system for the issuance of RCs and other documentation to Tibetans currently residing in India.'[16]

The Indian state's policy towards Tibetan nationals in India is often used as a yardstick (along with the Tamil Sri Lankan refugee community, discussed below) to evaluate how it fares with respect to other refugee groups. While it cannot be denied that Tibetan 'refugees' have been provided monetary and other forms of assistance while they live in India, their legal status is not clear, as is often made out to be. India's claims of non-*refoulement* need to be assessed in the context of such episodes of expulsion or the denial of entry to refugees who flee from the threat or actual persecution in Tibet.

Sri Lankan Tamil refugees

The official position of the Government of India towards the Sri Lankan Tamil refugees is articulated by the MHA as follows: '[The] Government of India's approach is to discourage the movement of people as refugees but if any refugees belonging to these categories [category 1 includes stateless persons who had not applied for Indian citizenship or those not yet conferred Sri Lankan citizenship and category 2 includes Sri Lankan citizens] do come, they are granted relief on humanitarian grounds. The ultimate objective is that they should be repatriated back to Sri Lanka. Relief is given pending such repatriation.'[17]

This humanitarianism, on the ground, involves a thorough process of enquiry and registration in the camps set up throughout the state of Tamil Nadu. According to the MHA, on arriving in India, '. . . refugees are quarantined and after complete verification of their antecedents, they are shifted to refugee camps. Pending repatriation, certain essential relief facilities are provided to them on humanitarian grounds. These facilities include shelter in camps, cash doles, subsidised ration, clothing, utensils, medical care and educational assistance.'[18]

A People's Union for Civil Liberties (PUCL) report of 2006 explains what quarantine and verification of the antecedents of refugees mean. PUCL visited camps in 2006 where an estimated 4,343 refugees arrived following the war between LTTE and the Government of Sri Lanka. The report states that refugees arriving in Tamil Nadu are first 'checked...by the Indian Navy, and then [by] the Special Branch enquiry at Mugandaraya Chatram and then enquiry and registration by police at Danushkodi Police station . . . .' Following this, 'they are being offered food provided by voluntary agencies.' In describing the practice of quarantine, the report further states, 'those newly arrived are quarantined under police custody at the Mandapam Camp. This is a prison house. When we visited, 39 people were confined to the quarantine (nearly 20ft/20ft) for males.' Giving the example of Bhavanisagar camp and Keelpathupattu camp, the report noted, 'Though registration cards are immediately provided to those in the camps, in many camps, there are many without registration. For example, in Keelpathupattu camp, 949 people belonging to 100 families live without refugee registration. They don't get any facility provided by the government. The refugee registration for children born to those who marry outside the camps are cancelled . . .'[19]

Sri Lankan Tamil refugees in India are considered to be the blue-eyed refugees;[20] they supposedly live decent lives, are able to access education and continue to receive subsidised food, housing and other facilities in the camps. Such description fails to account for the following questions: why do camps continue to exist in India almost 30 years after the first batch of refugees fled Sri Lanka in 1983? Why provision of essential supplies and fundamental services still remains contingent on registration in the camps (those who opt to live outside of the designated camps do not have access to free housing, subsidised food and other doles made available by voluntary agencies)? And, what happens to those refugees who are detained within the camps either for failing to be cleared by the security agencies or arrested for violating the Foreigners Act or other laws?

The Sri Lankan example suggests that refugee care and protection is preceded by an ineluctable surveillance mechanism. Although surveillance infrastructure (the intelligence, police and the administrative bodies, camps and detention centres) takes its legitimacy from the plenary powers of the state over immigration matters, these bodies nonetheless continue to be bound by laws. Little information is available on the functioning of the Q Branch, the local Police as well as other administrative bodies in the refugee camps. Thus, it would be worthy of further inquiry whether the infrastructure set in place adhere to both national as well as international norms for prison-like condition in the camps or the failure of authorities to register refugees. And if they do, to what extent? Camps are subject to the very same laws that apply to the rest of India and these include the Constitution which has extensively interpreted fundamental rights under Article 21 (right to life) and Article 22 (rights of an arrested person). International laws, some of which have attained the status of customary international law, also bind India, irrespective of whether it has ratified the convention, and these include the Universal Declaration of Human Rights (Article 5), the Convention against Torture and Other Cruel, Inhuman and Degrading Treatment, UNHCR's Guidelines on Applicable Criteria and Standards relating to the Detention of Asylum-Seekers adopted in 1999.[21]

UNHCR's role in tracking and counting asylum seekers, refugees and other persons of concern

No formal agreement exists allowing UNHCR to function or recognising its role or mandate in India; it functions in India through the United National Development Programme (UNDP). Under an informal system, basic information including the name, date of birth, sex and country of origin and biometric data including the face collected as part of the UNHCR's internal registration process is shared with the MHA of the Government of India on a monthly basis.[22] UNHCR maintains that the claims of individual asylum seekers remain confidential.

UNHCR has an extensive mechanism to register asylum seekers. In a document dedicated to the how, what and why of registration, it states that '. . . the recording, verifying, and updating of information on persons of concern to UNHCR' is carried out '. . . with the aim of protecting and documenting them and of implementing durable solutions.'[23]

The *Procedural Standards for Refugee Status Determination under UNHCR Mandate* (UNHCR Procedural Standards)[24] provides further insight into the purposes of registration. The UNHCR Procedural Standards is an important document that regulates the RSD mechanism, a vital function for the protection of refugees. It states that the purposes of registration 'is to gather standard information about all persons of concern to UNHCR, including Applicants for mandate RSD [Refugee Status

Determination] and other asylum seekers, refugees, returnees, internally displaced persons, and stateless persons. The registration information permits the UNHCR to make informed assessments of the number and profile of persons of concern and to design programmes for protection and assistance. The registration information also permits UNHCR staff to identify and assist persons with special needs, and to make decisions about whether the individuals should be referred to further UNHCR procedures. As Applicants for mandate RSD are persons of concern to UNHCR, UNHCR must maintain current standard registration information for each individual Applicant, including Applicants for derivative status.'[25]

As one protection officer of the UNHCR explains 'you can't serve a population if you don't know who they are, and registration is the first step toward that. All protection interventions stem from getting the people on our books – knowing who people are individually makes all the difference between being able to provide assistance or not. Registration and data management can help you do a plethora of good acts for the population we're dealing with. Sometimes you get staff doing registration with strongly technical backgrounds or you have people with protection backgrounds. If you can marry the two, the output for assisting people is very, very strong.[26]

The *UNHCR policy on refugee protection and solutions in urban areas* adopted in September 2009 (hereafter, Urban refugee policy)[27] envisages provision of basic services such as livelihood and self reliance, access to health care and education, fostering constructive relations between the local community and refugees as a joint effort by UNHCR and the host government. It stresses on the utility, function, importance and the mechanism of registration to meet these goals in the urban settings.[28]

Registration, UNHCR asserts, serves the goal of protection, provision of services and in expanding 'protection space', defined in the Urban refugee policy of 2009 as 'a concept employed by the Office to denote the extent to which a conducive environment exists for the internationally recognised rights of refugees to be respected and their needs to be met.'[29] Such assertion, however, needs to be subjected to thorough scrutiny. These include the question of ownership[30] of information, the connected question of identity and lastly whether the link between profiling and protection is as linear as is made out to be. Problematising this assertion in the light of these questions, it is argued, places the problem of profiling, protection and documentation in context and brings to the fore some of these concerns.

Sharing of information by asylum seekers and refugees with UNHCR or any other government agency is affected by the following factors: the ability of the asylum seeker to communicate effectively and clearly, the capability of the translator to translate clearly and accurately, the comfort level of the asylum seeker with the UNHCR officer, the asylum seeker's fear of authority owing to her experience in her country of nationality, the knowledge about the social, political and economic situation of the officer who is involved in registration and lastly, the asylum seeker's knowledge of the legal procedures. It is not uncommon to find incorrect information or misrepresentation by asylum seekers; this however does not imply that the refugee intends to lie or misrepresent. It is also not uncommon for asylum seekers to distrust anyone who seeks personal information, which she may not want to share either because of cultural factors or the low levels of trust (in her own community, the UNHCR or any other third party). These factors, cumulatively, can determine the outcome, i.e. accuracy of information and the willingness of the asylum seeker to part with the information.

Such profiling once again highlights the fuzzy nature of identity and identification of some as worthy of protection and others as not. For instance, in case of resettlement of refugees, governments often determine which refugee can be resettled, on the basis of her educational levels, family constitution, religion, health and a subjective determination of her ability to integrate. Refugees who do not fit the particular resettlement criteria have dim chances of being resettled. Even within the country of asylum, some of the most impoverished refugees are denied protection and services over long periods of time despite systematic collection of data.

Thus, the question remains whether such profiling and documentation has improved the conditions of refugees. In India, for instance, refugees are known to live in inhuman and degrading conditions (such as the Rohingyas and Chins from Burma, the Somalis and other groups).

Having stopped monetary assistance (subsistence allowance), refugees are left by the UNHCR to their own devices to provide for housing, healthcare, sanitation, water, education and other basic facilities. While it would be unfair to argue that no refugee or asylum seeker is provided for by the UNHCR, it is also not accurate or credible to suggest that profiling has changed the social and economic condition of refugees for the better. This brings us to a question of actual purposes served by the profiling. If a large number of refugees in urban areas remain outside the protective net of the UNHCR and its implementing partners, to what purposes and ends is the information collected?

The answer lies in the identification mechanisms that the state has embarked upon, in order to sort outsiders from insiders.

THE RECENT INNOVATIONS IN THE IDENTIFICATION MECHANISMS

In the last few years, the Indian state has embarked on new identification projects which are couched in the language of welfare and protection while at the same time addressing internal security concerns. Of relevance to migration are three projects, namely, the Aadhaar, compulsory registration in the National Population Register and the IVFRT. In what ways do these projects directly impact refugees and asylum seekers in India?

The Indian refugee management policy is conceived to allow for the most flexibility in addressing a particular population influx, as the cases of Tibetan and Sri Lankan Tamil refugees suggest. This flexibility is a factor of local political concerns, foreign policy or, as the case of migration in the north-east India suggests, the impossibility of 'controlling' borders. This flexibility is also manifested in India's outsourcing of some essential functions such as the Refugee Status Determination to UNHCR, in addition to protection programmes. Such posturing helps India to indicate its seeming adherence to international law while at the same time maintain a distance from the international agency and in doing so, to abdicate its responsibility under international law. However, since immigration is a central subject falling under Entries 17[31] and 19[32] of the Union List (List I) in the Seventh Schedule of the

Constitution of India, the central government has plenary powers over matters related to immigration. This implies that should the MHA or the Ministry of External Affairs decide, it can trump all decisions of UNHCR, a court of law or a law in force and decide the fate of a refugee. It is against this backdrop that the identification project of the Government of India needs to be studied. Access to services, protection and availability of welfare schemes for refugees is therefore not the primary or even a necessary component of the government's refugee policy. As suggested by the Tibetan and the Sri Lankan Tamil experience, it may be safe to infer that security concerns dominate India's population-mapping projects.

Aadhaar as unique identifier

A pan-India project to 'identify' each resident was formally inaugurated in 2009, with the establishment of the Unique Identification Authority of India (UIDAI) as an office attached to the Planning Commission.[33] Its mandate is to ensure a 'unique' number to every resident in India to facilitate easy access to government schemes and eliminate fraud such as duplication of identities resulting in significant savings to the state. The unique number would include an individual's demographic and personal information and biometric information – photographs, ten fingerprints and iris.

Although the UID is not mandatory and is demand-driven, since it is linked to services and benefits and the fact that the UIDAI has signed numerous Memoranda of Understanding (MoUs) with bodies, including banks, public-sector agencies, private companies and civil-society organisations, it forces the resident to apply for a number.

Though now projected as a number that would help ensure better access to services and benefits for the poor by assigning and authenticating identity, the origins of the project can be traced to a series of events in the 1990s and after, and debates within the government on the question of national security, terrorism and illegal immigration into India.[34] The Kargil conflict between India and Pakistan is considered to have triggered the idea for the need to ensure that 'terrorists' do not enter Indian territory. In a post 9/11 world, in the Indian context, the term 'terrorist' has assumed a flexible definition, and preceded profiling of individuals based on nationality, religious affiliation or region. Thus, a Sri Lankan Tamil is a suspect, a terrorist irrespective of whether he/she was involved in the conflict. A Muslim living in either West Bengal or Assam runs the risk of being branded as a 'terrorist' notwithstanding the fact that he/she may well be a local Bengali or an Assamese.

The Kargil Review Committee in its recommendations, among others matters, noted the 'gross inadequacies in the nation's surveillance capability. . .' in the section on 'Intelligence'. It further recommended – in the section on Civil Military Liaison – that '. . . steps should be taken to issue ID Cards to border villagers in certain vulnerable areas on a priority basis, pending its extension to other or all parts of the State. Such a policy would also be relevant in the North-East, Sikkim and part of West Bengal.'[35] Several committees/bodies were set up in the 1990s with a view to probe issues concerning internal security, border management, etc. and evaluate the aspects of national security.[36] The idea of the smart-cards system is not articulated explicitly anywhere except the Recommendations of the Kargil Review Committee but debates in the Lok Sabha between April and December 2001 see a number of questions being asked on smart-cards system to be used for various services.[37] In 2006, the national e-governance plan of the Ministry of Information Technology listed the 'National Citizens Database'[38] as one of the 27 Mission Mode Projects towards ushering in an 'era of e-governance' so that it improves 'the delivery of public services and simplify the process of accessing them.'[39] Later in 2007, the Working Group on Development Policy in the Planning Commission came up with a report titled 'Entitlement Reform for Empowering the Poor: The Integrated Smart Card Report (ISC)'[40] where the idea of the identity card was elaborated.

The National Identification Authority of India Bill, 2010 (hereafter, the UID Bill) does not mention the government's national security concerns. Only a passing reference is made in the confidential document published by UIDAI titled 'Creating a Unique Identity Number for Every Resident in India' where it notes that the inability to identify residents 'complicates government efforts to account for residents during emergencies and *security threats*.'[41] The UID Bill makes this clear in its Preamble where it notes that the objective is, 'to provide for the establishment of the National Identification Authority of India for the purpose of issuing identification numbers to individuals residing in India and to certain other classes of individuals and manner of authentication of such individuals to facilitate access to benefits and services to such individuals to which they are entitled and for matters connected therewith or incidental thereto.'

Thus, couched in the language of welfare, Aadhaar is conceived on the rationale that the lack of identification results in the denial of services to those entitled to it. The document, 'Creating a Unique Identity Number for Every Resident in India', notes, 'A crucial factor that determines an individual's well-being in a country is whether their identity is recognised in the eyes of the government. Weak identity limits the power of the country's residents when it comes to claiming basic political and economic rights. The lack of identity is especially detrimental for the poor and the underprivileged, the people who live in India's "social, political and economic periphery". Agencies in both the public and private sector in India usually require a clear proof of identity to provide services. Since the poor often lack such documentation, they face enormous barriers in accessing benefits and subsidies.'[42]

The UID Bill includes two other important points on the question of surveillance, profiling and safeguarding of the information so that there is no misuse. Section 9 of the Bill states that, 'The Authority shall not require any individual to give information pertaining to his race, religion, caste, tribe, ethnicity, language, income or health.'

Among the features of the UID, it is noted that it will not contain intelligence because 'loading intelligence into identity numbers makes them susceptible to fraud and theft. The UID will be a random number.' Lastly, Section 30 of the Bill ensures security and confidentiality of identity information of individuals. Section 33 makes an exception where it states that information can be disclosed if required by an order of a competent court [Section 33(a)] or in the interests of national security [Section 33(b)].

It has been argued that even though the Bill is silent and denies either profiling or centralising of information, 'convergence is a predictable and inevitable consequence of the UID project.'[43] Ramanathan goes on to show how the UID along with other initiatives such as the National Intelligence Grid (NATGRID) makes it clear beyond doubt that surveillance is one of the key objectives of the project. The Aadhaar, NPR and IVFRT have the dual goal to *identify* each resident with a unique number so as to facilitate welfare services (Aadhaar) and differentiate between an illegal migrant and a citizen (NPR and IVFRT).

The Bali process – Indications that asylum seekers/refugees constitute an important category of the identification exercise

The recently concluded Bali Process meeting held in New Delhi in April 2012 indicates that the Aadhaar number is considered an important tool to track illegal immigrants. Initiated at the *Regional Ministerial Conference on People Smuggling, Trafficking in Persons and Related Transnational Crime* held in Bali in February 2002, the Bali Process brings together 46 members including UNHCR and IOM (International Organisation for Migration) and 29 observers, to work on practical measures to help combat people smuggling, trafficking in persons and related transnational crime in the Asia-Pacific region. India chaired its latest and recently concluded Ad Hoc Group Workshop on 'Biometrics for Identity Integrity in Immigration' from 23-26 April 2012, in Delhi. The Government of India presented two case studies:[44] UIDAI and IVFRT (Cabinet Committee on Economic Affairs, Government of India, 2010). While Aadhaar seeks to 'identify' residents, the IVFRT[45] has as its objective the development and implementation of a 'secure and integrated service delivery framework that facilitates legitimate travellers while strengthening security.'[46]

The participants in the Ad-Hoc Workshop agreed to 'strengthen authorised migration', 'prevent or disrupt unauthorised or irregular migration' and lastly 'to consider developing a framework of voluntary minimum standards to facilitate sharing biometrics to strengthen immigration integrity within the legal framework of member countries' and 'review these arrangements within 12 months in an appropriate Bali Process forum.' In addition, the application of biometric technology in border and immigration process was shared. It was agreed that countries who are part of the Bali Process would 'co-operate amongst themselves in managing cross border risks and adopting common strategies for improving outcomes and maximise benefits of biometrics' with the shared understanding that biometric technology would improve security, service and savings. It was also stated that the biometric information will be shared with partners in tune with legislative and regulatory requirements and in a spirit of protecting privacy. The workshop appears to have acknowledged that adopting biometrics to strengthen its immigration would impact non-citizens; the absence of a legal authority, the question of trust (unknown use and sharing of the data collected) and the lack of awareness were raised as challenges. Lastly, it was recognised that in keeping with UNHCR's principles related to handling of data of asylum seekers/refugees, it needs to be ensured that personal data is not shared with countries from whom they seek protection.

UNHCR, in its statement,[47] noted that it agreed to share information with states subject to legal and confidentiality considerations. It notes in particular that any sharing of data of asylum seekers or refugees with the country of origin of the refugee directly or indirectly is prohibited. It has recommended that states have consent of the individual whose biometric data is to be collected, clarity of purpose for which it is gathered and security safeguards in place. In addition, it has pointed out that individuals should have the right to correct misinformation and redress. Further, data sharing among governments must be preceded by a legal framework for adequate protection of privacy and compliance with data protection principles. Additionally, sharing of data should be restricted to what is necessary and based on the assessment that the data will not be misused, by the party in question.

Aadhaar and IVFRT appear to complement each other, in which the former seeks to provide a number that will guarantee identity which in turn will aid the effective provision of services and ensure savings for the state, while the other seeks to bring a foreigner within the gaze of the state by registration and tracking, so as to address the state's security concerns. In doing so, both these projects tend to define 'identity' in a reductionist sense, presuppose the absence of any foul play in the use of the information gathered and essentially argue that the inability of people to access services is 'weak' identity.

Couching the problem in terms of access to services and security as the Aadhaar and IVFRT do, raises some concerns. To begin with, does the state's definition of identity acknowledge that it is essentially a fuzzy and fluid category which cannot be reduced to basic bio-data and biometrics? The difficulty in such a reductionist definition is that it runs the risk of exclusion, let alone the fact that biometric information has not yet been proven to be fault-free. For instance, clearly indicating that what the state identifies as an Indian citizen may not be an accurate or the only description of an Indian. *Business World* reported how an Indian citizen was denied a voters identification card for having stated that he spoke Nepali.[48] Secondly, while data protection and privacy have been agreed to in principle, it is not clear what safeguards are currently in place to ensure that data theft does not occur, information is not shared with the country of origin or that the privacy of an individual is adequately secured. Further, on what basis is it decided whether the information sought is necessary?

Moreover, the use of Aadhaar and the IVFRT as tools/systems to identify, classify, track and manage the asylum-seeking migrant population is not matched by the state's responsibility to set up a refugee protection law (and not a policy alone) in place. Differentiating between authorised migration and illegal migration or mixed migration requires a clear, certain and well-defined body of law that would not only recognise a refugee as a legal category but also provide safeguards for a refugee to stake her claim under existing laws. As far as mandate refugees are concerned, such a mechanism is absent.

While it may be argued that India is a generous host to millions of refugees, a number of examples corroborate the observation that an ad-hoc policy cannot be a substitute for a legal framework. For instance, although Rohingyas have been in the news for fleeing the Arakan state in Burma following the clashes with the Buddhist population, *The Hindu* in its report dated 2 September, 2012 noted the arrest of '60 undocumented' Rohingya 'migrants' in Manipur who were 'pushed back while trying to enter' the state.[49] In the absence of an opportunity to apply for asylum, for these 'illegal migrants' the risk of deportation or arrest for violation of laws remains real.

However, independent of the question of law and a legal mechanism to allow the legal migrant and deny entry to those whose presence is labelled as illegal, studies on forced migration in the Indian sub-continent have sufficiently pointed out that migration in the region is made possible by a host of factors, with the easy permeability of the borders being just one. The cartographic exercise divided the territories but failed to segregate communities that share ethnic, religious and cultural ties. The borders present a less sanitised space where a host of factors, including state authorities, are equally involved in making the border irrelevant – the economy that is generated and sustained at the borders being one of the most important factors. In addition, some borders are impossible to draw on the ground irrespective of the number of border security officers posted along legally imagined border areas. Cases in point are the borders in North-East India or the Pakistan-Afghanistan border where both human and natural reasons have rendered the borders irrelevant, if not notional. Thus, identifying a citizen becomes a difficult task precisely where migration becomes impossible to check.

A number of projects and programmes make the 'refugee' a central part of their existence; yet the current policy framework have the potential to throw up more confusing scenarios[50] and questions than they are likely to provide concrete answers to. The Aadhaar project, for instance, has been welcomed by the Tibetan refugee community so far. Tenzing Tsundue, a Tibetan activist, explains that Tibetans have taken an interest in the Aadhaar numbers. Some believe that an Aadhaar 'card' replaces the Registration Certificate and is a 'better' identity document than the Registration Certificate and an easier way to identify oneself.[51] Others such as the Hindus from Pakistan may also welcome such a project signifying that they 'want to be counted.'[52]

Assuming that refugees want to be counted, the absence of a legal framework that address issues of confidentiality, privacy and data protection highlights areas of concern. Asylum seekers are known to fear authority, including agencies like the UNHCR, the police, and the FRRO and this may explain their reluctance to share their biometric data. In countries such as India where refugees face hostility, they may consider finger printing/collection of other biometric information to be a badge of criminality.

On the other hand, identification practices have the potential of protecting the refugee population even if it is not the primary objective, as the cases of Tibetans and Sri Lankan Tamils illustrate. Thus, assuming that projects like Aadhaar would benefit every resident, would the benefit extend automatically to the refugee groups? Research on refugees in India has repeatedly pointed out that although refugees and asylum seekers (in the last two to three years) are assured of protection and assistance under the *UNHCR Policy on refugee protection and solutions in urban areas* adopted in September 2009[53], protection programmes for refugees and asylum seekers remain a half-hearted attempt, requiring more than just a policy document. Aadhaar and the technology that it relies upon are therefore unlikely to play a transformatory role in facilitating services more efficiently than the existing experience, in the absence of a mandate that is backed by clear laws and mechanisms designed to implement the policy.

Further, refugees and refugee advocates have for long insisted that India ratify the 1951 Convention on the Status of Refugees and/or adopt a law. The Government of India is disinclined to change the status quo.[54] In such a political scenario, what assures that a potentially technologically savvy government will want to do things any differently? Does this then lead us to conclude that the Aadhaar, the registration of citizens under the Citizenship Act, 1955, the IVFRT and the UNHCR Refugee Cards[55] primarily aim to profile individuals that are geared towards national security concerns than with making access to services and protection a reality?

The identity conundrum

Lastly, but no less important (and in fact a central argument of the Aadhaar project), is the question of the categories (legal-illegal, foreigner-citizen, BPL-APL etc) that these projects construct and sustain, ones that are perceived to solve problems of security and welfare. Migratory patterns in South Asia demonstrate sufficiently that it defies easy categorisation and a mono-chromatic narrative. This leads to the inference that although the identificatory projects may document refugees/asylum seekers, many others fall outside such mechanisms. Migration in South Asia highlights the layered nature of identity that is the hallmark of citizenship in South Asia. The north-east for instance is a kaleidoscope of movements of people across and within borders. These continually changing patterns of migration turn the received and valorised conceptions of nation-state and citizenship on its head, suggesting that distinctions made in law between the citizen and the alien, the insider and the outsider, and the excluded and the included, lose traction and meaning. The identities are fluid and not always hostage to the ones determined by the state; the allegiances towards 'brothers' and 'sisters' across borders continue to be strong, as the cases of Arunachal Pradesh or Mizoram indicate.[56]

CONCLUSION

Little public discussion preceded the implementation of the Aadhaar project and in any case little or no discussion is visible on the possible impact of Aadhaar or other surveillance mechanisms on refugees and asylum seekers. Independent of how these projects seek to implicate the non-citizen into the state mechanism of surveillance, the projected goals of the Aadhaar project have not been proved satisfactorily, leading one to ask what the real aim of creating such large databases without considering their potential misuse is. As people on the margins, asylum seekers and refugees are reluctant to part with information which they would have no control of. What has also not been proven beyond doubt is whether the availability of exhaustive information, in the Indian context, has led to a better and more efficient system of delivery of services, both in case of refugees and citizens.

NOTES

1. http://deity.gov.in/content/mission-mode-projects [Accessed on November 15, 2012]
2. Samaddar, Ranabir, ed., *Refugees and the State: Practices of Asylum and Care in*

India, 1947-2000, Sage: Delhi, 2003, p.77

3. The other being the Citizenship Act, 1955, which, in specific reference to the population-mapping project, requires all citizens to be registered in the National Population Register. The Unique Identification Authority of India Bill, 2010, strictly in terms of the law, would not apply, although the project is currently underway
4. See for instance, Mr. Bogyi *v* Union of India, CR 1847 of 1989 (Guwahati High Court), Dr. Malavika Karlekar *v* Union of India, WP 583 of 1992 (Supreme Court of India) where the court has held that refugees have a right to undergo refugee status determination and thus stopped their deportation, Digvijay Mote *v* Union of India, WA 354 of 1994 (Karnataka High Court) where the court directed that a destitute refugee may be provided with basic amenities, P. Nedumaran *v* Union of Indiam WP 12298 and 12313 of 1992 (Madras High court) where it was held that forced repatriation is not permissible
5. The reasons may be many including lack of information, the inability to travel to New Delhi to register with UNHCR or the decision not to formally seek asylum. See for instance SAHRDC, Survival, Dignity, and Democracy: Burmese Refugees in India, 1997, available at http://www.hri.ca/partners/sahrdc/burmese/fulltext.html [last accessed 27 June 2012] which notes that Burmese refugees who initially fled to India following the crackdown on pro-democracy protestors in 1988 opted not to apply for asylum because of their belief that their applications would be rejected by UNHCR
6. Human Rights Watch, "We are like forgotten people: unsafe in Burma, unprotected in India", 2009; http://www.hrw.org/reports/2009/01/27/we-are-forgotten-people [last accessed 10 August 2012]
7. It is not clear whether this issue has been resolved. Refugees argue that approaching the FRRO at the time of their arrival in the country puts them at a risk of being arrested for violating Section 3, Passport (Entry into India) Act (entering India without a passport), 1920, and Section 14, Foreigners Act, 1946 (continues to stay in India after the expiry of the period for which a visa was issued). Second, since the Refugee Status Determination process of UNHCR takes anywhere between six months to two years, they are not in a position to apply for Residence Permits at an earlier stage. It cannot be ruled out, however, that one of the reasons for imposing this fee may also have to do with checking the number of Burmese nationals officially seeking asylum.
8. Some amount of confusion continues with respect to this announcement. While the term 'long-term visa' has been used to describe the status of recognised refugees, officials at the FRRO in New Delhi have informed the author that this process would grant 'Residence Permits'. Under the law, a visa and a Residence Permit have different meanings
9. Bhattacharya, Suryatapa, 'India's Myanmar refugees get visas after month of protests in Delhi', *The National, May 17, 2012;* http://www.thenational.ae/

news/world/south-asia/indias-myanmar-refugees-get-visas-after-month-of-protests-in-delhi [last accessed 12 August 2012]; UNHCR, Summary conclusions of meeting with representatives of asylum-seekers from northern Rakhine State, Myanmar, http://www.unhcr.org.in/pages/showmainstory/10 [last accessed 11 August 2012]

10. Raina, Pamposh, "Thousands of Myanmar Rohingyas struggle for refugee status in India", *The New York Times*, India Edition, 18 May 2012; http://india.blogs.nytimes.com/2012/05/18/thousands-of-myanmar-rohingyas-struggle-for-refugee-status-in-india/ [last accessed 7 September 2012]
11. Ibid
12. Tibet Justice Centre, Tibet's stateless nationals II: Tibetan refugees in India, A report, September, 2011, p. 8; http://www.tibetjustice.org/reports/stateless-nationals-ii/stateless-nationals-ii.pdf [last accessed 8 August 2012]
13. Bureau of Immigration, Ministry of Home Affairs, Government of India, Information pertaining to Tibetan nationals, http://www.immigration india.nic.in/Instr_Tibetans2.htm [last accessed 7 September 2012]
14. Tibet Justice Centre, p.8
15. Ibid, pp.10-11
16. Ibid, pp.11-12
17. Ministry of Home Affairs, Government of India, Annual Report, 2011-2012, p.247; http://www.mha.nic.in/pdfs/AR%28E%291112.pdf [last accessed 7 September 2012]
18. Ibid, pp. 297-98
19. PUCL (TN & Pondicherry), Conditions in Sri Lankan Tamil refugee camps, 2006;
    http://www.pucl.org/Topics/International/2006/refugees-srilanka-report.html [last accessed 27 June 2012]
20. In a national consultation on the rights of children of refugees, migrants and stateless people in India organised by Haq: Centre for Child Rights and Development and Justice Initiative on 20 October 2012 in New Delhi, this is how an activist working with Sri Lankan Tamil refugees in Tamil Nadu, Ms. Florina Benoit, characterised the treatment and care of refugees by the state and central government.
21. UNHCR, Guidelines on Applicable Criteria and Standards relating to the Detention of Asylum-Seekers, February, 1999; www.unhcr.org/refworld/pdfid/3c2b3f844.pdf [last accessed 29 October 2012]
22. Interview with UNHCR India, 14 August 2012, New Delhi
23. UNHCR handbook for registration: Procedures and standards for registration, population data management and documentation, September, 2003;
    http://www.unhcr.org/3f8e9ce14.html [last accessed 10 August 2012]
24. UNHCR, Procedural standards for refugee status determination under UNHCR's mandate, September, 2005, Geneva; http://www.unhcr.org/publPUBL/4316f0c02.html [last accessed 27 June 2012]

25. Ibid, Unit 3: 3-1 to 3-31.
26. UNHCR, Q&A: Refugee registration takes UNHCR official across southern Africa, 30 March 2007; http://www.unhcr.org/460d08e34.html [last accessed 12 August 2012]
27. UNHCR Policy on Refugee Protection and Solutions in Urban Areas, September, 2009; http://www.unhcr.org/refworld/docid/4ab8e7f72.html [last accessed 12 August 2012]
28. Ibid, pp.9-11
29. Ibid, p.4
30. I wish to thank Patrick Hoenig who suggested that this aspect be taken into consideration in this analysis.
31. Citizenship, naturalisation and aliens.
32. Admission into and emigration and expulsion from, India; passports and visas.
33. The website of the UIDAI can be accessed at www.uidai.gov.in.
34. Mehmood, Taha, "Notes from a contested history of National Identity Card in India:1999-2007," *South Asia Citizens Wire*, 9 December 2008; http://www.sacw.net/article391.html [last accessed 5 August 2010]
35. "From surprise to reckoning," Kargil Review Committee, Executive Summary, 25 February 2000; http://nuclearweaponarchive.org/India/KargilRCA.html [last accessed 6 September 2012]
36. Mehmood, "Notes"
37. Ibid.
38. http://deity.gov.in/content/national-citizen-database [last accessed 8 September 2012]
39. See the webpage of the National e-Governance Plan, http://deity.gov.in/content/national-e-governance-plan [last accessed 8 September 2012]
40. Planning Commission of India, "Entitlement Reform for Empowering the Poor: The Integrated Smart Card Report (ISC)", http://planningcommission.nic.in/aboutus/committee/wrkgrp11/wg11_smtcard.pdf [last accessed 8 September 2012]
41. UIDAI, "Creating a unique identity number for every resident in India, Unique Identification Authority of India", Working Paper – version 1.1, November, 2009; http://wlstorage.net/file/creating-a-unique-id-for-every-resident-in-india-2009.pdf [last accessed 8 September 2012]
42. Ibid, p.10
43. Ramanathan, Usha, "A Unique Identity Bill," *Economic and Political Weekly*, XLV: 30, 24 July 2010, p.11
44. Representatives from Australia (co-chair), Islamic Republic of Afghanistan, Peoples Republic of Bangladesh, Indonesia, Malaysia, Maldives, Republic of the Union of Myanmar, Islamic Republic of Pakistan, the Philippines, Sri Lanka, Kingdom of Thailand, United States of America, and Vietnam as well

as representatives from the Office of the United Nations High Commissioner for Refugees (UNHCR) participated. Canada and the United Kingdom attended the meeting as observers; Bali Process, Final co-chairs statement, Ad Hoc Group Workshop on Biometrics for Identity Integrity in Immigration, New Delhi, India, 23-26 April 2012; http://www.baliprocess.net/files/Final-Co-chairs%20Statement%20Biometrics%20Workshop%202012.pdf [last accessed 8 September 2012]

45. A Mission Mode Project approved by the Cabinet Committee on Economic affairs in 2010. The National Institute for Smart Government (NSIG) was selected and tasked with the responsibility for generating a comprehensive e-Governance solution for the immigration, visa issuance and foreigners' registration and tracking functions, and to prepare a Detailed Project Report (DPR) for the same
46. Bali Process, Ad Hoc Group Workshop on Biometrics for Identity Integrity in Immigration, New Delhi, India, 23-26 April 2012; http://www.baliprocess.net/files/Final-Co-chairs%20Statement%20Biometrics%20 Workshop%202012.pdf [last accessed 8 September 2012]
47. Bali Process, UNHCR's Statement, Ad Hoc Group Workshop on Biometrics for Identity Integrity in Immigration, New Delhi, India, 23-26 April 2012. On file with the author
48. Mani, Jyoti Thapa, "In-Depth Citizenship issues plague Nepali-speaking Indians too", *Business World*, 14 March 2008; http://www.businessworld.in/index.php/Miscellaneous/Identity-Crisis.html [last accessed 10 August 2012]
49. "60 undocumented migrants pushed back while trying to enter Manipur" *The Hindu,* 2 September 2012; http://www.thehindu.com/news/national/article 3850239.ece?homepage=true&css=print [last accessed 15 November 2012
50. For instance, the recently announced policy of 'long term visas' to refugees is equally confusing. While it is termed as a 'visa', the FRRO states that they issue a 'Residence Permit' under Rule 7 of the Foreigners Order, 1948, a document that all foreigners have to apply for once they are in India on a valid visa and satisfy certain conditions of duration of stay. If it is only the Residence Permit that is issued to a refugee, this does not explain how and why the Ministry should carry out a parallel 'refugee status determination' (verifying whether the applicant is a refugee or an economic migrant, as stated by the MHA official).
51. Interview with Tenzing Tsundue at Dharamshala by the Centre for the Study of Culture and Society, Bangalore; undated. On file with the author
52. See the article by Bharat Bhushan in this volume.
53. UNHCR Policy on Refugee Protection
54. Interview with an official of the MHA, Government of India, 28 August 2012.
55. UNHCR started issuing refugee cards (replacing the Refugee Certificates) in

July 2011. These have been promoted by UNHCR as a safer and better option that would 'make a real difference to their lives'. "UNHCR distributes pioneering smart ID cards to refugees in India", 1 August 2011; http://www.unhcr.org/4e4bd1506.html [last accessed 12 August 2012]

56. Tun, Salai, "Border fence unnecessary, Mizoram authorities say," *Mizzima News,* 9 September 2010; http://www.mizzima.com/news/regional/4339-border-fence-unnecessary-mizoram-authorities-say.html [last accessed 15 November 2012]

V

Identifying Pakistani Migrants in India

Bharat Bhushan

Migrants from Pakistan came to India in three major waves – first, after the Partition of India in 1947, then after the 1965 India-Pakistan war and then again after the 1971 war. Except those who came to Jammu & Kashmir, the refugees who came to India after the Partition have full legal rights as citizens of the country. Those who came to Jammu & Kashmir are in a special category, as shall be discussed later, because of the special status of the state. Migrants from Pakistan, however, continued to cross over to India even after 1971 and their numbers saw a spurt during the dictatorship of General Zia-ul-Haq and the numbers are believed to have seen a spurt after 2005 and then again between 2009 and 2012.

HINDU MIGRATION FROM PAKISTAN

The story of Pakistani citizens seeking shelter in India is the fall-out of the continued faith of the majority in Pakistan in the two-nation theory. Even though the belief that religion could be the basis of a nation for all practical purposes should have been dispelled by the creation of Bangladesh out of Islamic Pakistan, it continues to power the imagination and actions of a large majority in that country. The gradual and continued Islamisation of Pakistan has had a direct impact on Pakistan's minorities – Hindus, Christians and the non-Sunni Muslims like the Ahmedis, and the Shias. They have become targets of religious zealots and they get little or no protection from the state which seems wary of taking on their tormentors.

Most of the Pakistani migrants to India are from the Hindu minority of Pakistan. The estimates of the Hindu population of Pakistan vary. According to the 1951 Census of Pakistan, the proportion of Hindus in the population was 22 per cent. However, that included the Hindus of East Pakistan, which became Bangladesh in 1971. There are no definitive estimates of the Hindu population of Pakistan after that till 1998. The Pakistan Hindu Council claims that Hindus form 5.5 per cent of the total population of Pakistan.[1] Others claim that they are only about 2.5 per cent, or 2,600,000, of Pakistan's population.[2] Yet others claim that Hindus form 1.6 per cent of Pakistan's population.[3] The 1.6 per cent figure – the population of Hindus is from the 1998 Census – is the last available census of Pakistan.[4] Hindus (upper castes or Jatis) are counted separately from the Scheduled Castes (lower castes) in the Pakistan Census – and the latter were 0.25 per cent of the population in the 1998 Census. That brings the proportion of the Hindu population to about 1.85 per cent of the total population of Pakistan. There are no estimates of Hindu population of Pakistan available since 1998.

What is well-known, however, is that a majority of the Hindus reside in Sindh (the third largest province of Pakistan located in the south-eastern corner of the country and sharing a long border with India) and they were 7.5 per cent – comprising 6.51 per cent Upper Caste Hindus (Jatis) and 0.99 per cent Scheduled Castes – of the total population of the province in 1998.[5] The Hindu minority is largely concentrated in the southern part of the Sindh province, especially the Tharparkar district which shares a border with the Indian states of Rajasthan and Gujarat. Up to 1970 the Tharparkar district of Sindh used to be a Hindu-majority district of Pakistan – with 70 per cent of its population believed to comprise Hindus. However, some estimates suggest that it has now come down to 30 per cent of the total due to migration to India.[6] Mirpur Khas, Sanghar and Umarkot are the other districts of Sindh with a sizeable Hindu population. The other areas of Pakistan with a substantial Hindu population are Hyderabad, Ghotki, Khairpur, Dadu, Badin, Sukkur and Karachi.

In the past, Tharparkar never witnessed inter-community or communal strife – not even in 1947 when the northern parts of India and Pakistan were burning. The relations between the Hindus and the Muslims have traditionally been one of tolerance towards each other. They share a common culture and worship common deities, although by different names. The Hindu Meghwals of Rajasthan and Sindh, for example, worship Baba Ramdevji, believed by some to be a fourteenth-century Tanwar Rajput King, while the Muslims of the region worship him as Baba Ramsaa, Ramaa Peer or Ram Shah Peer.[7] The area is influenced by Sufi traditions and there has never been any major anti-Hindu violence in Sindh. Yet, Hindus keep fleeing from Sindh. Each time there is a war or communal development in India such as the Babri Masjid demolition in 1992 or major communal violence such as the one in 2002 in Gujarat, the inter-community strife between the Muslim majority and the insecure Hindu minority of Pakistan increases and becomes more apparent. This results in an immediate majority backlash against the Hindus, forcing them to re-examine their situation as second-class citizens of Pakistan. The Sindhi migrants from Tharparkar come to India not because of any overt communal violence against them but because of a growing sense of insecurity. The destruction of the Babri Masjid, for example, led to the burning of Hindu temples in Sindh and Southern Punjab. The backlash against the Hindu minority in Pakistan even saw some killings which again resulted in a fresh spurt of migration to India.

The Pakistani migrants to India come largely from Sindh but not only from Sindh. They are also known to come in smaller numbers from Punjab – Hindus live in significant numbers in the districts of Rahim Yar Khan, Sadiqabad, Multan, Sialkot, Narowal, Mandi Bahauddin, Islamabad, Rawalpindi and Attock – and even from the Khyber Pakhtunkhwa province and Balochistan. Those from Sindh come to Rajasthan and Gujarat while those who come from West Punjab and from the other provinces try to settle down in East Punjab (that is, Indian Punjab), in Sirsa in Haryana or even Delhi which has some families of

Pakistani migrants near Majnoo ka Tila and Jehangirpuri. The Sindhi migrants to Rajasthan and Gujarat are largely Sodha Rajputs and Dalits from the Meghwal, Bheel, Koli and Charan castes. The Sodha Rajputs are from Tharparkar and they are a landowning caste. Their migration is virtually non-existent today. The Dalit migrants from Pakistan come from Upper Sindh as well as Southern Punjab.

While military conflicts between the two countries and the communal clashes in India led to waves of migration as the minority community is targeted in Pakistan, other factors are responsible for a slower but persistent migration of Pakistani Hindus to India. The factors which create insecurity among Pakistani Hindus are virtually the same across various provinces of the country. I. A. Rehman, eminent Pakistani political commentator and human rights activist, analysing the migration of Hindus, sums up the plight of Pakistani Hindus as follows: 'Pakistani Hindus have, by and large, displayed great qualities of forbearance by resigning themselves to their status as second-class citizens as long as they are allowed to pursue their vocations and live with some vestiges of dignity. It is the inability to realise even these modest expectations that has driven them to despair.' He identifies several reasons for their disenchantment with the Pakistani State: the seizure of Hindu shrines and their attached properties by the state and influential members of the majority community; ignoring their basic needs such as housing and their right to buy plots of land in officially sponsored housing estates; the snatching of land traditionally owned and cultivated by members of the Scheduled Castes by the local bigwigs and turning them into bonded labour; discrimination in access to state employment and educational opportunities; and not allowing them to freely run their private businesses. Worse, he notes, 'they began to be targeted for abduction for ransom, threats to their lives and property became more common, and the forced conversions and marriages of their girls took the form of campaigns organised by well-known clerics and political figures. On top of everything they got the feeling that the state did not even listen to their grievances.'[8]

This view is supported by the Pakistan Hindu Council. Its chairman, Ramesh Kumar Vankwani, told a newspaper that the reasons for the exodus of the Hindu community were 'abduction, rape and coerced conversion of our daughters, extortion, blackmailing and kidnapping of businessmen for ransom.'[9] Pakistani newspapers have also reported that Hindu traders of Punjab claim that members of the majority community often dishonour loans or business deals and get away by targeting them as blasphemers and Indian agents. The police are believed to be in cahoots with the 'extortion mafia' and help it to identify rich Hindu traders and businessmen for kidnapping and ransom.[10] Journalistic reports in Pakistan suggest that interior Sindh has seen a sharp increase in incidents of kidnapping for ransom of rich Hindu traders and their family members as well as in the abduction and rape of poor Hindu girls between 2009 and 2012. There is an increasing belief that even the courts will do nothing to help, and such is the fear that testifying against their kidnappers will cause harm to their family that abducted women refuse to do so in court and even refuse to recognise their kin in the courtroom.

The Hindus of Pakistan cite the 'Rinkle Kumari case' where even the courts which were 'their last hope of justice' did not provide relief to the Hindu victims.[11] Three Pakistani Hindu women – Rinkle Kumari, Lata and Asha – were kidnapped and forcibly married to their kidnappers. The kidnappers had the support of a Pakistan People's Party Member of National Assembly from Sindh Pir Abdul Haq Mian Mithu, who allegedly pressured and threatened the women if they went back to their families. When the Supreme Court gave them the 'freedom' to choose, not unsurprisingly, they chose to stay on with their kidnappers. Civil rights activists pointed out that the court did not take into account the circumstances under which they were asked to choose and some had not even been granted counselling time to weigh their options.[12] After the Supreme Court verdict, many Pakistani Hindus said that they had lost faith even in the judiciary.

The judgement clearly emboldened the extremist religious elements in Sindh, forcing the remaining Hindus to reconsider their stay in the province. After the Rinkle Kumari judgement a newspaper report claimed, 'the insecurity among Hindus increased after some extremists from another religion started a street campaign and made announcements using loudspeakers in different areas of Sindh to "choose and pick" Hindu girls for their forceful [*sic*] conversion.'[13] Except for a few Hindu policemen in Tharparkar in Sindh, Hindus are not present in the police forces of Balochistan, Khyber Pakhtunkhwa (earlier, the North West Frontier Province, or NWFP) and Punjab. So the minority Hindus can expect little help from the police. The 'War on Terror' has increased the presence of hardliner Islamists in Khyber Pakhtunkhwa. This has also increased the insecurity of the Hindus living in the province bordering Afghanistan. Many Hindu families are believed to have left their homes in Khyber Pakhtunkhwa, although it is difficult to say how many have fled because of the 'War on Terror'.

After a sharp spike in reports of migration of Hindus from Pakistan to India in 2012, when a group of about 250 of them set out for a pilgrimage to India, the Pakistan government made them give an undertaking that they would return.[14] These developments forced the Human Rights Commission of Pakistan to note in a statement that 'reports of Hindu citizens' migration to India have been coming from Sindh and Balochistan fairly regularly. Some spokespersons of minorities have argued that vested interests are threatening and frightening the non-Muslim citizens with a view of forcing them to migrate. Some of these elements are said to be religious extremists while others are said to have plans to grab their property. In any case there is little doubt that the minorities have been driven to despair.' The report argued that the continued migration of religious minorities 'from Sindh and Balochistan is a reflection of the state's failure to save these citizens from violence, discrimination and excesses such as forced conversion of young women. The live telecast of a recent conversion of a young Hindu man on television is a particularly reprehensible and indefensible manifestation of the attitude towards non-Muslims.'[15]

The Human Rights Commission of Pakistan has urged the government to demonstrate that it shares the distress of the minorities and for political parties to include in their manifestoes their vision for religious minorities in Pakistan. Others, like I. A. Rehman, have demanded the setting up of a high-powered commission to look into the condition of the minorities and their grievances. Such a commission, he argues, should ask the following questions:

> How many killers of minorities have been caught and punished? How many victims of abductions for ransom have won freedom through official efforts? What action has been taken against hate-preachers and those who have called for murder and arson? What steps have been taken to free executive officers and police forces of their communal biases?
>
> What is the answer to involuntary conversions and forced marriages? Why have redress mechanisms, from the so-called Minorities Commission to district commissions on minorities failed to deliver? And to what extent have political parties and other civil society elements defended minorities' rights?[16]

Whether such a commission is set up by the Pakistan government or not is a different matter; however, what these questions show is that there is an acute awareness among the Pakistan elite that the minorities are under threat. And as long as they feel threatened, they will continue to seek refuge elsewhere. For Pakistani Hindu migrants, the most obvious route is to India.

LEGAL STATUS OF PAKISTANI MIGRANTS IN INDIA

There are four different kinds of migration that have taken place from Pakistan to India: a) those who crossed over to the rest of India (excluding Jammu & Kashmir) in large hordes during a calamitous event like the wars such of 1965 and 1971; b) those who crossed over illegally post-1972 in an episodic manner to come and stay with their relatives in India hoping to stay on permanently – this has become increasingly difficult since the fencing of the border; c) those who come legally on short-term visas granted on their Pakistani passports, get them converted to long-term visas in the hope of finally applying for Indian citizenship; d) the migrants from West Pakistan and Pakistan Occupied Kashmir (PoK) who migrated to the Indian side of Jammu & Kashmir in 1947 and then again after the India-Pakistan wars of 1965 and 1971 from the villages in Chhamb and adjoining areas. What is the legal status of these four categories of migrants and what is it that they want from the Indian state?

LEGAL STATUS OF PAKISTANI MIGRANTS

The Government of India does not in general recognise Pakistani migrants to the country as refugees. It considers the migration of Hindus from Pakistan as an 'internal matter' of Pakistan – at least that is the position that the Ministry of External Affairs seems to have taken in an RTI query on 1 November 2011. In the same reply, the Ministry of Home Affairs said that it was not in a position to say how many of the Pakistani Hindus had immigrated to India.[17] India does not have specific refugee legislation – it is neither a party to the United Nations Convention Relating to the Status of Refugees (1951) nor to the Protocol Relating to the Status of Refugees (1967). As a result, the entire approach of India to different groups of refugees is *ad hoc* and determined by the immediate interests of the government of the day. Different refugee groups are treated differently depending on political and administrative exigencies – accepting some within the legal fold by giving them specific rights and criminalising others and denying them access to basic social services like education, healthcare, employment and residence.

The migrants from Pakistan have sometimes been treated as refugees and sometimes as illegal aliens. It is estimated that roughly 115,000 Pakistani migrants have arrived in India since 1965. Of these, an estimated 10,000 came after the 1965 war and another 70,000 to 80,000 Sindhi Hindus crossed over to India after the 1971 war. Similarly, after the demolition of the Babri Masjid, some 17,000 Sindhi Hindus crossed over to India.[18] Those who came in the wake of the 1971 war were lucky to be recognised by the Indian government as refugees. The government opened refugee camps for them which were run with the help of WHO. Most of the migrants who came to India before 1972 have been granted citizenship by now. The major complaint of these migrants who have now become Indian citizens is that they have not been given adequate or promised rehabilitation packages. They were promised, for example, that each family would get 25 bighas of land in canal-irrigated areas or between 50 to 70 bighas in non-irrigated barren land in the desert areas. Some have got only part of the land; some complain that the land meant for them was included in a desert national park, occupied by local people etc.[19]

Of the second category of migrants – those who crossed over illegally in the post-1972 period, there is no hard data available. One can only assume that most merged with the local population because of their extended families or relatives on this side of the border, hoping eventually to become legal. These are people who have entered India through the Rann of Kutch and Sir Creek areas without valid documentation. Since their entry is clandestine and surreptitious there is no correct estimate of such Pakistani migrants living in India.

In the third category are those who are in India on legal documents, who get their stay extended legally and want to be recognised as refugees and seek Indian citizenship. In 2005, there were about 17,000 post-1972 Pakistani migrants in Rajasthan and Gujarat. They were treated not as refugees but as oustees from Pakistan. They came on city-specific visas ostensibly to visit their relatives in cities like Delhi, Hissar and Hardwar but went to Gujarat and Rajasthan with which they had cultural and linguistic affinity but where their presence was illegal.[20] They were illegal because their stay in Gujarat and Rajasthan was without a visa and therefore they had to hide their identity. Most of them work as low-paid workers in agriculture, open petty shops, sell vegetables, bangles (*manihari*), etc or work in stone quarries. In 2005, most of them were given citizenship and basic rights through special camps organised by the government in the districts of Barmer, Jodhpur, Jaisalmer, Bikaner, Jalore and Pali. Of the 17,000 only 13,000 fulfilled the citizenship criterion – the rest had not been in India for five years or more.[21]

How do Pakistani immigrants get citizenship? The Indian Constitution and the Indian Citizenship Act of 1955 has special provisions for those who were born or whose parents were born in undivided India to apply for citizenship. The Citizenship Amendment Rules 2004 specifically allow Pakistani migrants to apply for citizenship in Gujarat and Rajasthan. The residence requirement for Pakistani migrants before they can apply for citizenship is five years – there are reports that this has been extended to seven years instead of shortening the residence requirement – as opposed to 12 years for other foreigners. The fee has been increased and many of the Pakistani migrants cannot afford to apply for citizenship for their entire families, coming as they do from very poor Dalit backgrounds.

The Pakistani Hindus, or for that matter, any migrant, has to follow a rather tedious procedure to get Indian citizenship. An application for grant of Indian citizenship is to be submitted by the applicant to the Collector/DM/DC within whose jurisdiction the applicant is ordinarily a resident. The Collector/DM/DC after satisfying himself regarding the eligibility of the applicant to become a citizen of India, forwards the application to the State Government/Union Territory administration. The State Government forwards the application, along with its recommendation, to the Ministry of Home Affairs. Hence, the grant of Indian citizenship is a multi-level and multi-agency activity. Still, no caste- or religion-based centralised data of such applications is maintained at the Ministry of Home Affairs.[22] Unlike the pre-1971 migrants who were recognised as refugees, the post-1971 migrants have not received any rehabilitation package and they are not recognised as refugees. Despite having received Indian citizenship, many of them still do not have ration cards or BPL cards and cannot benefit from the government's social welfare schemes. Then there seems to be a distinction between the post-1971 Pak migrants who came to Rajasthan where most have managed to get Indian Citizenship and those who went to Gujarat and have not as yet got citizenship. They number in several thousand but only a few hundred have got Indian citizenship.[23]

In the wake of the Babri Masjid demolition, a group of Pakistani Hindu families is also reported to have settled down in Haryana – especially in Sirsa. They too have not got citizenship, although many have married locally and have had children in India.[24] A group of 145 Hindus who arrived for pilgrimage to Delhi in December 2011 have refused to go back. They live in a make-shift camp near Delhi's Majnoo ka Tila and have managed to extend their visas. The Foreigners' Regional Registration Office in Delhi has reported that the number of Pakistani Hindus coming to India has shown a rapid increase from mid-2011.[25] However, consolidated data on the potential migrants is hard to come by. According to the Home Ministry between 1 January 2008 and 21 December 2010, 1,686 applications of Pakistani nationals were received for citizenship. Of these only 866 were granted citizenship. Between 2009 and 2011, 148 applications were received from Pakistani Hindus for citizenship, 16 were granted citizenship, 119 are pending consideration for want of requisite documents and 13 were rejected. In all 1,290 applications of Pakistani nationals were received from various state governments/Union Territories for grant of Indian citizenship by registration and naturalisation during 2009-2011. Indian citizenship was granted to 764 Pakistani nationals during this period.[26]

The Ministry of Home Affairs revealed in a Right to Information (RTI) query that as of 31 December 2009, the number of Pakistanis overstaying in India was 7,691. Most of them were believed to be Hindus and Sikhs.[27] The number of Pakistanis who were found to be overstaying in India on expired visas in 2011 had gone up to 8,319. They were booked, made to undergo prison term and deported back to Pakistan. The point the government makes is that the procedure of tracking them and locating them is poor as the Foreign Regional Registration Offices, intelligence agencies and local police are short-staffed and cannot keep track of those who have overstayed their visas. As of 30 June 2011, some 1,283 Pakistani nationals remained untraced or missing, having come to India on valid visas according to the Ministry of Home Affairs.

The trend amongst Pakistani visitors of overstaying their visa has been recorded in some detail in Rajasthan. Official statistics show that around 23,000 Pakistani citizens have come to Rajasthan since 2007; of these, 4,624 did not return on the expiry of their visas. Of these 4,273 applied for visa extension, four died during their stay and the rest seem to have melted away among the population of the state. The number of Pakistanis going missing is the highest for the year 2011: 2,471 Pakistanis arrived in Rajasthan on a valid visa, 1,851 went back, 620 opted to stay back despite the expiry of their visas. Of these, 309 applied for visa extension but 311 could not be traced.[28]

Many Hindus from Pakistan came to the Punjab in the wake of the Babri Masjid demolition. Over 1,000 families of such Hindus are settled in Punjab. The government apparently stopped extending their visas in 2004 and they have since then been living illegally in Amritsar, Jalandhar and Rajpura.[29] However, a large number of Pakistani migrants started coming again to Punjab from 2004 after the growth of radical Islamic activity in Pakistan's tribal areas of Khyber Pakhtunkhwa. As of now, an estimated 800 Hindu and Sikh migrants from Pakistan are staying in Punjab – a majority of them are in Amritsar while others are concentrated in Jalandhar and Khanna towns. They are mostly from Peshawar and Khyber Agency. Those from the cities claim that they had no problems with the Taliban activity as that was largely limited to the rural areas and that they came because their daughters could not get educated and their women could not move around freely in Pakistan.[30] These migrants are settled in clusters where they have relatives. Such areas include Peshawari Nagar, Tehsilpura or Khandwala Bazar in Amritsar. They are isolated from the mainstream though their culture is somewhat similar to that of the people of Indian Punjab. A majority of them is poor and illiterate. They sought shelter in Punjab because they expected to find some support amongst their relatives there. Many of them came to Punjab out of fear that their children would not get a suitable match within their religion and caste in Pakistan. However, earning a living is a difficult preposition for them as many of them do not get job due to their 'Pakistani' tag. 'No one wants to give us a job if we reveal that we are from Pakistan,' said a Hindu migrant living in Amritsar.[31] A few have set up small businesses, a lot of others have become vegetable and fruit vendors or are working as unskilled labourers.

The locals find it easy to identify the Pakistani migrants in Punjab because they have not given up their traditional way of dressing. The men invariably wear Pathan suits and women venture out only in clothes that cover them completely. They are mostly registered with the home department of the Punjab government and have permission to stay on extended visas, although some are said to be staying illegally as their visas have expired. There are some families in Punjab which have been waiting for citizenship despite being in India since 1999. They are made to apply several times and each time a lack of some document or the other is cited as the reason for the rejection of citizenship applications. The real problem arises when the migrants who are living on extended visas have to get their Pakistani passports renewed every five years. Earlier, the renewal could be done through the Pakistan High

Commission in New Delhi but now they are required to go back and apply from the cities they had left. Then they have to apply for a long-term visa from the Indian High Commission in Pakistan before they can come back to Punjab again.[32]

The Home Ministry estimates that overall about a thousand Pakistani Hindus come every month to India on valid visas to visit their relatives or attend family events such as marriage, birth and death ceremonies. The Home Ministry denies any knowledge of their condition or source of income once they are in India. It is believed that they do poorly paid jobs and are not treated well by their relatives in India once it is clear that they plan to stay here for good. India granted visas to 48,860 Pakistanis in 2010 and 51,944 Pakistanis in 2009 – though there is no break-up available religion-wise, it is estimated that a quarter of these visa-seekers were Pakistani Hindus.

STATUS OF MIGRANTS FROM PAKISTAN TO JAMMU & KASHMIR

In discussing the legal status of the Pakistani migrants to India, the category that stands out separately comprises migrants from West Pakistan and the Hindu and Sikh migrants from Pakistan Occupied Kashmir (PoK) to Indian Jammu & Kashmir. Essentially, there are two kinds of migrants in Jammu & Kashmir, namely those who came from West Pakistan and those who came from what is now referred to as PoK.

In 1947, because of the Partition of India, many Hindus and Sikhs crossed over from West Pakistan. These 'migrants from West Pakistan' had run for safety eastwards and as they had relatives in the Jammu reason, they sought refuge with them. Today, many of them think that they might have been better off going to states other than Jammu & Kashmir as those who went, say, to Punjab have got full citizenship rights but those who went to Jammu have not. The West Pakistan refugees in Jammu & Kashmir live around the border areas of Jammu, including Ranbir Singh Pura.[33]

The invasion of Jammu & Kashmir by tribals backed by the Pakistan army, forced those from what came to be known as PoK to also migrate to Jammu & Kashmir. These migrants came from Mirpur, Poonch,

Muzaffarabad and Kothi. The migrants from PoK were not given 'refugee status' because India considers PoK as legally its own territory and part of the Jammu & Kashmir state. Not being classified as migrants they could not get the benefits of refugees. They were not allowed to settle in the Valley because of opposition from local politicians. Some moved out of Jammu & Kashmir to other states while a large number still stay in camps. The total number of PoK migrants in the Jammu region vary between 200,000 to 300,000 at the lower end[34] to an astounding claim of 1,200,000.[35] The migrants from PoK are spread over the Jammu region and live in Digiana camp, Bhor camp, Simbal camp, Gadigarh, Bakshi Nagar, Rehari Colony, Karan Nagar, Keerian, Gangyal, Badyal Brahmana and Ranbir Singh Pura.[36] Not all the PoK migrants were able to settle down in Jammu & Kashmir and many have been forced to settle in states like Punjab, Rajasthan and UP.[37]

A second wave of migrants came after the 1965 India-Pakistan war. During the 1971 India-Pakistan war, some areas of Jammu like Chhamb became a part of Pakistan and people fled from there to the Indian side of Jammu & Kashmir. This was the third wave of migrants to Jammu & Kashmir. State Revenue Department sources claim that there are as few as 5,764 families of refugees from West Pakistan living in Jammu district and Akhnoor Tehsil of Jammu province, and their total number is around 22,000. However, Labha Ram Gandhi, who is president of West Pakistani Refugees Action Committee 1947, claims that there are almost 18,428 of West Pakistani Refugees families – almost three times the number given out by the government – living in Jammu district and Akhnoor Tehsil[38]. There are also no reliable estimates of the migrant families which came from PoK. Some scholars claim that the number of families registered with the government was 42,000 and is likely to have grown since.[39] Officials of the state government, again not on record, claim that some 31,000 families of PoK were living in Jammu but of these, several thousand left for the other states of India. Now only 24,000 families, they claim, are living in Jammu. None of the estimates are fully credible. Depending on their political predilections different sources and writers use different estimates. The state government seems reluctant to release any specific data officially as it considers it politically sensitive.

The West Pakistan migrants have Indian citizenship but have no right to vote in the Jammu & Kashmir legislative assembly and cannot get jobs as state government employees. They also cannot own property in the state because they are not considered permanent residents of the state of Jammu & Kashmir. They do not fulfil the criteria for being considered permanent residents as listed in the Constitution of Jammu & Kashmir which came into effect on 26 January 1957 and is recognised under Article 370 of the Indian Constitution. Article 6 of the Constitution of Jammu & Kashmir provides citizenship to only those who are 'permanent residents' of the state.[40] This rules out the West Pakistan migrants because the territories they came from were not a part of the state of Jammu & Kashmir. That is why even the Union government seems reluctant to address their demand for citizenship. Thus, for example, in a reply to a suggestion that West Pakistan refugees be given full citizenship rights, the Home Ministry told a Parliamentary committee on the Citizenship (Amendment) Bill 2011: 'The West Pakistan Refugees who migrated from Pakistan in 1947, and settled in Jammu & Kashmir, are citizens of India and are allowed to exercise their right to franchise in the Parliamentary Elections. As far as registration as a voter for elections to the Legislative Assembly of J&K is concerned, as per Section-140 of the Constitution of Jammu & Kashmir, 1957, only a person who is a permanent resident of the State (subject to fulfilment of conditions prescribed in that Section) is entitled to be registered as a voter in the electoral roll for the Legislative Assembly and subsequently, vote in J&K Assembly Elections. Further, as per Section-6 of the Constitution of Jammu & Kashmir, 1957, only a "State Subject" can be a permanent resident of the State. In view of the existing provisions of the J&K Constitution, "the West Pakistani Refugees are not State Subjects", and hence are not entitled to vote in the J&K Assembly Elections and also cannot apply for employment in the State Government. In so far as the issue of granting them State Subject status[41] is concerned, the State Government (J&K Government) has not been able to meet their demand as it has legal implications.'[42]

There are some in Jammu & Kashmir who believe that the West Pakistan migrants to the state should not be treated any differently from refugees who went to other states of India. Thus Balraj Puri argues:

'There is no justification for treating them differently from refugees from Pakistan settled elsewhere in India. Whether they should be given permanent citizen rights ["State Subject" rights] can be decided when tempers cool down. It may, however, be mentioned that total number of their families was 3,000 and they are [from] Scheduled Castes. Even making allowance for increase in their number, their number is too insignificant to affect the demographic composition of the state.'[43] According to Labha Ram Gandhi, the Jammu & Kashmir State cabinet passed an order in 1984 providing for three acres of land to some refugees. However, he claims that only 15 percent refugees got the benefit. They were provided evacuee land and property. The evacuee property belongs to Muslims who migrated from Jammu & Kashmir in 1947 to Pakistan. Most of this property has been given on lease for 90 years to politicians, their relatives and bureaucrats in Jammu & Kashmir. Gandhi says that the problem of the West Pakistan migrants will be solved only when they are given voting rights in Jammu & Kashmir. Although these migrants are allowed to vote for the Indian Parliament, they cannot vote for the state assembly and in the local body elections. He argues that because they are disenfranchised in the state, they do not even get the benefits of centre-sponsored development schemes whose benefits are passed on only to those who matter as local voters. However, Gandhi seemed willing to make a distinction between getting voting rights in the state of Jammu & Kashmir and being bestowed 'State Subject' status (which in any case cannot be granted retrospectively). Getting the right to vote locally, he argues, would empower the community because it would be able to elect its own representatives who would then represent their case in various elected bodies.

By contrast, the migrants from PoK have been given Indian citizenship and their rights as 'State Subjects' have also been recognised. The problems they face are of a different kind. Their claims to properties which they left behind in PoK were not registered by the government taking the plea that PoK is part of India illegally under the occupation of Pakistan and once it is liberated they would get their properties back. That has not happened in the last six-and-a-half decades and is unlikely to happen in the near future. A representative of SOS, an organisation of PoK refugees 'settled' in Jammu & Kashmir, Rajiv Chunni, described the confusion in the Union government about their status as follows: 'The Government of India is also confused over the status of PoK refugees and whether they are "refugees", "migrants", "displaced persons" or "internally displaced persons". In whatever category the PoK refugees are placed, there are specific benefits for each category to which these people are entitled as human beings. But we have been deprived of all such benefits. The Government of India is under an obligation to give all such benefits.'[44] He also notes how the PoK refugees were not allowed to settle in the Kashmir valley, saying, 'Refugees from Muzaffarabad desiring to settle in Kashmir valley were not allowed to settle there. Some 300 families of Muzaffarabad who had settled in District Kupwara of Kashmir valley were uprooted and pushed to Jammu.' In fact, he claims that the Jammu & Kashmir government did not want the PoK refugees to settle in the state at all and that those who were allowed to remain there did so because of the central government's pressure on the state.

The PoK refugees complain that they are treated worse than the Muslims who migrated to Pakistan from Jammu & Kashmir in 1947. The state government created a Custodian of Evacuee Property to safeguard the property of Muslims who had fled to Pakistan even though these migrants had been fully compensated by the Pakistan government for properties left behind in Jammu and Kashmir. The Hindu migrants from PoK have neither been compensated for property left behind nor were any attempt made to assess the value of the property they had left behind. In 1982, the state government in fact passed a law which would allow Muslim migrants from the state settled in Pakistan to come back and claim their properties.[45] The implementation of this law, however, was stayed by the Supreme Court subsequently.[46]

It seems that some of the PoK refugees have nevertheless settled down in rural areas on properties left behind by Muslim evacuees. The original Evacuee Property Act has a limitation of 12 years within which the evacuee can come back and claim the property left behind but this period has long since expired.[47] They have been given State Subject rights; they participate in voting of Assembly and Parliament. They have been also provided 10 lakh *kanals* of land.

The Government of India seems to be finally waking up to the plight of the migrants from Pakistan to Jammu & Kashmir. In August 2012, there were reports that the Union government is considering constituting a high-level committee to be monitored by the Prime Minister's Office or the Union Home Ministry for examining all outstanding issues – except the issue of 'State Subject' – for all categories of displaced people in Jammu & Kashmir. The attempt apparently is to work out a package for their one-time settlement. However, this has met with stiff opposition from the Kashmir separatist leadership, with the Syed Ali Shah Geelani faction of the All-Party Hurriyat Conference claiming that this was 'part of the plan to change the demography of the state.'[48] Whether the problems being faced by the West Pakistan migrants would finally be resolved, however, remains to be seen.

Meanwhile, it might be worth noting what the Asian Centre of Human Rights had to say about the discrimination being practised by the majority community in Jammu & Kashmir against the West Pakistan migrants: 'International human rights law is unambiguous about the prohibition of citizenship based on "*jus sanguinis*" i.e. based on the nationality of their parents instead of where they are born. The UN Human Rights Committee and UN Committee on the Elimination of Racial Discrimination directed a number of States like Cambodia, Japan and Germany not to practise citizenship based on "*jus sanguinis*". The grant of permanent residentship to about 250,000 lakh victims of partition cannot change the demographic character of the Kashmir valley where Muslims are in a majority. According to the 2001 census, the population of Jammu & Kashmir was 10,143,700.'[49]

QUEST FOR OFFICIAL IDENTITY AMONG PAK MIGRANTS – WILL UID HELP?

There is little doubt that what the Pakistani migrants to India seek is full citizenship. The question then is: Can the attempts of the Unique Identification Authority of India (UIDAI) to give an identity to these migrants be of any use to them?

The UIDAI mandate is that any person usually residing in India in the area demarcated by the Registrar General of Citizenship for the purpose of the National population register is entitled to and can choose to apply for Aadhaar (the 12-digit individual identification number issued by the UIDAI[50]) by providing their demographic and biometric information in the manner specified by the UIDAI. The mandate also says that the UIDAI project will include all residents who are in India and who may want to avail of social services. The UID cards pose no dilemma for the pre-1971 Pak immigrants who have already got Indian citizenship. They also pose no problems for those post-1971 migrants who have been conferred Indian citizenship. It is an additional identification – one more layer on top of their citizenship identification. However, what does the UIDAI do for those who are either (a) illegally staying on and (b) those who are staying on legally through the extensions of their visas?

It is pertinent to note that the decision about the legal status of immigrants is not within the ambit of the UIDAI but lies in the domain of other Government Departments. This creates a gray area for Pakistani Hindu migrants who are in India on legal visas or by illegal migration and decide to apply for an Aadhaar card. The Aadhaar card requires: One, proof of identity containing name and photo (one of 17 documents listed); two, proof of address containing name and address (one of 29 documents listed); and three, date-of-birth proof giving name and date of birth (one of 4 documents listed).[51] The Pakistani migrants who are illegally here or on valid visa do not have any of these documents. Although it is not clear whether a Pakistani passport would be considered a valid document for all three requirements – it is unlikely to be considered a valid proof of anything except of the Pakistani citizenship of the holder. It would not be a valid address proof as that has to be an Indian document. So, how does a non-citizen resident, and a Pakistani to boot, apply for Aadhaar?

There is a provision that in the absence of any identity or residence documents, one can still get Aadhaar if an existing Aadhaar-holder acts as an 'introducer' for the applicant. The provision reads: 'In the case of people who do not have documents for proof, there is an introducer system. The Registrar for enrolment can designate individuals who can vouch for the validity of a person's information. Introducers can be government agencies, banks, teachers, village postmen, elected representatives and NGOs. Introducers will be enrolled first and given training. Their UID will be mentioned among the details of the person who gets enrolled.'[52] In this way, the Indian family member of a Pakistani migrant can possibly act as an 'introducer' to get the latter the Aadhaar. This number allows one to open a bank account and it hopes to be the single source of identity verification for access to other services, such as obtaining a passport or a driving license.

However, officials of the Ministry of Home Affairs say that UIDAI is a purely voluntary exercise and by no means would the Aadhaar make anybody's case stronger for Indian citizenship. However, they caution that the 'introducer system' is a big security risk as anyone without any documents can get the Aadhaar. On the other hand, as each person will give his biometrics for getting the Aadhaar card, the numbers allotted to those who get the cards through the introducer system could lead to the detection of illegal migrants as well. Hindu Singh Sodha of the Seemant Lok Sangathana or Border People's Organisation based in Jodhpur and Daulat Ram Sharma of Thar Jagrut Nagrik Manch Chohatan in Barmer believe that Pak migrants should be given UID cards. They feel that there is no negativity attached to covering the Pak migrants under UID. They think that once the migrants have Aadhaar cards, they can do all those things which they cannot do for lack of an ID proof. Sodha feels, 'The refugees are not going to be harmed. They are not infiltrators. They have come legally with valid documents.' His point is that those who have come on legal documents are already under surveillance – their records exist with Immigration officials, the FRROs, local police stations if they have police reporting visas, some have residence certificates given to them by the Home Ministry.[53] Lastly, the case of the West Pakistani migrants to Jammu & Kashmir: they have been given Indian citizenship rights but they also want the right to vote in the state legislature and local-body elections. Although they have the right to vote for parliament they are excluded from local politics, which is largely communal in nature by virtue of Jammu & Kashmir being the only Muslim majority state of India. The special status of Jammu & Kashmir under Article 370 means that unless the local government decides to give them permanent residents' status in the state, they will remain disenfranchised in Jammu & Kashmir. This is something on which even the Union government refuses to take a call. Getting a UID card would mean little to these people as they already have some kind of a local address proof because they have a Voter's ID card for voting in parliamentary elections. The West Pakistan Refugee Action Committee has also issued its own official ID-cards to the refugees and their children. Apparently, they are a great help in proving the domicile of the children while seeking admission in schools.[54]

Who might the UID harm? Perhaps the illegal immigrants if they were to get Aadhaar cards made – by increasing surveillance over them.

NOTES

1. Population of Hindus in Pakistan, Pakistan Hindu Council; http://pakistanhinducouncil.org/hindupopulation.asp [last accessed 15 November 2012]
2. Baabar, Mariana, "Sindh's stolen brides," *Outlook*, 23 January 2006 http://www.outlookindia.com/article.aspx?229886 [last accessed 15 November 2012]
3. Hindus of Pakistan, World Directory of Minorities; http://www.faqs.org/minorities/South-Asia/Hindus-of-Pakistan.html [last accessed 15 November 2012]
4. Population by Religion, Population Census Organisation, Government of Pakistan;
   http://www.census.gov.pk/Religion.htm [last accessed 15 November 2012]
5. Ibid
6. Sikand, Yoginder, "Pakistani Hindu migrants to India: Demanding to be heard," *Pakistan Hindu Post*, 30 December 2009; http://pakistanhindupost.blogspot.in/2009/12/pakistani-hindu-migrants-to-india.html [last accessed 15 November 2012]
7. Baba Ramsaa Peer, http://babaramsaapeer.com/history.html [last accessed 15 November 2012]
8. Rehman, I. A., "Perils of intolerance," *Dawn*, 16 August 2012
   http://dawn.com/2012/08/16/perils-of-intolerance/
   [last accessed 15 November 2012]
9. Ebrahim, Zofeen, "Why are Hindus from Pakistan Crossing Over to India?" Inter Press Service, 24 August 2012; http://www.ipsnews.net/2012/08/why-are-hindus-from-pakistan-crossing-over-to-india [last accessed 15 November 2012]
10. Hussain, Kashif, "A Tale of Migrating Hindus," *The Daily Times*, 20 August 2012, http://www.dailytimes.com.pk/default.asp?page=2012%5C08%5C20%5Cstory_20-8-2012_pg7_10 [last accessed 15 November 2012]
11. Ibid

12. Joshua, Anita, "'Forcibly converted' Hindu women choose to stay with husbands," *The Hindu*, 18 April 2012; http://www.thehindu.com/news/international/article3328893.ece [last accessed 15 November 2012]; and Marvi Sirmed, "Rinkle Kumari: A Test Case for Jinnah's Pakistan," *The Friday Times*, 25-31 May 2012; http://www.thefridaytimes.com/beta3/tft/article.php?issue=20120525&page=6 [last accessed 15 November 2012]
13. Hussain, "A tale of migrating Hindus"
14. Ibid; also, and Ebrahim, "Why Are Hindus"
15. "HRCP's outrage at minorities' flight," Human Rights Commission of Pakistan (HCRP), 10 August 2012; http://www.hrcp-web.org/showprel.asp?id=292 [last accessed 15 November 2012]
16. Rehman, "Perils of Intolerance."
17. Vij-Aurora, Bhavna, "No Country for Pakistani Hindus," *India Today*, 27 April 2012. http://indiatoday.intoday.in/story/pakistani-hindu-refugees-feel-betrayed-by-india/1/186304.html [last accessed 15 November 2012]
18. "Report of Refugee Populations in India, November 2007," Human Rights Law Network, New Delhi, p.10; http://www.hrln.org/admin/issue/subpdf/Refugee_populations_in_India.pdf [last accessed 15 November 2012]; and Sikand, "Pakistani Hindu migrants"
19. Sikand, "Pakistani Hindu migrants"
20. Ibid
21. Ibid
22. Citizenship to Hindu Migrants from Pakistan, Ministry of Home Affairs, 22 August 2012; http://pib.nic.in/newsite/erelease.asx?relid=86509 [last accessed 15 November 2012]
23. Sikand, "Pakistani Hindu migrants"
24. Roy Choudhury, Shreya, "Pak Hindus narrate 'citizenship' woes," *The Times of India*, Pakistan, 28 December 2010; http://articles.timesofindia.indiatimes.com/2010-12-28/pakistan/28255011_1_tourist-visa-long-term-visas-refugee-status [last accessed 15 November 2012]
25. Vij-Aurora, "No country for Pakistani Hindus"
26. This was stated by Mullappally Ramachandran, Minister of State of Home Affairs, in written reply to a question by Bharatsinh Prabhatsinh Parmar and Parshottam Khodabhai Rupala in the Rajya Sabha on August 22, 2012, Press Information Bureau, Ministry of Home Affairs, Government of India; http://pib.nic.in/newsite/erelease.aspx?relid=86509 [last accessed 15 November 2012]
27. "Over 7,500 Pakistanis overstayed in India: RTI" *Jagran Post*, 14 November 2011; http://post.jagran.com/Over-7500-Pakistanis-overstayed-in-India-RTI-1321253851 [last accessed 15 November 2012]

28. Mishra, Sudhanshu, "Pakistanis in India with expired visas under security scanner," *Mail Today*, 26 August 2012; http://indiatoday.intoday.in/story/security-on-alert-for-pakistanis-in-india-with-expired-visas/1/214759.html [last accessed 15 November 2012]
29. Deol, Rajesh, "Pakistani Hindus in India unwilling to return," *Deccan Herald*, 5 September 2012; http://www.deccanherald.com/content/86879/pakistani-hindus-india-unwilling-return.html [last accessed 15 November 2012]
30. Shiv, Pakistani Hindu migrant living in Amritsar; interview with a Hindu migrant from Pakistan living in Amritsar, 5 August 2012.
31. Ibid
32. Davinder Singh, Pakistani Sikh migrant living in Amritsar; interview with the author, 5 August 2012
33. Dey, Ishita, and Sucharita Sengupta, "An Interview with Ved Bhasin on Forced Migration in Jammu & Kashmir," *Refugee Watch*, Issue No. 36, December 2010; http://www.mcrg.ac.in/rw%20files/RW36/9.Interview.pdf [last accessed 15 November 2012]
34. Ibid; Ajay Kumar, "Impact of Internal Displacement in Jammu & Kashmir: Study of Pakistan occupied Kashmir Refugees," *Indian Streams Research Journal*, vol. 2, issue. 3, April 2012, pp.1-4; http://www.isrj.net/PublishArticles/695.pdf [last accessed 15 November 2012]; and Shailendra Pandey (text and photographs), "An uncertain refuge – three lakh refugees left their homes behind only to find they have restricted rights in J&K," *Tehelka*, 5 May 2012. http://www.tehelka.com/story_main52.asp?filename=hub050512UNCERTAIN.asp [last accessed 15 November 2012]
35. Suba Chandran, D., "The forgotten people of Jammu & Kashmir – 'Refugees' from PoK," Institute of Peace and Conflict Studies, 8 January 2007. http://www.ipcs.org/article/india/the-forgotten-people-of-jammu-and-kashmir-refugees-from-pok-2182.html [last accessed 15 November 2012]
36. Kumar, "Impact of Internal Displacement" p.2
37. Suba Chandran, "The forgotten people"
38. Labha Ram Gandhi, President, West Pakistani Refugees Action Committee; interview with the author, 4 August 2012
39. Puri, Balraj, "Refugee problem in Jammu & Kashmir," *Kashmir Newz*, http://www.kashmirnewz.com/a0002.html [last accessed 15 November 2012]
40. "Hindu and Sikh refugees from Pakistan: Majority Kashmiris have a case of extreme discrimination to answer!" *Human Rights Report Quarterly*, Asian Centre for Human Rights, issue 2, Oct-Dec 2010; http://www.achrweb.org/ihrrq/issue2/hindu_and_sikh_refugees.html [last accessed 15 November 2012]
41. "State Subject Definition Notification dated the 20th April, 1927," Legal Document No 44; http://www.kashmir-information.com/LegalDocs/44.html [last accessed 15 November 2012]

42. "One Hundred and Forty-Ninth Report on the Citizenship (Amendment) Act 2011, Department-related Parliamentary Standing Committee on Home Affairs (Presented to the Rajya Sabha on 28 March 2012. Laid on the Table of Lok Sabha on 28 March 2012.) Rajya Sabha Secretariat, New Delhi, March 2012; http://www.prsindia.org/uploads/media/Citizenship/SCR%20Citizenship%20Amendment%20Bill%202012.pdf [last accessed 15 November 2012]
43. Puri, "Refugee problem"
44. Suba Chandran, "The forgotten people"
45. Ibid
46. "Court extends stay on J&K Resettlement Act," *The Hindu*, 21 February 2008. http://www.hindu.com/2008/02/21/stories/2008022151381300.htm [last accessed 15 November 2012]
47. Puri, "Refugee problem"
48. "Permanent settlement of Pak refugees: Hurriyat (G) sees red," 24 August 2012 http://kashmirwatch.com/index.php/2012/08/24/permanent-settlement-8217-of-pak-refugees-hurriyat-g-sees-red.html [last accessed 15 November 2012]; also, Bashaarat Masood, "Will oppose settlement of Pak refugees, says Geelani," *The Indian Express*, 24 August 2012; http://www.indianexpress.com/news/will-oppose-settlement-of-pak-refugees-says-geelani/992342/ [last accessed 15 November 2012]
49. "Hindu and Sikh refugees from Pakistan," *Human Rights Report Quarterly*
50. "What is Aadhaar?" UIDAI, Planning Commission, Government of India; http://uidai.gov.in/index.php?option=com_content&view=article&id=57&Itemid=105 [last accessed 15 November 2012]
51. "Documents needed for enrolment," 8 August 2011; http://uidnumber.org/aadhaar/628/documents-needed-for-enrollment/ [last accessed 15 November 2012]
52. Ibid.
53. Hindu Singh Sodha, Chairman of Seemant Lok Sangathana, Jodhpur; interview with the author, 26 June 2012
54. Labha Ram Gandhi, interview with the author, 4 August 2012

VI

Political Will and the Success of Aadhaar in Tripura

Jayanta Bhattacharya

INTRODUCTION

Amid the controversy that digitisation of identity which has been introduced under the 'Aadhaar' project by the Government of India is an erosion of the right to privacy and introduction of intrusive surveillance on the people, Tripura's Marxist government[1] has successfully implemented this project covering over 90 per cent of the population with a hope that it would help taking the various government schemes to the downtrodden who live mostly in remote areas. The project (a 12-digit Unique Identification number or UID number) was started on pilot basis in Mandwi Block in West Tripura district in November 2010 and later extended to all over the state. By January 2011, over 90 per cent of the population of the state was enrolled under UID project. In recognition of covering the highest percentage of targeted population, Tripura was awarded Aadhaar Excellence Award, 2011 and the Chairman of the Unique Identification Authority of India (UIDAI), Nandan Nilekani, gave the award to the Tarun Kanti Debnath, State Nodal Officer, on 29 September 2011.

The UIDAI introduced the project to provide each resident of India a unique identity number (Aadhaar). It is an electronically generated unique number which is created after several processes are followed, starting from field-level data collection to de-duplication check. This is a biometric-based identity of a person and apart from the demographic data and photograph of the resident, 10 finger prints and iris scan are also being recorded. This data is stored in a secure server of UIDAI, namely CIDR, in encrypted form and thus the secrecy of the public data is maintained. Any state government would be permitted to use this biometric database to authenticate the identity of a resident for various purposes. The objective of the project is to offer various government services like the public distribution system, different pension schemes, wages payment, gas connection, electricity connection and other beneficiary-based schemes in a better and effective way to the targeted population by weeding out fake identities.

In Tripura, the state government declared the Rural Development (RD) department as the nodal department for implementing the project. The work for enrolment started from Mandwi Block on 18 November 2010 and concluded on 15 January 2012. So far, 3,277,109 people of the state's total population of 3,671,032 have been enrolled under the project and the Aadhaar generated numbers are 2,842,329. This paper would like to probe how this phenomenal task was implemented in a landlocked state like Tripura, bordered by Bangladesh on three sides. Why the government happily implemented the task and what could be its possible impact on the migrant population.

GOVERNANCE & FINANCIAL INCLUSION IN TRIPURA

Encircled by Bangladesh on three sides, Tripura is a mountainous state of the North-Eastern region which shares an 856-Km international border with the neighbouring country. An erstwhile princely state, Tripura merged with the Indian Union on 15 October 1949, as a Group-C state and became a Union Territory on 1 July 1963. It was elevated to the status of a full-fledged state on 21 January 1972. Partition of the British India into India and Pakistan saw the movement of more than 15 million people. This massive displacement caused great suffering which in turn brought about major socioeconomic and political changes in the state.

Partition flooded Tripura with migrants who came to outnumber the indigenous people of the state within a decade and permanently changed the demography of the state. The demographic change paved the way for the eventual conflict between the tribals and Bengali migrants which devastated the state for more than three decades. In addition, the state's traditional links with the rest of the country was broken by the Partition too and Tripura became a geographically isolated and landlocked state with poor infrastructure. 'With majority of the population living below the poverty line, the state has inherent limitations in mobilisation of financial resources from within. Lack of physical infrastructure also adversely affected the pace of industrialisation in the state.'[2]

The state has come a long way since it attained statehood in 1972. Yet, in recent years, the state has witnessed a massive change from conflict to harmony. Riots, ethnic conflicts and massacres appear to be a thing of the past. The schools in the hills, now that they have been vacated by the security forces, are full of children again. The doors of government offices and banks have been thrown open to the public. The Primary Health Centres (PHCs), which had not seen doctors for years, are been manned once again. And the old relationship of trust is being re-established between the plains people and the hill people. Things began to change once a combination of political firmness, stringent security measures and determined development efforts were initiated. The motor was provided by the state government's proactive attitude.

The Tripura Tribal Areas Autonomous District Council (TTAADC) was set up in 1982 initially under seventh schedule of the constitution and was brought under the sixth schedule of the constitution for protecting and safe-guarding the socioeconomic and cultural interests of the tribals who constitute one-third of the population. The tribal council area comprises 68 per cent of the state's territory. With the formation of this council the indigenous people started enjoying the fruits of development. More than 117,000 tribal families (roughly about 585,000 tribe's people) have thus been rehabilitated under the Schedule Tribes and other Traditional Forest Dwellers Act, 2006.[3] Despite all limitations, it has moved towards and made considerable development for socioeconomic development of the state. The state adopted a strategy based on mobilisation of the people and their active participation in a three-tier Panchayat (local self-government) structure to facilitate the development process. 'Development of Human Resources and physical infrastructure were made the major planks of development. With active cooperation of peace-loving people and sincere efforts of the security forces, the state has been able to tackle the insurgency situation effectively and keep law and order under control, which has facilitated the implementation of developmental plan and programmes.'[4]

The state has made considerable progress in building infrastructure and promoting economic and human resource development since it attained statehood in 1972. Infrastructural development like building roads, railways and air connectivity was achieved satisfactorily. The national Highway was extended up to Sabroom, the southern most town of the state from where the Chittagong port in Bangladesh is just 75 Km and final survey for constructing a bridge on the river Feni in Sabroom has been completed by the joint survey team of India and Bangladesh. The Chittagong port would be connected by roads with Tripura following the construction of the bridge. India completed the final survey for the 11.5-Km line to lay the rail link between Akhaura in Bangladesh and Agartala, the state capital, a project which New Delhi plans to implement for linking railways between the two countries. The Railway Ministry started making the Detailed Project Report (DPR) for the plan and the central government has sanctioned Rs.2.52 crore for laying the railway track to connect West Bengal and Tripura through Bangladesh. During Bangladesh Prime Minister Sheikh Hasina's visit to New Delhi in January 2010, India and Bangladesh have agreed to lay the tracks between Akhaura and Agartala. Agartala airport is now second busiest airport in the North-East after Guwahati with about 176 flights operating every week.

As regards power availability, the state is soon going to be a power-surplus state. The 726 MW gas-based thermal power project at Palatana in Gomati district started producing power on trial basis and on completion of the transmission line with the national grid at Bongaigaon, full-fledged generation would be started. It was set up by ONGC Tripura Power Corporation (OTPC) and 2.6 MMSCMD gas per day is required for the power project. The total project cost is Rs.3,500 crore. The Prime Minister had laid the foundation stone for the project at Palatana, 60 Km from Agartala in 2005. Four north-eastern states – Assam, Mizoram, Meghalaya and Manipur – will buy power from the power plant and the Northeast Power Trading Company has already started erecting transmission lines from Palatana to Bongaigaon in Assam. Tripura will also emerge as the biggest on-land natural gas-producing state in the country by 2014 with the capacity of producing 50 lakh cubic meter natural gas (5 MMSCMD) per day. Oil and Natural Gas Corporation (ONGC) Executive Director, Tripura Asset, K Satyanarayana has said. 'Now 18 lakh cubic meter gas (1.83 MMSCMD) is produced daily from the operational wells in Tripura. We have fixed a target of producing 50 lakh cubic meter natural gas (5 MMSCMD) per day by 2014.'[5]

Tripura is the fourth highest literate state in the country after Kerala, Mizoram and Lakshadweep. According to the report of the census-2011 the literacy rate in the state has gone up from 73.19 per cent in 2001 to 87.75 per cent, as against the national average of 74.04 per cent in 2011.

While agriculture and allied sectors continue to grow, the secondary sector has also started picking up. The share of secondary sector of Gross State Domestic Product (GSDP) has increased from 14.1 per cent in 1998 to about 26.4 per cent in 2010. Bodhjungnagar near Agartala is developing as the flagship industrial cluster of Tripura, spread over an area of over 700 acres. The trade with Bangladesh which started in 1995, has already reached the level of about Rs.330 crores per annum.

The state has attached the highest priority to providing all the basic amenities for the people to enable them to live a life of dignity and to make progress. The Government has been allotting land and providing houses to the landless and homeless people. Up to the year 2012, government land has been allotted to about 97,827 families and IAY houses has been provided to about 2.06 lakhs families. The state government has also been pursuing the goal of safe and adequate drinking water to all families as also 100 per cent sanitation coverage in the state. The government has been making special efforts for the uplift of the weaker section of the society; special schemes have been taken up for their educational and economic development. The state has been in the forefront of implementation of Schedule Tribes and Other Traditional Forest Dwellers (Recognition of Forest Rights) Act, 2006. This is a major initiative for the development of tribals in the state. So far, 120,062 Forest Dwellers have been given 168,839.61 hectares of forest land which constitute about 16.1 per cent of the total geographical area of the state.

For the religious minorities, Special Action Plan has been taken up for development of areas with concentration of minorities. The government has been striving to provide transparent and pro-people governance. That good implementation and good governance is good politics is seen in the results of the elections for the TTAADC which were held on 3 May 2010. The Left Front bagged all 28 elective seat, further consolidating its traditional base among the indigenous people, with 63.80 per cent of the votes, brushing aside the Congress and its former poll ally, the Indigenous Nationalist Party of Twipra (INPT), headed by Bijoy Kumar Hrangkhawl, an insurgent-turned political leader.

TRIPURA HAS EARNED MANY LAURELS FOR GOVERNANCE[6]

The Agartala Municipal Council was awarded Nagar Ratna Award in recognition of its performance, transparency and accountability for the year 2011. The award comprising a certificate and a trophy was given by the then President of India Pratibha Patil to Agartala Municipal Council Chairperson Prafullajit Sinha in a function held at New Delhi on the 8 July 2011.

The President's Colour was awarded to the Tripura Police for their outstanding success in combating the three decade-old insurgency in the state and for ensuring that there was no human rights abuse. Tripura is the fourth state after Jammu & Kashmir, Punjab and Tamil Nadu to receive this rare distinction. Presenting the President's Colour (Flag) to Shri Sanjay Sinha, Director General of Police, in a colourful march past and ceremony held at Agartala on the 11 January 2012, the Vice-President of India observed that 'it is a rare honour for the Tripura

Police. Our President and the entire country view it as a mark of pride and bravery.'[7]

Excellence Award for the implementation of Mahatma Gandhi National Rural Employment Guarantee Scheme (MGNREGS) was given to North Tripura district for the year 2008-09. The award was given to the district in recognition of its achievement in generation of Mondays, coverage of women, transparency, etc in implementation.

The Prime Minister's award for Excellence in Public Administration in the team category for the year 2010-11 was given to a four-member team of the undivided North Tripura district for the project 'Village Health and Nutrition in complete convergence mode'. Implementation of a number of schemes like National Rural Health Mission, Integrated Child Development Scheme, Accelerated Rural Water Supply Programme, Total Sanitation Campaign, Mid-Day Meal, etc were taken up on a convergence mode by pooling fund, manpower with active involvement of the Panchayati Raj Institution and mobilisation of the target group through generation of awareness, effective monitoring and feedback system.

Implementation of e-Panchayat Mission Mode Project for 2011-12 was awarded to Tripura. The prize, comprising a citation and cash prize of Rs.50 lakhs, was handed over to Manik Dey, Minister for Panchayat, Tripura, by Jairam Ramesh, Union Minister for Rural Development, on the 24 April 2012, in the Plenary Hall, Vigyan Bhavan, during the National Conference to celebrate the National Panchayati Raj Day, in presence of V. Kishore Chandra Deo, Union Minister for Panchayati Raj, and Paban Singh Ghatowar, Union Minister for Development of North Eastern Region (DoNER). Also, the e-Panchayat Award, 2010-11, comprising of a trophy and cash prize of Rs.30 lakhs, was handed over by Vilash Rao Deshmukh, Union Minister for Panchayat to R. K. Vaish, Principal Resident Commissioner, Government of Tripura, New Delhi on the 24 April 2011, in the Plenary Hall, Vigyan Bhavan, New Delhi during the National Conference held to celebrate the National Panchayati Raj Day.

Construction of dwelling units at a cost of Rs.1673 lakh under Basic Services for Urban Poor (BSUP) programme was taken up at Kunjaban by the Agartala Municipal Council. The project, with 256 dwelling units along with related amenities, roads, storm water drains, water drains, water supply, UGT/pump house, sewerage, electrification, substation, street light, boundary wall, park/garden, community centre, etc, was completed on the 30 June 2010. The complex named 'Vivekananda Awasan' is being maintained by the Ramakrishna Mission.

Tripura was chosen for launching of the Aadhaar project of the Government of India. As has been noted earlier, in recognition of covering the highest percentage of targeted population, Tripura was awarded Aadhaar Excellence Award, 2011.

Tripura Vision Centre project, an information technology-based intervention, was taken up in the state for provision of primary and preventive eye-care services in the rural and interior areas. This project was implemented jointly by the State Health Department, IL&FS-ETS and Arvind Eye Care Hospital. The project was launched in Melaghar Block in April 2007 and later extended to the other Blocks. This project has got a number of awards.

The Fiscal Responsibility and Financial Management (FRBM) Act was enacted in Tripura in the year 2005 and was meticulously followed up to achieve the objectives and targets set under the Act. In recognition of the financial discipline and achievement of FRBM's target, the state government was rewarded with a debt waiver of (i) Rs.22.25 crore for the year 2005-06,(ii) Rs.22.25 crore in 2006-07, (iii) Rs.22.25 crore in 2007-08 and (iv) Rs.11.12 crore in 2008-09, a total of Rs.77.87 crore under the State Debt Consolidation and Relief Facility scheme of the Government of India.

The Ministry of DoNER has given an award of Rs.20 crore to Tripura in the year 2011-12 for the successful implementation of projects sanctioned under the Non-Lapsable Central Pool of Resources (NLCPR).

Tripura was awarded the Best State Award for Water & Sanitation under the category of the Small States on 23 February 2011, at New Delhi. This was decided by a Jury headed by Bimal Jalan, Ex-Governor, Reserve Bank of India, based on the primary survey done by the International Consulting Group-KPMG.

FINANCIAL INCLUSION IN TRIPURA

Financial Inclusion is the process of ensuring access to appropriate financial products and services needed by all sections of the society in general and vulnerable groups, such as weaker sections and low-income groups, in particular at an affordable cost in a fair and transparent manner by mainstream institutional players. 'In advanced economies, Financial Inclusion is more about the knowledge of fair and transparent financial products and a focus on financial literacy. In emerging economies, it is a question of both access to financial products and knowledge about their fairness and transparency.'[8]

Financial inclusion or inclusive financing is the delivery of financial services, at affordable costs, to sections of underprivileged and low-income segments of society. Unrestrained access to public goods and services is one of the components of an open and efficient society. It is argued that as banking services are in the nature of public good; the availability of banking and payment services to the entire population without discrimination is the prime objective of this public policy. The term 'financial inclusion' has gained importance since the early 2000s. Financial inclusion is now a common objective for many central banks among the developing nations. Most of the banks in many states have taken significant strides in the opening of no-frills accounts through the BC (Banking Correspondent) model because government – be it central or the state – prefer transfer of payments under various government schemes through bank accounts for transparency in transfer of benefits, to avoid pilferage and for quicker implementation. 'Tripura presents an example where a proactive state government, apart from covering all the villages (with above as well as less than 2000 population) in the first phase itself gives an incentive of Rs.100/- per no frill account opened per job card under MGNREGA. This incentive is given only to Tripura Gramin Bank (TGB) – the only RRB in the state – and to Tripura State Cooperative Bank (TSCB). Riding on this incentive which TGB shares in the ratio of 10:90 with its company BCs, the bank has gone for a massive drive for opening of no frill accounts thus covering nearly all households in the unbanked villages having more than 2000 population. Hence, in the parlance of bankers in Tripura, no frill accounts are known as NREGA accounts."[9]

The TGB has 123 branches in Tripura of which 91 branches are in rural areas and the bank has appointed 185 Business Correspondent Agents in different parts of the state through two NGOs for giving banking services at the door steps of poor people and opened 185 Customer Service Points (CSPs) in remote areas. The TGB has made payments of NREGA wages through 351,000 people in the state in the current Financial Year.[10] 'Indepay Networks', an enabler of Rural Payment Infrastructure, launched its RBI guidelines based BC programme for Tripura State Cooperative Bank Limited (TSCB) on 4 February 2011. The programme was inaugurated by State Minister for Rural Development Jitendra Chowdhury at Kalachara Gram Panchayat. Indepay, a payment processor, is enabling benefits of rural programmes such as MGNREGS to reach the rural masses through innovation in payments technology. By extending its infrastructure to the last mile in the rural areas, Indepay, through the use of biometric technology, is ensuring that benefits of governmental programmes reach the people they are intended for. Tripura, with an annual MGNREGA allotment of over Rs.500 crores, has close to a million MGNREGA beneficiaries who receive employment through the programme. In addition to MGNREGA beneficiaries the state has a further quarter of a million beneficiaries of National Old Age Pension (NOAP), Social Security Pension (SSP) and other similar programmes. Indepay with its biometric enabled, UID compliant MicroATM infrastructure is addressing these opportunities through partners such as TSCB by leveraging its nationwide rural payments infrastructure. The programme, which was successfully piloted for over a year at certain branches of TSCB in North Tripura, is being scaled throughout the state through the disbursement of biometric-enabled smart cards to MGNREGA beneficiaries, starting with Kalachara and Manubazar branches in Satchand block. Indepay completed the enrolment of all MGNREGA beneficiaries in North and South Tripura Districts through enrolment camps held at each panchayat with the help of over hundred trained enrolment agents supported by the respective District Magistrates and Block Development Officers (BDOs) and the necessary state machinery. Rural development Minister

Jitendra Chowdhury, who inaugurated the programme, said, 'Infrastructure of the Indian banks is rapidly expanding and the visible benefits of ICT in day-to-day banking are well known. Common man is becoming quite used to ATMs and internet banking etc, are gradually finding its acceptance. RBI has been placing a lot of emphasis on financial inclusion covering no-frill accounts, rural bank branches, BC/ BF models etc. Further, many pilot projects have been initiated in various states using smart cards for opening & operating bank accounts with biometric identification at people's doorsteps. Here, in Tripura, we are at the forefront of such advances with programmes like UID and BC models being deployed on a state-wide basis. Indepay have deployed manpower to make you equipped with the technology so that you can encash your money as per your requirement in North and South Tripura district and it will benefit the NREGA beneficiaries.'[11]

'Tripura State Cooperative Bank, in furtherance of fulfilling its social responsibility of ensuring faster inclusive growth of weaker and poor sections of the society, wishes to extend banking services to the identified beneficiaries of the MGNREGA through the Business Correspondent like M/s Indepay Networks Pvt. Ltd, by opening of no-frill accounts and by issuance of a biometric-enabled smart card in the name of the beneficiaries through which the benefits of MGNREGA are to be passed to them,' said Haripada Chakrabarty, President, TSCB, who presided over the function.[12] Adding to Chakrabarty's statement, S. K. Saha, Managing Director, TSCB added, 'The bank will also extend financial assistance such as small credit to fulfil other credit needs of the beneficiaries and other banking services, micro insurance, financial products and non-financial services as may be required by the beneficiaries/ card holders through its wide network of branches/ offices in the state through the Bank's duly appointed Banking Correspondent(s) as per the guidelines of the RBI.'[13]

Krishan Sujan, Director, Indepay Networks, said that 'Indepay has carried out extensive evaluation of Rural Banking systems and plans to address the problems associated with last-mile infrastructure, connectivity in rural locations and the issues related to citizens being non-literate and non-numerate through its innovative infrastructure offering. Indepay wishes to enable and operate, an extended Rural

Banking Branch in each village and panchayat in the state where banking services will be extended to each citizen of the state within a few kilometres of their residence as per RBI guidelines for the BC model. This infrastructure will also help to act as points for sourcing Rural Credit and Micro Housing Finance for the citizens of the state in addition to including the unbanked into the Banking system. Indepay has made significant investments in the state and plans to deploy real time, online, UID-enabled infrastructure throughout the state and make Tripura a model state for the rest of India to follow. The Indepay ecosystem of BCs will enable non-financial services such as Rail/Air Ticketing, Utilities Bill Payments including Electricity, Telephone and Municipal Taxes in addition to airtime recharge, making the BC model viable and scalable through the state of Tripura as they have done in other states.'[14]

Tripura State Cooperative Bank was registered under the Tripura State Cooperative Societies Act, 1358 in 1957. The bank has 44 branches and extension counters all over the state. The Tripura state government is the major share holder of the bank and being the apex bank of the state, TSCB has its full-time commitment to rural economy and has the highest CD Ratio in the state. Indepay Networks is a third-party payment processor and enabler of Rural Banking, Micro Credit and various Non-Financial Services that touch the common man in their daily lives and makes their lives change for the better. Indepay operates a nationwide financial payment and transaction processing business that includes comprehensive point-of-sale services, card issuance and master merchant acquiring services for debit/prepaid/credit cards, rural banking, government disbursements, electronic distribution of content, money transfer and utility bill payment services. Indepay enables infrastructure for banks to offer rural banking and access at village level on a sustainable model. Indepay infrastructure is placed at rural and retail outlets and allows the retail of content services, Public Call Office (PCO) services, card payments, distribution of financial services, remittances and basic/rural banking services across the counter. Indepay has setup operations in various parts of Tripura with a state-level office in Agartala. Indepay have employed over 100 personnel to take care of state-wide operations where they are carrying out enrolment programmes for NREGA beneficiaries for the State Co-operative Bank.[15]

So, financial inclusion had already started working in Tripura and the Business Correspondent model had also been introduced before the UID project was implemented. The former factors, in fact, helped in the implementation of the UID project in the state.

AADHAAR NUMBER

Tripura set a target of enrolling all its residents under UID project free of cost by 31 March 2011 and finished the task at least two months before the schedule. The District Magistrates (DMs) and Collectors, Sub-divisional Magistrates (SDMs) and Block Development Officers (BDOs) as well as the elected representatives like village heads were sensitised. While the DMs and Collectors were the overall in-charge for implementing the project in their districts, the main work was done by the BDOs. The DMs issued detailed instructions within the overall ambit of the operational guidelines. As per the operational guidelines, intensive enrolment was done in one block which took about 25 days to finish. The enrolment agency prepared an enrolment plan in consultation with the R&D Department at the state level following the key principle that the enrolment agency formed adequate number of teams and gathered equipments in the particular Gram Panchayats (GP) or the village Committees. The enrolment took place at the respective GP/VC offices. The respective BDOs checked the adequacy of space in the GP/VC office for deploying suitable number of teams as finalised in the enrolment plan. In many cases there was shortage of space in the GP/VC offices; to address this, temporary structures having GCI sheet roofing were constructed by the BDOs. In some cases locations other than GP/VC offices were selected by the respective Blocks for convenience of the residents and this information was disseminated properly in the locality. It was ensured that the selected enrolment centres had proper power supply for the machines required for enrolment to function and if needed new electrification and wiring was done to set up new power connections, switch boards, etc. Places where there was no electricity supply, the Enrolment Agency provided generator sets at their own cost. Even in electrified offices, the Agency kept standby generator sets for uninterrupted enrolment process. BDOs ensured that adequate quantity of drinking water was stored at the enrolment stations. The BDOs also ensured availability of toilets.

THE PRE-ENROLMENT AND ENROLMENT PROCESS

The enrolment for Aadhaar numbers included capturing basic demographic data as well as biometric data of each individual. The biometric data consist of ten fingerprints, iris scan and digital photograph of the individual which were captured by the operators of the Enrolment Agency in the enrolment station and the demographic data consist of KYR (Know Your Resident) data as well as KYR + data.

KYR (Know Your Resident) data included the following: Name; Gender; Date of Birth/Age; Pin code; Building/House number; Street/ Road/Lane/Ward/Para; Land mark; Area/ Locality/ Revenue Mouja; GP/ADC Village/Village/Town/City; District and State; Mobile/ e-mail; Proof of Address (POA) & Proof of Identity (POI) document; Relationship: Parent/ Guardian (in case of child); Existing bank account details/Opening of Aadhaar enabled new bank account (optional).

KYR+ data included the following: Electoral Photo-Identity Card (EPIC) number; MGNREGA job card number; Driving licence; Permanent Account Number (PAN); TIN number of the Census; Pension number; Bank account number associated with MGNREGA job card; Ration card number; Serial number in the ROR maintained by GPs/VCs as well as Nagar Panchayats & AMC; Name of GP/ADC village/Nagar Panchayat/Municipality.

In general each enrolment centre had five enrolment stations. Each station had a set of equipments to capture the demographic and biometric data which were operated by trained operators of the Enrolment Agency. In each enrolment centre there was at least one Technical/Station Supervisor deployed by the Enrolment Agency. Though it had been expected that enrolment of one individual should take 8-12 minutes, in reality it took about 20-25 minutes for an individual.

A large quantum of KYR and KYR+ data was available at the GP/VC level either in the ROR or MGNREGA card holders registers. The Enrolment Agency team deployed its data entry operators in advance to the concerned GP/VC for entry of all available data. The respective Panchayat Secretaries, RPS, Village Secretaries had extended all possible help in data entry by making available the record as well as assisting the data entry operators.

For the purpose of enrolment, residents had to produce POA and POI documents. The following documents were accepted as proof of address (POA): Entry made or Serial number in the ROR; Address mentioned in the Voter ID Card; MGNREGA job card; Bank statement; Electricity bill, etc. The following documents were used as proof of identity (POI) in order of priority (The order of priority is indicated only for the convenience of enrolment process.): EPIC; MGNREGA job card having photograph; Citizenship Certificate with photograph issued by the SDMs; SC/ST/OBC Certificate issued by SDMs; Permanent Resident Certificate issued by the SDMs; Passport. In addition, an exhaustive list of eligible POI documents is also given.

The KYR data includes data related to 'age' or 'date of birth' (DoB). In case the resident brought proof of DoB, his/her DoB was verified in the software and the document was scanned and uploaded in the database being prepared by the Enrolment Agency. Following documents were treated as proof of DoB: Date of Birth Certificate issued by the registrar of births; and the school-leaving certificate. In case the resident did not bring the proof of DoB, his approximate age was inserted in the software without verifying the DoB. It is recommended that residents having DoB certificate should bring the same and get their DoB verified.

At the enrolment centre, the supervisory teams checked the application forms and verified all the entries including the spelling of the name. They also checked the POA and POI produced by the residents and matched the details in the application forms. An awareness was created among the Local people to bring POA, POI, proof of DoB (if available), NPR form number given by census team, MGNREGA job card, EPIC, KYR+ documents like bank details, ration card, PAN card etc which are optional. The Enrolment Agency either kept a photocopy of POI, POA and DoB documents or preserved them electronically for later use. A campaign was made before the appointed day of enrolment by beating drums or by putting up posters in localities so that the people visit the enrolment stations.

The enrolment stations had generally three separate teams: (i) Station Supervisor for checking POA and POI and the application forms, (ii) operators at the enrolment centre who collected biometric data and also demographic data and (iii) Station Supervisor-ii to check if the data entered in the enrolment centre was correct as per the corrected application form.

The responsibilities of the enrolment agency as formulated by the UIDAI were as follows: procuring certified biometric devices; procuring other hardware & infrastructure for enrolments; ensuring that enrolment software was installed on laptops; loading pre-enrolment residents data; ensuring that UIDAI processes & standards were followed; assisting the Registrar to develop enrolment schedules; assisting the Registrar in enrolment publicity & awareness; ensuring the availability of certified operators & supervisors at enrolment centres; ensuring that adequate quantity of stationery is available; ensuring adequate backup arrangement at enrolment centre; setting up enrolment stations; capturing demographic and biometric data; handling exceptional cases during the capture of data; obtaining consent letters and making corrections in the data recorded; providing acknowledgement slips to residents; handling issues and concerns of operators and residents; ensuring that audit feedback, if any, is incorporated in process; enabling successful data transfer to CIDR; filing, creating back-up & storing enrolment data as per UIDAI guidelines; and taking corrective action in case of process/ quality deviations.

The machineries set up in the enrolment stations included: Laptop, USB hub port, UPS, 2MP Webcam, Iris scanner, Fingerprint capturing device, LCD monitor, Printer cum photocopier, White background and lamp to capture photograph well, Generator set, Required stationery articles, namely paper, pen, stapler etc. Existing facilities of the enrolment centre may be used by the Enrolment Agency for enrolment exercise. If any additional facilities and amenities are required for smooth exercise of the process those will be arranged by the Enrolment Agency.

When the state managed to enrol more than 90 per cent of the population under the UID project, it became compulsory to provide various government services to the people. A meeting of the UID implementation committee headed by the Chief Secretary S.K. Panda was held on 17 April 2012 in presence of the Director General of UIDAI R.S. Sharma which observed that 10 per cent of the population could not be covered for issuing UID number which was extremely important. So, the meeting decided that permanent enrolment centres could be set up in block or sub-divisional headquarters to provide UID number using the same process as before. These centres might also be used for updating of demographic and biometric data.

Since such a large number of people had already enrolled for Aadhaar, there is a good opportunity for deriving the benefits of Aadhaar by using Aadhaar in various applications like MGNREGA, Pension and Scholarship payments. For this purpose, Aadhaar numbers needed to be seeded in the respective database. UIDAI Regional office at Guwahati developed a tool for semi-automatic seeding of Aadhaar numbers in various databases and extended full support to the state government in this exercise.

As we have seen, Tripura had already operationalised Business Correspondent model for payment of MGNREGA wages in different Panchayats of the state. Since such an infrastructure already existed, it became very easy to convert this 'Offline BC Model' into an 'Online Aadhaar Enabled BC Model' in all such panchayats of the state where broadband or mobile connectivity was available. Financial Inclusion Team of UIDAI provided the necessary technical and managerial support to the banks involved in this exercise. The savings against the enrolment grant given by the UIDAI to the state government were utilised for payment of commission to the banks for operationalisation of the 'Online BC Model'.

EXPERIENCE IN MANDWI BLOCK

Mandwi had once hit the headlines of newspapers for the riots that took place in the month of June, 1980, between the tribals and non-tribals. This rural block not only witnessed the killing of people, torching of houses, army's flag-march and huge displacement of people, it was also witness to the breakdown of trust between the two communities – tribals and non-tribals. It again came to the limelight when the work for enrolment of Aadhaar number started from this Block on 18 November 2012, and concluded on 15 January 2012. The block covering 225.16 sq km has a population of 59,888 of which 55,844 people are from tribal community. It is a 100 per cent literate block. Here, old-age pension could be distributed to the people through Aadhaar-enabled payment system for the first time in the country on 18 October 2012. A group of journalists, including the author, was present in the Burakha village of the block to cover the occasion.

Rampati Debbarma, a 71-year-old tribal woman of this sleepy village in West Tripura district, pressed her finger on a micro-ATM carried by a 'Business Correspondent' and a print-out came out from the device confirming the amount of her old-age pension and she was paid the pension in cash. Rampati was not alone, and hundreds of old-age pensioners of this village collected their pensions in the same way after the Aadhaar-enabled payment system was introduced here. 'Earlier I used to walk about 10 km from my village to Mandwi Block headquarters for withdrawal of my pension from Gramin Bank, but today I got it at my doorstep. It is important because I cannot walk much now,' Rampati told the group of visiting journalists.[16]

The UIDAI in collaboration with the United Bank of India and the Tripura Gramin Bank undertook this field trial of Aadhaar enabled payment system with online authentication of biometrics of the beneficiaries in Mandwi Block. 'Our endeavour was successful today,' said Dinesh Mushahary, the Chairman of the TGB, who was present during cash transfer. 'Tripura is one of the frontrunners in the field of taking banking facilities to the doorstep of the common masses. Mandwi block is a rural block where all most all the residents are tribal and backward, but the process of giving Aadhaar number started in this block first not only in Tripura but in the entire north-eastern region. My officials and I are trying to motivate common people to register their Aadhaar numbers with the banks so that people can get their money directly and no middleman can cheat them. Tripura Gramin Bank too has become the first rural regional bank in the country to provide services based on Aadhaar,' he added. 'The Unique Identification (UID) project is a flagship project of the Central government which aims to provide old-age pensions, wage of NREGA etc directly to the beneficiaries where de-duplication is not possible. Payment of wages through banks and post office has made wage corruption quite difficult,' said Kiran Gitye, the District Magistrate of West Tripura.

The BDO of Mandwi, Manohar Biswas recounts his experience, 'It was a matter of confidence for us that we wanted to pay old-age pension to 194 people and we could do so without any problem. Earlier during the test run we could not pay much because the SIM of GPRS system inserted in the Micro-ATM operated by the Business Correspondents did not work well. There were problems of internet connectivity. But when we used Y-Max data card of BSNL we got good connectivity and could complete our works without any problem.' Biswas stated that payment through Aadhaar-enabled system for providing houses under Indira Awas Yojna (IAY) and NREGA and Total Sanitation Campaign (TSC) for construction of latrines would be started in November. 'We have 24 villages in the block of which online connectivity through Y-Max data card works in 22 villages without hindrance. So we have decided to provide payments of the two villages in the nearby villages. We have identified that there is no connectivity in Harbang and Khamtingbari villages, so the payments of Harbang could be made in adjacent Dinkobrapara and the payment of Khamtingbari could be made at Bhrigudaspara which are within a 2-Km radius of the villages.'[17] Aadhaar enrolment is a continuous process. So far, 38,912 people in the block have got their Aadhaar numbers and total eligible number for enrolment is 44,571. So 5,659individuals are yet to be enrolled. The process for new enrolment would begin soon.

For making online payment through Aadhaar core banking service is important. In the block under discussion there are a total of seven banks of which TGB has five branches with core banking facilities. 10,560 people have NREGA job cards but only 10,271 people have bank pass books. So, attempt is being made to convince them to make bank pass books in TGB so that NREGA payments can be made to them. Past experience says that off line BC model is not free from corruption. It was observed that many fake names could be inserted into the micro-ATM. So, it has been decided that Electronic Fund Management System (EFMS) would be introduced for Aadhaar-enabled payment for NREGA job card holders.

The claim of checking corruption through UID is made on the premise that payments are still being made in cash. In Tripura when BC model was introduced and payments were made by biometric cards, embezzling of funds could not be brought to end because there was huge scope for fudging attendances. It is generally done either by adding names of people who had not worked, or by inflating the attendance of those who had worked. When the payments are made through Aadhaar-enabled payment system it becomes difficult to misappropriate funds. There are a lot of evidence and video footages to show that direct cash payments were made for NREGA wages. But when it is made on-line the chances of misappropriation of funds reduce.

However, three potential channels of siphoning off money remain open – extortion, collusion and deception. Extortion means that when 'inflated' wages are withdrawn by the labourer, the middleman turns extortionist and takes his share from him or her. Collusion means that the labourer and the middleman agree to share the inflated wages that are credited to the labourer's account. Deception means that middlemen open and operate accounts on behalf of the labourers, withdraw the inflated wages from these bank accounts. 'Biometric-enabled UID to authenticate identity can help to prevent "deception", but is of little use in preventing collusion or extortion,' said Manohar Biswas, the BDO of Mandwi. The UIDAI's note on NREGA also shows a poor grasp of many other aspects of the implementation of NREGA. The following paragraph is an amusing example of this: 'The village level social audit committee can be selected after authentication with the UID database. The social audit reports filed by the village level committees can be authenticated by the biometrics of the committee members and the social audit coordinator.'[18]

The UIDAI is correct in its assessment that social audits are important in NREGA. Contrary to the UIDAI's understanding that the problem in social audits lies in the selection of members of the social audit committee, or social audit reports being filed by people other than those who are actual members of the committee, the issue is that social audits threaten vested interests and are therefore vehemently opposed by them. There is no obvious problem of 'identity fraud' in NREGA that UID is waiting to resolve. There is no evidence, for instance, of fake job cards being a major problem. An NREGA job card is not like a PDS ration card, which automatically entitles the holder to subsidised grain. To get benefits under NREGA, the job card holder is required to work. So, a fake job card is of little use. Claiming benefits without working requires collusion between non-working job card holders and implementing officials. If the two parties collude, some job card holders can have wages credited to their bank accounts, by being on master rolls. UID purports to prevent this through 'biometric attendance at the worksite', but the practicality of this imaginative idea is far from clear – it could easily create more problems than it resolves. And some forms of collusion can persist even with biometric attendance at the worksite. Facilitating 'doorstep banking' through banking correspondents (the 'BC model') is supposed to be another benefit of the UID. At the moment, labourers often have to go long distances to withdraw their wages. Banking correspondents (intermediaries who extend banking services to remote villages) are supposed to enable disbursal of wages at their doorstep. Here again, however, there are issues of practicality and effectiveness, and need to consider alternatives. Modernising and computerising post offices would also contribute to making banking services accessible.

People are now so familiar with the online BC model in 'our block that now they are demanding the facilities for transferring money to their children studying outside. Following people's request, money was transferred from remote Patni village of the block on 10 October 2012 to a number of students studying outside,' Biswas adds.

CONCLUSION

Strong political will of the CPI(M)-led Left Front government, bureaucratic alacrity and the virtual non-existence of any opposition from other political parties can be accepted as the reasons behind the success of the implementation of Aadhaar project in Tripura. The project ran smoothly because there was no opposition from any political party in the state. The main opposition Congress has no ground to oppose it because it was a flagship programme of the Congress-led United Progressive Alliance government in the centre. The Indigenous Nationalist Party of Tripura (INPT), a tribal-based opposition party which is an electoral ally of the Congress government, also did not oppose. Other parties like Bharatiya Janata Party have hardly any political standing in the state. Neither did any NGO oppose the project in the state.

The strong political will of the government is in evidence when the state minister for rural development, which is the nodal department for implementation of the project, says, 'As per UIDAI guidelines, implementation of UID project is optional for the states. Considering the immense benefits of the UID number, Government of Tripura has opted to implement the project in Tripura in first phase.'[19] 'It envisages empowering the poor and the marginalised and enhancing their access to public service. The UID (Aadhaar) number is a revolutionary idea taken up to avoid duplication of information, based on biometric features covering ten finger prints and iris scan in addition to photographs. It scores over other identity documents which can be duplicated.' The Aadhaar enrolment is a huge project. On being asked whether he thought government servants need lot of enthusiasm to implement it properly, the minister responded: 'It is a huge and diversified project. Government servants' enthusiasm and attachment is required to implement it properly. State Government has taken up the project enthusiastically for which Tripura could cover highest percentage of enrolment in the country.'[20] In these words, the rural development minister made it clear what accounted for the huge success of UID enrolment in Tripura – the iron-clad will of the state government which is turn ensures utmost bureaucratic alacrity.

NOTES

1. Tripura has been governed by the Communist Party of India (Marxist) (CPI(M))-led Left Front from 1978 to 1988 and then again continuously from 1993. In the last elections held on 23 February 2008, the Left Front won 49 out of 60

seats in the Assembly, 46 of which went to the CPI(M). From 1998, Manik Sarkar has been the chief minister of the state. He is also a CPI(M) politburo member

2. "Tripura Marching Ahead (1972-2012)," Government of Tripura, http://tripura.nic.in/portal/More_Info/document/Planning/Tripura%20Marching%20Ahead%20%281972-2012%29%20 English.pdf [last accessed 15 November 2012]
3. Speech of Manik Sarkar at the 59th North Eastern Council (NEC) Meeting, which is the 10th Meeting as the statutory Regional Planning Body for the North Eastern Region, held on 28 September 2010, at the Parliament House Annexe, New Delhi. The Meeting was chaired by the Union Minister of Mines and Development of North Eastern region (DoNER) and Chairman NEC, B.K. Handique
4. Interview of Manik Sarkar with the author
5. "Tripura's natural gas production to reach 5 mmscnd by 2014," 30 July 2012; http://www.goodreturns.in/news/2012/07/30/natural-gas-production-reach-5-mmscmd-on-135071.html [last accessed 15 November 2012]
6. Details of all awards have been taken from, unless otherwise indicated: "Tripura winning awards and recognitions," Tripura State Portal; http://tripura.nic.in/portal/More_Info/document/Planning/Tripura%20Winning%20Awards%20and%20Recognitions%20%28English%29.pdf [last accessed 15 November 2012]
7. Ibid, p.7
8. IAS100, A Civil Service Chronicle Initiative; http://ias100.in/basix_archive_details.php?id=213 [last accessed 15 November 2012]
9. Bakshi, Prakash, "Financial Inclusion- BC/BF Model- what's new?" *Bank Quest*, 83:2, June 2012, p.7; http://iibf.org.in/documents/IIB-Bank-Quest-april-june-12.pdf [last accessed 15 November 2012]
10. Interview with Chairman of TGB, Dinesh Mussahary on 2 November 2012
11. "Indepay empowers rural banking with biometric technology in North East India," *i-Newswire*, 3 February 2011; http://www.i-newswire.com/indepay-empowers-rural-banking/87960 [last accessed 15 November 2012]
12. Ibid
13. Ibid
14. Ibid
15. Ibid
16. For a gisted version of this and the following statements by Dinesh Mushahary and Kiran Gitye, see, "Aadhaar-enabled micro-ATM delivers money to villagers," *The Economic Times*, 18 October 2012; http://articles.economictimes.indiatimes.com/2012-10-18/news/34555541_1_aadhar-payment-system-pension [last accessed 15 November 2012]

17. For a similar take on the matter by Manohar Biswas, see Das, P., "Tripura tops UID Applications," *Seven Sisters Post*, 7 September 2012; http://sevensisterspost.com/tripura-tops-uid-applications/ [last accessed 15 November 2012]
18. "Social Audit," in UID (Aadhaar) and MGNREGA – Mahatma Gandhi National Rural Employment Guarantee Act (last edited by npn junction; 22 February 2011 at 05:28 pm); http://www.indiasemiconductorforum.com/showthread.php/883-UID%28Aadhhar%29-and-MGNREGA-Mahatma-Gandhi-National-Rural-Employment-Gurantee-Act?s= 209527fbfd55e4cf289286471110ec3e [last accessed 15 November 2012]
19. Interview with State Rural development Minister Jitendra Chowdhury, conducted by the author
20. Ibid

VII

UID's Augean Task? Assam and 'Illegal' Migrants

Samir Kar Purakayastha

INTRODUCTION

In Assam, 'identity' is a word that is divisive in character, fraught with inherent contradictions. Any attempt to profile identity – digital or otherwise – is, therefore, a tricky proposition. More so since enumeration processes have in the past triggered many a mutiny in the state. In fact, it was the preparation of a revised electoral roll for the Mangaldai parliamentary constituency that set the tone for the historic six-year-long anti-foreigners agitation in the state in 1979, and that shaped the contours of Assamese sub-nationalism. Not too long ago the state witnessed a violent uprising when a pilot project for updating the National Register of Citizens was launched in Muslim-dominated Barpeta district. Four persons were killed and 50 others injured on 21 July 2010 in Barpeta town when police opened fire on activists of the All Assam Minority Students Union (AAMSU) who tried to thwart the NRC updating work.[1] The protest was so intense that the beleaguered state government was forced to shelve the pilot project and take a fresh look at its approach towards the entire process. In another instance, introduction of electoral photo identity card (EPIC) in the state was stonewalled by the All Assam Students Union (AASU). These are indicators of the sense of threat that pervades the state's general psyche during any attempt to provide identity proof to its residents. It was thus natural to have very few takers even within the government when the proposal to issue UIDs to all the residents of the state was mooted.

Two days after the infamous Barpeta incident Assam government set up a state-level empowered committee under the chairmanship of Chief Minister Tarun Gogoi[2] and State UID Implementation Committee under the chairmanship of Chief Secretary N.K. Das[3] to oversee the implementation of the UID project in the state. After the formation of the twin committees, the Assam government on 26 July 2010 signed a memorandum of understanding (MoU) with the Unique Identification Authority of India (UIDAI) for implementation of the project. On behalf of the UIDAI, the MoU was signed by Davinder Kumar, deputy director general of the identification authority. Subhash C. Das, the then principal secretary, home and political department, was the signatory to the MoU on behalf of the state government. There are two views put forward for the state government's uncharacteristic decision to give a nod to the project in a hush-hush manner. It is stated that the compulsion of the Congress-led state government to toe the policy of the United Progressive Alliance (UPA) government at the Centre forced the signing of the MoU. The proponent of this theory, among others, is former chief minister and Asom Gana Parishad (AGP) president Prafulla Kumar Mahanta.[4]

A senior Assam government official who was then posted in the home department and was privy to the UID project on condition of anonymity, however, recalled that when the government entered into the agreement, enhancement of efficiency in delivery of government benefits and setting up of uniform standard process for verification and identification of beneficiaries were foremost in its mind and it somehow overlooked the project's potential to rekindle the identity debate. In its instruction to bidders for selection of an enrolment agency, the Panchayat and Rural Development Department of the Assam government on 24 December 2010 declared: 'The Government of India (GoI) has embarked upon an ambitious initiative to provide a Unique Identification (UID) to every resident of India and has constituted the Unique Identification Authority of India (UIDAI) for this purpose. The timing of this initiative coincides with the increased focus of the GoI on social inclusion and development through massive investments in various social sector programmes, and transformation in public services delivery through e-governance programmes. The UID has been envisioned as a means for residents to easily and effectively establish their identity to any agency, anywhere in the country, without having to repeatedly produce identity documentation to agencies. The enrolment is voluntary.' According to this official, the state government's decision was influenced by the fact that an Aadhaar card is merely a proof of identification and does not establish citizenship. It hoped that once the UID number started rolling out, the apprehension against the project would gradually die down. Accordingly, it decided to initially kick-start the project in the upper Assam districts of Jorhat, Dibrugarh, Sonitpur, Sivasagar and Tinsukia where there was not much presence of 'illegal migrants'. The first phase of the UID exercise in Assam was supposed to be completed by 31 March 2011.[5]

Lack of political will to push the project was evident in the absolute no-show of urgency on the part of the state government to take it to the people even after a lapse of several months since the signing of the MoU. According to Assam Home Secretary G. D. Tripathi there was 'zero progress' in the issuance of UID numbers in the state.[6] The state further developed cold feet in going ahead with the contentious project when the AASU raised objections to it. The powerful students' body, according to Das, insisted that the NRC should first be updated to determine the number of illegal migrants in the state. As objections against the project started trickling in, the state government slowed down its implementation. In fact it was so laid back in implementing the project that it took almost five months since after signing of the MoU for bidding by selection agencies to carry out the project. Dispur's lack of conviction about the initiative was apparent from Chief Minister Tarun Gogoi's suggestion to UIDAI Chairperson Nandan Nilekani to try to evolve a consensus in the state on the UID-drive. Das quoted Gogoi as saying to Nilekani: 'I am convinced about the benefit of the project. But you need to convince the people and other pressure groups about its utility back in Assam.' Following deliberations with the chief minister in New Delhi, the authority had even decided to conduct a seminar on Aadhaar in 2011 to dispel any misconceptions about the project.[7]

In the meantime, much to the relief of the Assam government, several other quarters, including the home ministry started raising security concerns over the project. Opposing the UID scheme, Bharatiya Janata Party (BJP) spokesperson Ravi Shankar Prasad said: 'Can the issue of development be diverse from national security? In many parts, especially in the Northeast, illegal immigrants have manipulated documents like ration cards and voter I-cards, and got several rights. If we give them UIDs, they will say they are citizens of India.'[8] Earlier, the then Home Minister P Chidambaram even went to the extent of writing a letter to Deputy Chairman of the Planning Commission Montek Singh Ahluwalia articulating his reservation over the project.[9] The data collected by multiple registrars of the UIDAI does not meet the degree of assurance required under the NPR from the point of view of internal security. The possibility of inclusion of non-usual residents in the local register and the creation of false identity profiles is also real, Chidambaram reportedly warned. To iron out the differences between the home ministry and plan panel over the issue, a cabinet committee on 27 January 2012 worked out a compromise granting permission to UIDAI to carry out the enrolment under Aadhaar in 16 states.[10] It was decided that in these states the home ministry for its NPR project, conceived by the BJP-led NDA government after the Kargil War, would accept the biometric data collected by the UIDAI. In the remaining states, including Assam, it would collect its own data through the Registrar General of India. Under the new arrangement, it has been decided that the UID number will be issued in Assam on the basis of the NPR. Explaining the changed *modus operandi*, Assam Home Secretary G.D. Tripathi, who is also the nodal officer overseeing the project, said that the UID number would be issued only to those registered in the NPR. Unlike, for the Aadhaar card, registration of names for the NPR is mandatory. 'Another significant difference between the two projects is their approach towards registration. In case of the UID, the 12-digit unique number can be procured by applying for it. But NPR is prepared through house-to-house enumeration and verification, thus considerably reducing security concerns,' Tripathi said.[11]

Notwithstanding such explanation and the much-hyped tussle between the home ministry and the plan panel over the twin initiatives, both these projects are identical and are not meant to determine citizenship. As such the concern of various quarters in the state over the possible issuance of UID to illegal migrants has not been addressed even by the NPR-linked UID process. In the words of Mahanta, 'The two projects are replicas of each other in the sense that both are not detrimental to influx of illegal migrants from across the border.' The apprehension is that even if the UID and the NPR are not to assign citizenship, they could be a supporting document to claim citizenship. 'Is a ration card proof of citizenship? It is a vital document to acquire citizenship,' Mahanta said.[12]

To deal with such apprehensions and to prevent any further roadblocks to the initiative by ethnic Assamese organisations, the state government has decided to conjoin the UID project with the updating of the NRC. It will now simultaneously take up the process of updating the NRC to tackle the contentious issue of illegal migrants. According to Tripathi both the projects are expected to be completed by 2015. A decision about the need to update the NRC to settle the problem of illegal migrants was taken during a tripartite talk between AASU, the Centre and the state government in May 2005. Accordingly, the state government in June 2010 initiated a pilot project to update the NRC of 1951 in Chaygaon and Barpeta. The process had to be stalled following violence in Barpeta. The violence was triggered by AAMSU's opposition to the manner in which the exercise was undertaken. To avoid a recurrence of Barpeta-like incidents, the government treading with caution, prepared the modalities of the NRC updating process after several rounds of marathon meetings with the stake holders like AASU and AAMSU. After preparations of the modalities by a cabinet sub-committee headed by Revenue Minister Prithbi Majhi on how to go about the task, the state government in August submitted it to the Centre for approval. The modalities were prepared after consultations with the AASU, AAMSU and other organisations.[13]

The Assam government for once is confident that the double initiative will be the answer to the state's long-pending problem of illegal migrants. The confidence stems out of the fact that there is also a broad consensus in the state on the need to update the NRC – although there is still some differences on how to go about it – to settle the problem of illegal migrants. Against this backdrop, any study on the impact of digitisation of identity on the migrant population in Assam should take into account the problem of immigrants in the state. It is also imperative to assess the impact on the basis of the two initiatives the state government has taken for profiling its residents as well as citizens, as the two projects are interlinked.

GENESIS AND PROBLEM OF MIGRANTS IN ASSAM

Legal or illegal: migrants all – is how a political commentator once described the demographic makeup of Assam. A noted Assamese litterateur and politician, late Gauri Sankar Bhattacharya, in one of his columns in 1999 too made a similar observation, stating that since life in its human form did not originate in Assam all its inhabitants are one-time migrants.[14] Migration is not a new phenomenon in Assam. It has been a melting pot of migrants of diverse ethnicities and cultures even before the concept of nation-state or citizenship was defined. But the pot started to stir once Assamese nationality began to take shape following the signing of the Yandaboo Treaty in 1826 and the British taking over reins. In order to run the administration the British brought with them officers, lawyers and clerks from Bengal, thus sowing the seeds of antagonism between the Ahom nobility and the British bureaucracy represented at the grassroots level by Bengali officials. The subsequent imposition of Bengali as the medium of instruction in schools in Assam further drove a wedge between the two communities – which had far-reaching consequences in the post-colonial era.

The Assamese community began viewing Bengali Hindus as cultural imperialists, who given the opportunity, would assimilate the Assamese.[15] This sense of threat was further entrenched by the Administrative Reforms of 1874, which transferred Bengali-dominated districts of Goalpara (undivided Goalpara is now divided into four districts), Cachar and Sylhet to Assam. The transfer of the three districts significantly affected the demography of Assam and opened the floodgates of migration of Bengalis into the state, soon transforming Assam into a

Bengali-majority province. Another factor that caused a demographic shift in the early nineteenth century was the British policy of encouraging the immigration of landless Bengali-Muslim peasants to Assam, to till fallow land and 'grow more food'. To quote E.H. Pakyntein, Superintendent of Census Operations, Assam: 'From 1901 onwards the men of Mymensingh began to advance into Assam, apparently by pressure on the soil at home. They were joined by the people of other East Bengal districts in lesser numbers. These immigrants settled in clear lands of Goalpara from the Bengal districts of Mymensingh, Pabna, Bogura and Rangpur. The population of Goalpara which increased only by 1.4 per cent in 1881-91, and by 2 per cent in 1891-1901 shot up by 30 per cent in 1901-11. The *thanas* most effected were in the west of the district. The percentage rate of increase was 70.1 in South Salmara, 61.8 in Lakhimpur and 88.6 in Bilasipara. The extent of immigration can readily be estimated from the fact that the growth in the natural population was only 15.6 per cent.'[16]

The settlement of these landless peasants from East Bengal districts was not, however, restricted to Goalpara. Migration to other parts of the province like Nowgong, Darrang, and Kamrup also received momentum, bringing these migrants into direct confrontation with the indigenous population. During 1911 and 1921, Assam recorded a decadal population growth rate of 20.47 per cent. In order to quell the tension, and in response to the demand of the indigenous people, the British administration in 1920 introduced the Line System in certain parts of Assam, demarcating areas for settlement of migrants. The system was subsequently extended to other parts of the Brahmaputra valley. This was the first administrative measure taken to check infiltration.

The system, however, proved to be ineffective (like various other measures adopted since then to abate migration), and only created greater rift between the immigrants and the indigenous people. In order to find a solution to the turf war, the Assam Assembly set up a committee headed by F.W. Hockenhull in 1937 to devise a land settlement formula that would be acceptable to the two contending parties – Bengali migrants and indigenous tribals. A year later, Hockenhull in his report was to advocate for continuation of the Line

System, even while pointing out that tribals by themselves would not be able to develop the wastelands.[17] The Hockenhull Report also stressed on the need for stringent measures to prevent alienation of tribal land. Interestingly many Assamese landless peasants too were given permission for new settlement on tribal lands by the Congress government headed by Gopinath Bordoloi before partition.

The Congress' war directive that forced the Bordoloi-government to step down in November 1939 gave a new dimension to the migration of Bengali Muslim peasants into Assam. The new Muslim League-backed government led by Syed Mohammad Saadulla that took over encouraged migration on religious lines as it was the avowed policy of the League to make land available to all immigrants from East Bengal, even scrapping the Line System. The much-talked-about land development scheme was subsequently scrapped in March 1942, during the short period of Governor's rule clamped in the state after the fall of the Saadulla ministry in December 1941. After returning to power in August 1942, the Muslim League-supported government in Assam gave a renewed thrust to its policy of opening up the state's reserve land for settlement of migrants from Bengal. Soon a large number of migrants came to settle in the grazing reserve areas and wastelands of Nowgong, Darang, and Kamrup districts in order to grow more food and generate more revenue to help the war economy of the British government.

Another wave of migration of Bengalis to Assam was witnessed after the partition of India in 1947. The unanticipated spurt in influx of population from East Pakistan frightened the Assamese leadership who were under the impression that exclusion of Sylhet would rid Assam of Bengali over-presence. So, almost the whole of Sylhet was transferred to East Pakistan, ignoring cautious voices like that of Rohini Kumar Choudhury. Choudhury, a member of the cabinet headed by then premier of Assam, Gopinath Bordoloi, while opposing the referendum in Sylhet held in July 1947 had said, 'Problems would persist, not land.' Incidentally, although Sylhet was sliced away from Assam, as a result of the Radcliffe Boundary Commission award a portion of the district comprising Ratabari, Patherkandi, Badarpur and half of Karimganj thana (present Karimganj district) came back to Assam.

The sense of relief the transfer of Sylhet to the then East Pakistan brought to the state's leadership was ventilated in the historic opening address of Governor of Assam Sir Akbar Haidari at the first Assembly session after Independence. Underlining his government's policy towards shaping the future of Assam he had said: 'The natives of Assam are now the masters of their own house. They can take whatever steps are necessary for the propagation of Assamese language and culture. The Bengali has no longer the power, even if he had the will, to impose anything on the people of those hills and valleys which constitute Assam. . . . The basis of such feeling against him as exists is fear, but now there is no cause for fear. I would, therefore, appeal to you to exert all the influence you possess to give the stranger in our midst a fair deal provided, of course, he in his turn deals loyally to us.'[18]

The sense of relief was short-lived. Rohini Choudhury's words proved prophetic. The partition forced Bengali Hindus to flee their homeland. Because of participation in the referendum thrust on them, explicitly on Hindu-Muslim lines, their stay in East Pakistan was at risk. The slice of Sylhet which had been transferred back to Assam by the boundary commission as also Bengali-dominated Cachar district, which had been retained in Assam, gave immediate footing to the Hindu refugees rendered homeless as a consequence of the referendum. Assam witnessed the largest ever increase in urban population in Assam from 1941-50, largely due to the inflow of partition victims, primarily from Sylhet district. However, in the colonial era, apart from Bengalis, a large number of migrants from Chhotanagpur plateau, Bihar, Orissa and other parts of the country were also brought to Assam as plantation labourers for the tea gardens. Many Nepalese and people from other Indian communities, notably Biharis and Marwaris, too came to Assam from time to time in search of better livelihoods. No doubt there have been the occasional resentment and also conflict between the Assamese and other migrant groups, but the Assamese society have by and large been mainly concerned over migration of Bengalis because of the latter's numbers and dominant presence in administration.

Several post-Independence developments further shaped the demography of Assam and pattern of its politics. The communal riots on either side of the border in 1950 saw both inflow and outflow of

Bengalis from Assam. While Hindus trickled in from East Pakistan, many Muslims of the then undivided Goalpara district and Barpeta ran away to Pakistan. Due to the mass exodus of refugees from East Pakistan, the issues of immigrants began dominating the socio-political space in Assam and soon the state witnessed a violent uprising. Subsequently, the Immigrant (Expulsion from Assam) Act 1950 was passed in Parliament which mentioned that only those people who were displaced because of civil disturbances in East Pakistan could migrate to India. The Act, however, failed to quell the tension as periodic riots took place in 1951 and 1961. Interestingly, in the 1950s, Assam witnessed a sharp increase in the number of Assamese-speaking people as Bengali-Muslim settlers in Brahmaputra valley registered their mother tongue as Assamese in the 1951 census. This group started to be referred as NaAsamiya or Neo-Assamese. The number of Assamese speakers rose from 31.4 per cent in 1931 to 56.7 per cent in 1951, while the percentage of Bengali speakers declined from 26.8 per cent in 1931 to 16.5 per cent in 1951. The Assamese intellectuals at that point of time were more than accommodating to Bengali Muslims.

According to Myron Weiner, '[A]fter 1947 the Bengali Muslims became *de facto* allies of the Assamese in their conflict with the Bengali Hindus. Bengali Muslims have been willing to accept Assamese as the medium of instruction in their schools, and have thrown their votes behind Assamese candidates for the state Assembly and the national Parliament. They have declared Assamese as their mother tongue. In return, the state government has not attempted to eject Bengali Muslims from lands on which they have settled in the Brahmaputra valley, although earlier leaders had claimed that much of the settlement had taken place illegally. . . . There is thus an unspoken coalition between the Assamese and Bengali Muslim against the Bengali Hindu.'[19]

Another significant development during that phase was the signing of Liaquat-Nehru Pact on 8 April 1950. The pact facilitated the return of many Muslim families who had left Assam in the wake of communal riots after Partition. According to one estimate 40,000 families had returned to Assam by 31 March 1958. According to the Assam chapter of the National Confederation of Human Rights Organisation, 212,000 Muslims came back to claim their properties and were given Indian citizenship. Assam recorded the highest ever population growth of 34.97 per cent during the ten years spanning 1951-61. Assam witnessed a fresh spurt in influx of Bengali Hindus during the communal tension in East Pakistan in 1964-65. Alarmed by the steep increase in population, the Bimala Prasad Chaliha-headed state government, against the wishes of the Central government, launched an all-out drive in the early sixties against immigrants who had settled in Assam since January 1951. Prime Minister Jawaharlal Nehru wanted Assam Chief Minister Bimala Prasad Chaliha to go easy on deportations and even stop them. Chaliha refused, saying that the problem was so critical that Assam's demography and culture would be permanently changed.[20]

The Assam government detected and deported several thousand foreigners to East Pakistan during 1964-69 by setting up foreigners' tribunals under the Foreigners Tribunal Order, 1964. In an official letter dated 11 July 1969, the then joint secretary of the political department, home, Madan Prasad Bezbaruah informed the then Assam Jamiat president late Sheikh Ahmed Ali that there were no foreigners in Assam. Subsequently, Chaliha declared on the floor of the Assam Assembly that there were no more foreigners left in Assam and as such the foreigners' tribunals should be wound up.

Another important post-Independence development that influenced Assam's polity was Bangladesh's liberation movement. During that period it is stated that about a crore of refugees took shelter in India, many of them in Assam. Although many returned after the creation of Bangladesh, a large number stayed back and this once again rekindled the issue of foreigners, with the state registering a decadal population growth of 34.95 per cent during 1961-71. The simmering tension flared up into a major agitation in 1979 when the electoral roll was revised for a by-election in Mongoldoi parliamentary constituency, following the demise of Janata Party MP Hiralal Patowary. In the early months of 1979, Hiralal Patowary, the then MP from Mongoldoi constituency of Assam expired all of a sudden. The Election Commission announced by-elections and accordingly started updating the voter list in April, which continued till May. Soon complaints began pouring in, with many alleging that illegal foreigners had been included in the list and demanding that the suspected citizens' names be deleted. Out of the 600,000 names in the voters list objections were raised against 70, 000. Significantly, the Election Commission reviewed the list and found 68.28 percent of the allegations to be true. It directed the state government to verify the complaints and chief minister Golap Borbora set up a tribunal which declared 45, 000 as foreigners, sending shock waves across the state. Muslim leaders like Golam Osmani and Zahirul Islam objected to the deletion of names.

The AASU in its annual conference from 7 to 10 March 1979 discussed the 'alarming' situation and called for detection and deportation of foreigners. The anti-foreigner movement culminated in the signing of the Assam Accord on 14 August 1985, by the AASU, the state government and the Centre. As per the accord, it was agreed that those who had come to Assam on or before 25 March 1971, the day Bangladesh was created, would be treated as Indian citizens and the rest would be deported. It was easier said than done. Determining pre- and post-25 March 1971 migrants became a bone of contention between the Assamese and the Bengalis. The issue came full circle when the then Assam Chief Minister late Hiteswar Sikia, in response to a query from AGP leader Prafulla Kumar Mahanta, told the state Assembly on 10 April 1992 that there were three million Bangladeshis illegally residing in the state. Although he retracted his statement two days later at a public meeting, the remark reinforced the fear of Assam being swamped by migrants. It was further accentuated when the then Governor S.K. Sinha in a 42-page report to President K. R. Narayanan on 8 November 1998, underlined the threat the unabated influx of illegal migrants from Bangladesh was posing to the demography of Assam. Sinha in his report stated: 'The unabated influx of illegal migrants from Bangladesh into Assam and the consequent perceptible change in the demographic pattern of the state, has been a matter of grave concern. It threatens to reduce the Assamese people to a minority in their own state, as has happened in Tripura and Sikkim.'[21]

From past events it is apparent that the overwhelming presence of Bengalis in Assam has always evoked a sense of marginalisation among the Assamese intelligentsia and therefore their discourses on migrants are predominantly Bengali-centric. According to Gauri Sankar

Bhattacharya the ever increasing influx of population from East Bengal (later East Pakistan and ultimately Bangladesh) that started from the beginning of twentieth century frightened the Assamese people.[22] The attempt to group Assam with East Bengal during partition and the subsequent utterances of some Bengali intellectuals like Professor Humayun Kabir and others in favour of inclusion of Assam within Bengal only added legitimacy to the fear. Kabir in his monthly review *India* had in 1914 commented: 'One can easily visualise a Bengali state comprising about ten million people and living in a compact area. Such a state would include the present administrative province of Bengal and some of the outlying districts of Assam and Bihar. In fact the province of Assam may be wholly incorporated in it.'[23] These statements are often viewed as a manifestation of a covert attempt to convert Assam into a Bengali state through a silent demographic invasion.

Governor S K Sinha in his report had also observed: 'There is a tendency to view illegal migration into Assam as a regional matter, affecting only the people of Assam. Its more dangerous dimension of greatly undermining our national security is ignored. The long cherished design of Greater East Pakistan/ Bangladesh, making inroads into the strategic land link of Assam with the rest of the country, can lead to severing the entire landmass of the North East, with all its rich resources, from the rest of the country. This will have disastrous strategic and economic consequences.'[24] To underline the gravity of the situation Sinha in that report to the president even referred to the pre-partition assertion by Moinul Haque Choudhury, M. A. Jinnah's Private Secretary, who after Independence became a minister in Assam, of presenting Assam to Jinnah on a 'silver platter'. Sinha also extensively quoted another Bengali leader, Shiekh Mujibur Rahman, or Bangabandhu as he is popularly known. Mujibur Rahman in his book *Eastern Pakistan: Its Population and Economics* had justified the merger of Assam with East Pakistan for getting additional living space and achieving economic prosperity as Assam had enough land and abundance of forest and mineral resources.

The higher growth rate among Muslims, mostly of Bengali origin, in Assam further deepened this fear and created a sense of insecurity among the Assamese and local tribal communities. This sense of insecurity blurred the definition of migrants, which often became synonymous, in common parlance and usage, to foreigners – Bangladeshis or illegal migrants. Consequently, almost the entire Bengali population of the state became a suspect nationality, undermining the fact that many Bengalis in Assam – both Muslims and Hindus – are as much indigenous, if not more, as an Assamese Brahmin or a Kalita.

The fallout of such distortions was the indiscriminate profiling of Bengalis as foreigners and 'doubtful' voters (in short 'D' voters). The latter tag is again an Assam-specific innovation engineered by the Election Commission of India to weed out non-citizens from the voters list. The commission vide its letter No. 23/AS/96 Vol-III on 12 November 1997 directed that names of all such persons whose cases are referred to the appropriate tribunal may be provisionally included in the voter list, but before final publication the letter 'D' may be indicated against such name in the voter list to denote that their citizenship status is doubtful or disputed. The fate of the 'D' voters was sealed by a subsequent EC directive issued on 5 January 1998 which stated that all persons against whom 'D' had been marked shall not be allowed to cast their votes as long as their citizenship status is not determined by the appropriate tribunal in his/ her favour. The same directive also debarred such persons from contesting elections.

According to government statistics, between 1997 and 31 January 2011, a total number of 221,936 'D' voters' cases were referred to the tribunals and out of these only 83,471 cases were disposed of by the tribunals. And out of 83,471 only 5,577, that is about 6.5 per cent, 'D' voters were found to be foreigners, liable to be deported. A recent RTI report revealed that out of 1,004 cases of 'D' voters judged by the foreigners' tribunals in Goalpara, 948 persons were found to be genuine Indian citizens. At present three categories of cases are pending in the state's 36 foreigners' tribunals.

(i) Cases transferred from IMDT to Foreigners Tribunals after the striking down of the controversial IM(DT) Act by the Supreme Court on 12 July 2005.
(ii) Cases referred to foreigners tribunals directly by the police
(iii) 'D' voters referred to the tribunals from 1997 onwards.

As per a statement submitted by the government at Gauhati High Court on 8 March 2011 (WP(C) No 1334/09) a total of 406,451 cases under the three categories were registered with the tribunals between 1996 and 31 December 2010.

According to State Home Secretary G.D. Tripathy, since 1996 the government could deport only 2,400 persons identifying them as foreigners.[25] After the AGP came to power following the signing of the Assam Accord in 1985, the police at the behest of its political master lodged a complaint against 287,625 persons. But after proper scrutiny and verification, the tribunals declared only 8,694 persons as foreigners. There are innumerable cases of even prominent members of Assamese society, like Syed Abdul Malik, becoming victims of indiscriminate drives against illegal migrants in the state. The most vulnerable against such a drive, according to Hafiz Rashid Choudhury, a prominent minority leader of the state, are the poor and illiterate who moved out of their areas of original settlement in search of livelihoods by working as construction labourers, vegetable vendors, rickshaw pullers, so on and so forth. 'Whenever some hand-to-mouth Bengalis from Assam are seen living together – be it in New Delhi, Mumbai or Guwahati – they are branded as Bangladeshis,' Choudhury said.[26] Often they are pushed back to Assam in hordes from neighbouring states like Meghalaya, Nagaland, Arunachal Pradesh, Mizoram and Manipur, even after they have produced ample proof of their domicile in Assam.

A large number of these internally displaced people are Muslims of East Bengal descent, settled in the shifting sandbars of the Brahmaputra and its tributaries called *chars* or *chaporis* since over a century. The gushing Brahmaputra regularly inundates and erodes its densely-populated river bank and river islands, rendering thousands homeless and jobless. Mass migration of these impoverished flood and erosion victims to Assam's hinterland raises the spectre of illegal Bangladeshis. Their presence in new areas is viewed as a proof of fresh influx of illegal migrants from Bangladesh. According to a state government estimate over 4.5 lakh hectares of river bank have been eroded, affecting over 21 lakh people in the state so far. Most of these affected areas are densely populated with Bengali-speaking Muslims.

Serman Ali, the AIUDF legislator representing Bagbar, the state's largest *char* area, while highlighting the predicament of the flood victims pointed out that the hardest blow the deluge strikes to the migrants is by destroying their documents of residency.[27] As a result their identity, which they need to carry around like insignias in order to avoid being labelled as illegal migrants from Bangladesh and at times even as Muslim terrorists, becomes a suspect. The flawed approach in typecasting a community is aptly captured in the following narration by journalist Pamela Philipose: 'Take the political and media discourse on what has come to be termed the "Bangladeshi problem". Here the genuine displaced person/environmental refugee has become synonymous with the jehadi terrorist. The distortion that now characterises the discourse, the general conflating of terms like refugee/migrant workers/displaced people/infiltrators, has had two unfortunate consequences. It has not only prevented the government from framing an ethical response to a very human predicament of vast number of people, but ironically also from evolving a legal and rational framework with which to deal with what are sometime justified concerns, relating to nation's security and its social and economic well-being, that arise out of such mass displacement.'[28]

Prejudice over contested identity has also succeeded in polarising any debate on illegal migrants in Assam and complicated the process of finding a solution to the vexed issue. Worst, it has also pushed the migrant lobby into a perpetual denial mode on the problem of infiltration. Such a trend also negates the state's demographic plurality. In the protracted campaign against illegal migrants in the state, the pro-migrant lobbyists see a mindset that perceives all Bengalis of Barak Valley and East Bengal origin as the diabolic Other who could be a great threat to Assamese and tribal dominance. This mindset was purportedly in play in the July 2012 violence in Kokrajhar and its adjoining districts that left over 4.8 lakh people, mostly Muslims of Bengali origin, homeless. The discrimination, according to Choudhury, has been prevailing since the branding of Bengalis as 'strangers' by the first state government after Independence.

'It is an irony of fate that every Bengali-speaking person living in Assam is doubted to be a foreigner in his native state. This exaggerated emotional picture gave birth to such an atmosphere that thousands of innocent Bengali-speaking people were butchered at Nellie, Gohpur, Mukulmua and other parts of Assam,' said CRPC in its approach paper for the national convention it organised in New Delhi on 6 September 2011 to highlight the plight of Bengalis in Assam. Endorsing the CRPC's contention, both Choudhury and Ali claim, during the course of interviews with them in Guwahati, that talks of large-scale influx from Bangladesh changing the demographic pattern of the state is a grossly misplaced theory. According to them, there could be illegal migrants in the state but the figure is definitely not as high as radical groups perceive.

The irony of Assam's problem of contested citizenship is clearly reflected in a bizarre episode concerning a neo-Assamese, Ashfaq Ahmed of Nagaon district. Ahmed was pushed back to East Pakistan by the Assam police via Latu (Karimganj) border in the sixties for being a foreigner. Managing somehow to return to Assam he moved a writ under Article 226 in the High Court. The court upheld his stay. To mobilise public opinion on such *suo moto* expulsion, two social activists of Karimganj – Parthapratim Moitra and Maloy Dey – also made a short-length movie *Ashfaq Alir Swadesh* on the issue. Apart from highlighting the indiscriminate targeting of religious and linguistic minorities as foreigners, the episode clearly indicates the ease with which international borders can be transgressed, thereby also justifying claims of unabated infiltration to the state. Any attempt so far to find a solution to the conflicting claims invariably became controversial, as was the case with the now-scrapped Illegal Migrants (Determination by Tribunal) Act, with one section or the other rubbishing it as a complete sell-out of their interest.

The absence of any precise estimate of the number of illegal migrants in the state as also a mechanism to identify a legal migrant from an illegal migrant compounds the prevailing sense of competitive victimhood. Interestingly, the protagonists on either side randomly quote the same census figures to justify their contesting claims [See Table 1]. There is a broad consensus that these claims and counter-claims could be set to rest by devising a mechanism to determine the nationality of all residents of the state through a fool-proof headcount. In rare unison, protagonists on either side of the spectrum advocate the immediate need for such an arrangement. According to AGP, such an arrangement would succeed in establishing the exact number of unauthorised persons living in the state,[29] while for All Assam Minority Students' Union this would be an effective deterrent against harassment of genuine Indian citizens as foreigners.[30]

Table-1

Comparative Data of Population growth: India and Assam (1901-2011)

Year	India		Assam		Above (+)
	Number (lakh)	Rate of Growth (%)	Number (lakh)	Rate of Growth (%)	Below (-) India
1901	2383		32.90		
1911	2520	5.73	38.49	16.99	+11.26
1921	2512	-0.30	46.37	20.47	+20.77
1931	2789	11.00	55.61	19.92	+8.12
1941	3185	14.23	66.94	20.07	+6.14
1951	3610	13.31	80.29	19.94	+6.33
1961	4391	21.64	108.37	34.97	+13.33
1971	5479	24.80	146.25	34.95	+10.15
1981	6809	20.60	182.21*	24.59	+3.99
1991	8463	23.85	224.14	23.01	-0.84
2001	10,269	21.38	266.39	18.85	-2.49
2011	12,100	17.64	311.00	16.93	-0.71

* In 1981, census was not held in Assam because of AASU's objection. Figure is taken from Assam government's projection.

Sources: (a) Relevant Census reports
(b) Statistical handbooks, Government of Assam

Much before the UID project was conceived, former governor S. K. Sinha in his much-talked-about report to the President recommended similar mechanism suggesting issuing of multi-purpose identity cards to the residents of the state as one of the solutions to the vexed problem. 'I also recommended that as the Bangladesh government, including Sheikh Hasina, did not accept the fact about illegal migrants, it was not possible to deport them. They should be declared stateless citizens with no voting rights nor [sic] be allowed to acquire immovable property,' Sinha wrote in the *Asian Age*, while also advocating for multi-purpose identity cards.[31]

Will the NRC and a multi-purpose identity card or the UID number put an end to the endless harassment meted out to the migrant workers from Assam, both within and outside the state? Will such citizenship invent the answer to Assam's problem of contested citizenship? These are some pertinent questions foremost in the mind of policymakers and common citizens alike, even as a besieged Assam government gave a fresh impetus to update the NRC and issue UID numbers in the aftermath of violence in the BTAD areas in July. Chief Minister Tarun Gogoi met Union Home Minister Sushil Kumar Shinde on 15 September 2012 in New Delhi seeking to expedite the process of updating the NRC. Needless to mention, Gogoi's Congress-led government in Assam believes that handing out of UID numbers can be a natural extension of the NRC revision. An attempt has been made through this study to find an answer to these all-pervading questions.

THE SOLUTION

From the genesis of the conflict, it is apparent that at the core of Assam's problem of illegal migrants is the dispute over who actually the illegal migrants are and what is their exact size. Once these core issues are settled, more than half the problem would be resolved. Herein is the importance of the identification exercises that the government has embarked upon. It is expected that once the NRC is updated and the NPR prepared, a credential figure about the number of illegal immigrants in the state will be established. More importantly, there would also be a biometric database on them.

But before analysing any likely impact of the two projects on the vexed issue of illegal migrants it is important to know how the government plans to go about implementing the ambitious initiatives. As per the existing plan, biometric and demographic information pertaining to all residents will be collected for preparing an NPR, a comprehensive identity database. An inventory of residents has already been prepared by the state government based on the population census report of 2011. Once the biometric database is put in place all registered in the NPR will automatically be eligible for an UID number for accessing benefits and services under government schemes and programmes, irrespective of citizenship status. In the meantime, along with the nationwide UID-NPR project, the Assam government is taking up a parallel initiative to update the 1951 NRC in order to establish the citizenship status of all its residents enlisted in the NPR.

Going by the provisions of the Assam Accord, the revised NRC will include the names of all those who have entered Assam on or before 25 March 1971, provided they can furnish relevant documents. While existing rules, applicable across the country, provide for preparation of the NRC strictly through house-to-house enumeration, the Citizenship Act rules have been suitably amended exclusively for Assam – in order to enable the updating of its citizenship register by inviting claims from direct descendents of those figured in the 1951 NRC or any electoral rolls prepared up to 1971. At this stage the state government is not forthcoming on elaborate details of its plan, given the sensitivity attached to any drive in Assam that is even remotely connected with identification of its residents. But it is apparent from the information gathered by probing several officials involved with the projects that in the long run Dispur intends to legalise the stay of existing illegal migrants as *de facto* citizens by providing residence-based entitlements.

'For all practical purposes, the NPR-linked UID will allow residents, legal or illegal, to procure benefits from government welfare schemes and programmes. But since it would not be a proof of citizenship, those holding UID numbers but not enlisted in the NRC, would be divested from voting and other rights reserved exclusively for Indian citizens. In other words, their status would be that of a stateless citizen. On the contrary, a place in the NRC as it is will be conclusive proof of one's Indian citizenship,' explained an Assam government official on condition of anonymity.[32] Going by his explanation, the projects will achieve two objectives. First, the guessing game over the exact number of illegal migrants in the state will be set to rest – those whose names would not figure in the NRC would naturally be foreign nationals or illegal migrants. Second, by linking the UID project with the NPR the government will also have ensured collection of biometric digital records of all its residents, and not just a select few who opt for it. This will create a digital wall against any further infiltration. As mentioned earlier, the registration of names for the NPR is mandatory and not optional as in the case of the UID.

Another significant gain of the initiatives will expectedly be an end to harassment of genuine Indian citizens. In order to avoid being dubbed as illegal migrants, poor and illiterate Bengali-speaking migrant workers often have to carry a sheaf of documents (ration card, birth certificate, land *pattas* etc). A UID number will save them from the cumbersome process of moving around with so many documents. They will have to now just remember a 12-digit number. 'Presently a marginalised migrant worker has to present a multiplicity of documents in order to prove his residency as his language and religion make his citizenship a permanent suspect in Assam and rest of the country as well. In the process of roaming around with documents many often lose or damage them and this run the risk of going through the ignominy of being labelled as a foreigner in his own country. Once the UID and NPR care are doled out, such harassments will definitely be minimised,' another minority leader Abdul Khalique, press secretary to the chief minister and a former MLA, pointed out.[33] With the UID there will be no fear of loss or damage.

Another common problem many of these migrants, particularly those living in the *char* areas, confronts is acquiring duplicate copies of the documents once they are lost or damaged in floods or erosion. In the absence of these identification documents, these marginalised people not only run the risk of being marked as foreigners, but are also deprived of benefitting from government schemes. The NPR-UID is again billed as a possible shield against such eventualities.

No doubt, some objections may be raised over giving resident-based entitlements to illegal migrants. But in the given scenario, considering the fact that Bangladesh never admits the illegal presence of its nationals in India and it is next to impossible to forcibly deport anyone to that country, it is the best option. At best, as Dilip Patgiri suggested, once the illegal migrants are identified, if they cannot be deported to their country of origin, they should be 'equally distributed' among all Indian states instead of burdening only Assam with what is perceived as 'unwanted guests'.[34] The biometric database of the residents will in fact give a lot of leverage to India to present its case before Bangladesh in the event of any future influx. And with India's eastern neighbour already having biometric databases of its citizens in future the two countries may also use their respective records to settle any dispute over nationality of any intruder.

True many questions may still be raised about the feasibility and utility of the projects as many doubts have been raised about the accuracy of the biometric mechanism. It is said that even the best designed biometric systems will be incorrect or indeterminate in some cases, and both false matches and false non-matches will occur. The sources of uncertainty include variations in biological attributes both within and between persons, sensor characteristics, feature extraction and matching algorithms. Traits captured by biometric systems may change with age, environment, disease, stress, occupational factors, socio-cultural aspects of the situation in which data submission takes place, changes in human interface with the system and, significantly, even intentional alterations. This would be so particularly in the case of the poor engaged in labour-intensive occupations such as farming, where hands are put to rough use causing weathering of finger and hand prints. Recently, it has also been shown that the three 'accepted truths' about iris biometrics involving pupil dilation, contact lenses and template aging are not valid. Kevin Bowyer and others from the University of Notre Dame, US, have demonstrated that iris biometric performance can be degraded by varying pupil dilation, by wearing non-cosmetic prescription contact lenses, by time lapse between enrolment and verification and by cross-sensor operation and that all these factors significantly alter the matching done to identify an individual uniquely.[35]

In Assam's context vis-à-vis its problem of illegal migrants, there is no gainsaying that the present initiatives, even after considering possible shortcomings, are likely to return with the best possible answer that is acceptable to all. More so as the only alternative solution we hear from intellectuals, policymakers and social thinkers is legalising illegal migrants by giving them work permits. As a matter of fact the Atal Bihari Vajpayee-led National Democratic Alliance government too had once toyed with this idea. The concept, however, cannot be hard-sold as it has some basic flaws. One, it will facilitate import of more migrant workers while not actually addressing the issue of alleged presence of a vast number of illegal residents in the state. Secondly, such permits would be easily misused. One could be entering the state with the permit and then could go missing. Considering that many Bangladeshi nationals have become untraceable after entering the country with valid papers, there is a high possibility of misuse of such work permits. There are over 12 lakh Bangladeshis who have entered India with valid documents but have gone missing and there are no records of their return, former BSF DG A Mitra had said in 2008 after quoting a report of West Bengal Intelligence.[36]

As far as the present moves are concerned, there will be no such concerns: primarily because if the government is armed with biometric information of its residents it will be easier to trace any stranger. Even those provided with resident status will find it difficult to fake their citizenship status once their biometric and demographic information are recorded. The information collected for the NPR-UID can also be accessed in the central database from anywhere in the country.

Many would perhaps opine that the NRC would have been enough to deal with the problem. The answer to such a contention is, however, both yes and no. The citizenship register, no doubt, itself is adequate to settle the issue of who an illegal migrant is. But an NPR-UID will empower the relevant agencies with vital biometric and demographic digital backups to prevent further intrusion and faking of identity by detected illegal-immigrants. The benefits of these projects, therefore, lie in their integration and not isolation.

NOTES

1. "Four student activists killed in police firing in Assam," *The Times of India*, 21 July 2010; http://articles.timesofindia.indiatimes.com/2010-07-21/india/28292131_1_student-activists-nrc-assam-assembly [last accessed 15 November 2012]
2. Assam government notification No PLB 34/2009/144 dated 23 July 2010
3. Assam government notification No PLB.34/2009/143, dated 23 July 2010
4. Interview with Prafulla Mahanta, Guwahati, 12 September 2012
5. Interview with Subhash Das, Guwahati, 13 September 2012

6. "UID work to start in Assam," *The Sentinel,* 13 January 2011, available at *followuidai: Anthropological inquiry into India's new biometric identification program*; http://followuidai.wordpress.com/2012/01/24/uid-and-bangladeshi-migrants-worries-from-an-assam-newspaper/ [last accessed 15 November 2012]
7. Interview with Subhash Das, Guwahati, 13 September 2012
8. "UID poses national security threat: BJP," *Times of India,* 22 January 2012; http://articles.timesofindia.indiatimes.com/2012-01-22/india/30652633_1_uid-bill-national-population-register-bjp-demands [last accessed 15 November 2012]
9. "Home Minister P. Chidambaram wants cabinet panel meet on UID," *The Economic Times*, 19 November 2011; http://articles.economictimes.indiatimes.com/2011-11-19/news/30419509_1_ uid-data-uidai-npr-project [last accessed 15 November 2012]
10. "UIDAI's mandate expanded," *The Hindu*, 27 January 2012; http://www.thehindu.com/news/national/article2837329.ece [last accessed 15 November 2012]
11. Interview with G.D. Tripathi, Guwahati, 12 September 2012
12. Interview with Prafulla Mahanta, Guwahati, 12 September 2012
13. Jaiswal, Umanand, "Move to empower NRC directorate," *The Telegraph*, 12 September 2012; http://www.telegraphindia.com/1120912/jsp/northeast/story_15966703.jsp#.ULSXZWcbFa8 [last accessed 15 November 2012]
14. Bhattacharya, Gaurishankar, "Assam's problem of foreign infiltration," Headlines, *North East News Agency*, Vol.2 Issue7-8, 22 June to 6 July 1999; http://www.nenanews.com/OT%20June22-%20July6%20,99/oh3.htm [last accessed 15 November 2012]
15. Weiner, Myron, *Sons of the Soil: Migration and Ethnic Conflict in India*, Princeton University Press: Princeton NJ, 1978, p.118
16. Census of India Vol. III (1961) Assam, General Report, p.213
17. Report of the Line System Enquiry Committee, vols. 1 and 2 (Hockenhull Committee), Shillong, 1938
18. Ahmed, Kamaluddin, *Assam's 'Doubtful Citizens': Fact or Fiction?* Pharos Media & Publishing Pvt Ltd: New Delhi, 2011, p.19
19. Weiner, *Sons of the Soil*, p.124
20. Hazarika, Sanjoy, *Rites of Passage: Border Crossings, Imagined Homelands, India's East and Bangladesh*, Penguin Books: India, 2000, p.60
21. "Report on Illegal Migration into Assam" submitted to the President of India by the Governor of Assam. D. O No GSAG 3/98 dated 8 November 2012.
22. Bhattacharya, "Assam's problem of foreign infiltration"
23. Phukon, Girin, *Assam, Attitude To Federalism*, Sterling Publishing Private Limited: New Delhi, 1984, p.23
24. "Report on Illegal Migration into Assam" submitted to the President of India by the Governor of Assam. D. O No GSAG 3/98 dated 8 November 1998.
25. Interview with G.D. Tripathi, Guwahati, 12 September 2012

26. Interview with Hafiz Rashid Choudhury, Guwahati, 13 September 2012
27. Interview with Sarman Ali, Guwahati, 12 September 2012
28. Philipose, Pamela, "Writing Displacement Creativity and Objectivity," in Nilanjan Dutta ed., *Forced Migration in North East India: A Media Reader*, frontpage: London & Kolkata, 2012, p.170
29. Interview with Ramendra Narayan Kalita, Guwahati, 13 September 2012
30. Interview with AAMSU president, Guwahati, 14 September 2012
31. Sinha, S.K., "'Stateless' remedy to illegal problem," *The Asian Age*, 15 August 2012; http://www.asianage.com/print/180829 [last accessed 15 November 2012]
32. At least ten officials directly or indirectly associated with the projects now and in the past were interviewed at Guwahati during 12-14 September 2012
33. Interview with Abdul Khalique, Guwahati, 12 September 2012
34. Interview with Dilip Patgiri, Advisor of the Asom Jatiyotabadi Yuba Chatra Parishad, Guwahati, 12 September 2012
35. Ramachandran, R., "How reliable is UID?" *Frontline*, vol. 28, issue 24, 19 November - 2 December 2011; http://www.frontlineonnet.com/fl2824/stories/20111202282402500.htm [last accessed 15 November 2012]
36. 12 lakh Bangladeshis missing after entering India: BSF, *Indian Express*, 11 September 2008

VIII

The Idea of Identity Card(s) and Experiences from Subaltern Mumbai

Manish K. Jha

In spite of it being a metropolitan/cosmopolitan city with an overwhelming migrant population, in Mumbai paradoxically the parochial sentiments have thrived and been asserted over decades. Over the years, the migrants have had experiences of encountering a variety of governmental technology to identify them and calculate their numbers. The history of Mumbai (Bombay) as a modern city with vast masses of migrants has its colonial roots. Confronted by what they perceived to be a maze of land rights, the British in Bombay sought to impose a uniform system of land tenure based on private property.[1] In order to consolidate its influence, the colonial regime required detailed information through land surveys and attempts were made as early as in the seventeenth century to do cadastral surveys, but with limited success. In nineteenth and early twentieth century extensive cadastral surveys of Bombay were done in the years 1811-27, 1865-72, and 1915-18. The survey sheets, maps, plans, and accompanying reports provided the authorities with valuable land use information[2] that enhanced political control and improved the processes of colonial governance. An array of statistical and information-gathering exercises, which existed in Britain, was also employed in India during colonial rule.

With increasing work opportunity in the mills, docks and other employment avenues, the inflow of migrant into Bombay increased substantively in the nineteenth century. This resulted in extensive increase in the number of migrants and the overall population of the city. John Fryer, in the 1670s, estimated the population of Bombay to be approximately 10,000 persons, mainly kolis or fisherfolks, kunbis or farmers, agris or salt-pan workers, and bhandaris or toddy tappers along with a few Portuguese fazendars or landholders, Jesuit priests, Pathare Prabhus, and Konkani Muslims.[3]

By the 1780s, Bombay's population had increased to 113,713 and by the 1872 census it reached to 644,405.[4] Recounting the history of migration in the city, Sujata Patel also affirms 'The expansion of trade and the lure of wealth attracted migrant groups to the city. When the British established their base in the city their indigenous partners and collaborators had migrated with them. These were the Parsis and Gujarati traders. Soon Bombay become the home of migrants from the north ... In addition, Bombay attracted distress migration that occurred as a result of famine and floods. Displaced peasants and agricultural workers as well as artisans migrated to the city to become workers in the port and other transport facilities being developed in the city.'[5] Whereas initially migration to the city was incentivised, in the wake of food scarcity in late eighteenth and early nineteenth century plans were made to restrict inflow of distress migrants and it was suggested that town should be cordoned off from undesirable elements such as 'vagrants, beggars and fakirs'.[6] However, due to the requirement to recruit a large number of people in the Company's battalion, the plan to restrict migrants could not be effectively pursued. Further, another spate of high rate of migration was experienced in the city during the years preceding and succeeding the year of independence. This was also the time when the economy of the city diversified and its cosmopolitanism was firmed up.

At present, in Mumbai, out of the total population of 13 million about 54 per cent constitute its slum population, who occupy about 12.85 per cent of the city's total land area. However, the recent census data states that the slum population has crossed 60 per cent of the total population of Mumbai. More than half of the city's population lives in slums, characterised by the illegal occupation of land and absence or shortage of basic civic amenities such as water, sanitation and electricity.[7] In spite of the dismal situation and inhuman condition in which the poor live, the access to housing and the lack thereof has become one of the most contentious issues for the migrant poor in Mumbai. Claiming and struggling for housing becomes the foremost concern for the vast majority of the migrant masses. On the other hand, though settlement of population is one of the oldest activities of the state, the power to decide for and against the right to settle for migrant masses has become a predominant preoccupation for the modern state. However, when one traces the history of migrants in the city of Bombay, one realises that migrants were incentivised to come and settle in the city. Through her archival work of colonial era, Dossal emphasises 'To populate Bombay Island, promote trade and agriculture, and develop the settlement into a profitable venture, the Bombay Government offered a wide range of incentives to attract labourers, artisans, traders, and financiers to leave their "native place" and settle in Bombay.'[8]

IDEA OF NATIONAL/UNIQUE IDENTITY CARD

The national identity card has been envisaged and managed in different countries by different names, such as Social Security number in the US, National registration identity card in China, Identification card number in Hong Kong, Israel, Iran, etc. The purposes are varied and so are the processes; however, the prime motive has been to identify and differentiate citizens and legal migrants from the illegal migrants. In India, the UIDAI's stated mandate is to issue every resident a unique identification number linked to the resident's demographic and biometric information, which he/she can use to identify him/herself anywhere in India, and to access a host of benefits and services.[9] Through the promotion and propagation of the UID or Aadhaar scheme, it seems that the state envisages this database to become the lynchpin of official identity, welfare, development, life, death, marriage and citizenship. The UID which claims to be unique, universal and ubiquitous is being projected necessarily for streamlining welfare and service delivery, though officially it declares that 'UID will only guarantee identity, not rights, benefits and entitlement.' The rationale for such a massive exercise is legitimated by the promise that this identity would make the poor and the marginalised visible to the state. The UID number is expected to plug leakages, including in the public distribution system (PDS), ease payments to be made under the Mahatma Gandhi National Rural Employment Guarantee Scheme (MGNREGS), and enable achievement of targets in consonance with the right to education. Service delivery is a central theme in its promotional literature.[10] However, numerous questions concerning the social consequences of the biometric technology-based Aadhaar come to the fore. Is it driven by a certain kind of political economy? Will it really improve the lives of people? Is a centralised system of identification, and regulation, compatible with the dispersed forms of governance structure, a hallmark of modern democracy? Will the private sphere liquefy under the system of an all-encompassing centralised repository of digitised database?

Historically, recording, documentation and statistical information are employed to consolidate control over population and territory; nevertheless, it is expressed in the language of care and concern for the population. Though the process of making people 'legible' does not allow claim-making and entitlement-security, yet UIDAI has been advertised and been crafted in the language of development policy and programme. This ambiguity makes it necessary to understand and analyse the experiences of people. The enthusiasm to get the Aadhaar card issued among the people residing in the slum locality and among informal-sector workers, homeless population, etc. draws attention to the complexity of the migrant situation. Though social activists of different ideological orientation are suspicious of a 'hidden agenda', 'veiled threat of targeting poor adversely', 'anxiety of misuse of profiling' and 'heightened securitisation as threat to the poor', etc., nevertheless, they respond to the 'here and now' exigency of getting these identity proofs issued for their respective constituency. There is confusion, contradiction and differences even among the sangathans' activists vis-à-vis their disposition to UIDAI. Some of the social activists have been raising doubts about motives and ideology of the NGOs that are involved in ensuring housing for the poor. It is alleged that some of these NGOs are being used to divide and weaken the people and render them incapable of launching united people's struggles for equality and dignity. Their constant effort is to subvert, misinform and de-idealise people so as to keep them away from class struggles.[11] Das further stresses that the effort of these NGOs is to divert people's attention from the larger political evils of imperialism to merely local issues that confuses people.

The practices of identification simultaneously secure and undo identities. The exercise of identification, though it has become technical and digital in the modern times, has always been an obsession of the state. However, the tools and strategies were continuously changed and improvised so as to govern better. The colonial state's efforts for statistical information-gathering were subsequently supplemented by use of ethnography to know India better. The ethnographic state was driven by the belief that India could be ruled using anthropological knowledge to understand and control its subjects, and to represent and legitimise its own mission.[12] In order to augment the grip on its subjects by overcoming the prevailing documentary regulation, the fully digital unique national identity card has been perceived by the state as panacea. Computerised biometrics, like its paper-based predecessors, is driven by the fantasy of administrative panopticism – the urgent desire to complete and centralise the state's knowledge of its citizens.[13] The image of the 'panopticon' refers to Bentham's design for a prison in which individual prisoners could be seen at all times by a centrally located guard who was invisible to them. Same is true with the centrally deposited database. Biometric technology is perceived to be a solution to the limits of documentary regulation and thereby strengthen the state's grip over identity, movement and regulation of population.

The majority of the population encounters the state through documents such as passport, ration cards, variety of identity cards, court papers, birth and death certificates, First Information Reports (FIRs) filed in the police stations, Inner Line Permit, the Aadhaar card, etc. 'These documents bear the double sign of the state's distance and its penetration into the life of everyday.'[14] The idea of penetration into life and fascination for legibility has been convincingly elaborated by Scott: 'An illegible society, then is a hindrance to any effective intervention by the state, whether the purpose of that intervention is plunder or public welfare … A thoroughly legible society eliminates local monopolies of information and creates a kind of national transparency through the uniformity of codes, identities, statistics, regulations, and measures.'[15] Michel-Rolph Trouillot suggests that the legibility effect is the 'production of both a language and a knowledge for governance and of theoretical and empirical tools that classify and regulate collectivities.'[16] This state-created and controlled identity information has the potential to be used and misused by mapping, zoning and profiling of individuals and population. The attraction for such data reveals what Zuboff (1988) calls 'power of information panopticon'.[17] Such systems can become information panopticons that, 'freed from the constraints of space and time, do not depend upon the physical arrangement of buildings or the laborious record keeping of industrial information ... [or] the presence of an observer.'[18] These information and records influence the ideas of subjects and citizens and are appropriated by those who act as the repository of this information. On the other hand, subaltern migrants do wish to manipulate these documents to make certain claims on the state. State-deployed techniques of measurement and mapping the incommensurable are marred by the possibility of trickery and offsetting. There are enough instances that depict the limits of making population legible and arrange-able. Whereas the state relies on its confidence, predictability and authority to make population legible, the element of deception based on practical skills is often underestimated. These practical skills, indigenous knowledge and folk wisdom have been explained by Scott as metis.[19] Considering the way several other documentation and recording processes (such as PDS card, Voter ID card, PAN card, etc.) were forged, duplicated, altered and manoeuvred in the past, one needs to factor in this localised metis with individuals and communities that might undermine the state's overconfidence of making population legible. This overconfidence is to be analysed in the light of the underwhelming track record of the country during its earlier experiments with identifying population.

At a time of skewed regional development and increasing urbanisation, space crunch as also configuration and re-configuration of space has become a crucial issue. With large swathes of land being occupied or squatted upon, identity proof has become a major point of reference either to stake claims or to refuse claims. Enumeration, mapping and documentation of migrants living in slums and resettlement colonies as also on pavements are critical processes both for the state, individuals and communities residing therein, albeit for different reasons. At a fundamental level, the management of movement of populations requires two instruments: a robust database of identities to know who all should be asked to move out and who all to be settled, and a highly efficient state machinery to facilitate the process. The recent, or perhaps not so recent, obsession of the state to transform the 'invisibility' of the marginalised category of migrant poor that are either homeless or stay in 'peripheral' urban spaces into a countable and documentable population highlights the fact that the state is increasingly recognising the need to factor in their existence and to manage them better. This certainly necessitated the process of converting their identity into governmental database. Active surveillance and tracking of migrants by the state depends heavily on information and knowledge production. This knowledge production for the purpose of control has always been redefined, improvised and modernised. Control depends on information to make society 'legible' so that the state can act and implement policy.[20]

The practices and promises of these documentation and digitisation have been experienced by different section of migrant population differently. The migrant lives on the threshold of legality/illegality, security/insecurity, insider/outsider, wanted/unwanted, etc; and their experiences of accessing or inability to access services of the state revolves around the strength and limits of their citizenship emanating from identity proof or the lack of it. More often than not, legal recognition eludes the migrant. The legality demands identity, an identity that is authenticated as governmentalised identity proofs, so that they can plead for their right to move and settle. UIDAI claims that it will enable authentication 'anytime, anywhere, anyhow'. It, thus, aims to give migrants mobility of identity. Though history is replete with instances and strategies of recording, documenting and providing migrants with identity markers,[21] the entire process has taken a gigantic and exceptional dimension in the digitised age of the neo-liberal regime the world over.

Referring to slave branding for Dutch West India Company and drawing parallel through use of modern technology, Browne explains 'Current biometric technologies and slave branding are not one and the same; however, when we think of our contemporary moment where "suspect" citizens, trusted travellers, prisoners and others are having their bodies informationalised by way of biometric surveillance – sometimes voluntarily and sometimes without consent or awareness – and then stored in large-scale databases – some owned by the state and some owned by private interests – we can find histories of these accountings and inventories of the bodies in slave registers, slave branding and the slave vessel manifests that served insurance purposes.'[22] Premised on the logic of 'surveillance for security' and 'making welfare smart', the aspiration for documentation and digitisation has been articulated by the state as a process of providing identity to the unidentified and the unidentifiable.

However, the identification of population is often projected as an onerous task due to increasing migration from one place to another. Regional imbalances in development within India, along with widespread unemployment, have recently led to a significantly accelerated pace of internal migration.[23] The process of migration, though mainly defined and analysed in terms of poverty, land alienation, income opportunity, etc, the impact of disaster, displacement and forced migration have received scant attention. While profiling the destination for migration, it is observed that metropolitan cities like Mumbai and Delhi are considered favoured places. The profiling of source, through census data, reveals that Uttar Pradesh and Bihar alone constitute one-third of inter-state out-migration. Though the phenomenon of migration has a long and chequered history, post-1991 liberalisation policies have enhanced the pace of internal migration of skilled, semi-skilled and unskilled workers from rural to urban areas. Vast majority of these migrants are engaged in unorganised sector work and live a life of insecurity, vulnerability and are susceptible to 'illegality'. Monteiro describes the unorganised sector generally as comprising a large number of unregistered persons.[24] Typically, born in village homes without birth certificates, dropped out of school at some stage without leaving certificates, forced to migrate to distant cities for work, the migrants live in unauthorised slum dwellings, often without any identity card. For many such persons, their name on a voter list is the only record of their existence as an Indian citizen. Informal staying arrangement for people engaged in informal and unorganised work limits their claim to citizenship. In order to extend the net of mapping migrant workers, UIDAI has signed a Memorandum of Understanding (MoU) with National Coalition of Organisation for Security of Migrant Workers, a consortium of over 20 civil society organisations. Efforts have been made to include poor and marginalised persons, including street/ orphaned children, widows and other disadvantaged women, migrant workers, the homeless, senior citizens, nomadic communities, including tribals, and the differently-able under Aadhaar card.

ENUMERATION FOR HOUSING: SEARCH FOR 'IDENTITY'

'The political economy of the city depicts that urban governance in Mumbai is meticulously planned and carefully crafted based on a very detailed information and knowledge about the inhabitants of the city; that include high taxpaying citizens (including corporate houses, entrepreneurs, employees of corporate and government, etc.) and people living in chawls[25], slums, resettlement colonies, pavements (sidewalk ways) and engaged in lowly-paid employment avenues and involved in informal and unorganised sector. The government employs diverse apparatuses for generating information and knowledge about population and thereafter accordingly decides to render docile the unruly domains over which government is to be exercised, to make government possible.'[26] Governmentalities both extend the concerns of rulers to the ordering of the multitudinous affairs of territory and its population in order to ensure its wellbeing, and simultaneously establish divisions between the proper spheres of action of different types of authority.[27]

There are multiple digital and manual databases, such as, Passport, Census, Election Commission, BPL (Below Poverty Line) card, Ration card, Driving License and Border area ID card, etc. These are already in use in India. The experiences of the Mumbai migrant expose the duality of the state where identity that is linked to entitlement is vehemently denied whereas identity that is premised to map and calculate for the sake of addition in database for security and governing process is easily facilitated. A case in point for the former is PDS card and the latter is certainly UID/Aadhaar card. This essay locates the experiences of documentation and digitisation of the migrant poor in and around the housing issue and of those who live in a state of homelessness. As far as housing policy in the city of Mumbai is concerned, it vacillated between slum clearances to improvement to resettlement. In the first two decades after independence, the state government and the municipal corporation of Mumbai sought to demolish slum and clear land that had supposedly been 'encroached' upon by the urban poor. The public perception of slum dwellers principally revolved around the notion of the 'other' that was perceived as a 'nuisance'. 'The contribution of slum dwellers to the city's economy – as industrial workers, construction labour, domestic servants, rag-pickers and in a whole range of petty trades such as vegetable and fruit-selling – remained unacknowledged.'[28] In due course of time, the idea and policy of clearing slums seemed unsustainable and by 1970s slums began to be considered as solution of housing scarcity. Subsequently, legislation was enacted and policy framework developed to provide basic civic amenities in the slums. For this, the need to count and verify the eligibility of slum dwellers was felt necessary by the government.

The housing rights activists in Mumbai claim that the first unofficial enumeration was done in Janta Colony, where eviction threat was looming large in 1973. 'Doing an enumeration – counting and listing all the houses, the electricity poles, the telephones, the shops, the businesses, the people who have ration cards – was to show to the courts how well established the settlement was ... If you do not do an enumeration, you cannot stand in the courts to prove your legality ... File a petition in court and you include the documentation as evidence – the telephone poles, the number of land lines for telephones, the water connections, the number of licensed establishments and other enterprises.'[29] A subaltern community enumeration and documentation process got grounded in the slums of Mumbai that documented the history of settlements along with profiling of household. However, the first official census of slums was carried out by the State Government in January 1976 (Government of Maharashtra, 1995) and 902,015 huts in 2,335 pockets were identified.[30] All those who had been counted in 1976 were eligible for slum improvements, redevelopments and relocation. The government at that time decided that further encroachments would be effectively and ruthlessly stopped. After a census of huts was conducted in 1976, photo-passes were issued to all those who were found eligible on the basis of the fact that they could establish that they were living in the slum at the time of the census. This was in a way the first official mapping and documenting of slum-dwellers. It is interesting to observe that for most of the slum-dwellers who received photo-passes, these documents became their most prized possession. Interestingly, though the original photo-pass was in a book form with spaces for entry of rent payment to Municipal Corporation for availing civic amenities, it is mentioned on the document that it should be framed in the glass frame. The assumption that this photo-pass would become crucial as identity proof seems to have guided the idea of framing the document. However, slums on central government and privately owned lands were excluded from the exercise of counting and issuing photo-pass.

A second enumeration was carried out in 1983. 1,930 settlements with a population of 43 lakhs were counted.[31] Of 678,381 huts surveyed up to 1984, about 50 per cent were located on private land, 16 per cent on state government land, nine per cent on land belonging to the Maharashtra Housing Board and 18 per cent on Bombay Municipal corporation lands.[32] Besides, initiative to enumerate pavement dwellers, unrecognised by the state, was undertaken in the year 1986 for the purpose of asserting their identity and existence in the city. The enumeration of the pavement dwellers included details of where they lived, the name of the street, which part of the street, how many huts, how many electricity poles; and it comprehensively mapped the makeshift addresses for asserting their citizenship rights.[33] These enumeration processes became markers for deciding illegality and illegality of claims of the migrant poor over housing rights in particular and on city-citizenship rights in general. Subsequently, the state government also introduced legislation that protected the slum dwellers who could establish that they were living at a particular place as of 1 January 1995. The homes of 'eligible' slum dwellers thus could not be demolished without their first being resettled.[34] 'Any squatter family that owns its structure and can prove that it has been there since 1 January 1995, will be given a new home at no cost if their community is targeted for a government aided project.'[35] This meant that all slum residents and pavement dwellers who could establish that their names were on the electoral rolls on 1 January 1995 were protected in a manner by which they are to be rehabilitated if their homes are demolished for the project. Those who cannot furnish documentary proof will automatically fall outside the purview of any consideration. The 'cut-off' date determines whether the state is going to tolerate the urban poor within its limit or not. The entire enumeration process undertaken by agencies like the MMRDA[36] and the issuance of identity numbers are the proof of peculiar forms of classification and surveillance which keep the insecure poor always on tenterhooks.

James Scott's influential book, *Seeing Like a State*, attempts to understand statecraft as a process of rendering populations 'legible'. Scott argues that this has been achieved through a series of disparate state practices of surveillance and control, including sedentarisation, the creation of permanent names, the establishment of cadastral surveys and population registers, the invention of freehold tenure, the standardisation of language and legal discourse, the design of cities and the organisation of transportation. These practices have functioned 'as attempts at legibility and simplification'.[37] However, the process of identifying project-affected persons became a gigantic and contentious process. Slum dwellers are largely deprived of access to land ownership, basic infrastructure and amenities and formal employment opportunities. And to access these as rightful citizens rather than as a burdensome population, one needs proof of identity. These magical dates determining their entitlement become vital for the city's migrant population. Since the agencies of government consider the slum population after a particular date as illegal occupants and encroachers, they are therefore undeserving of entitlement, security and rights.

MIGRANT MASSES AND THEIR PERCEPTION OF AADHAAR

The Aadhaar, though it does not guarantee any rights or entitlements, however promises, through its propaganda, a variety of entitlements, security and rights. A gigantic process which is highly technical and digital, by way of usage of biometrics and fingerprints, stokes aspiration and raises expectation that the possession of this digitised identity card would mean much. The twelve-digit Aadhaar number becomes a magical one and subaltern subjects scramble to get it hoping to use it as identity proof or to make claims for housing, or to make their existence legal. While referring to the 'issues relating to the subjects of digital technology', Taylor and Harris quote de Certeau: 'We witness the advent of number. It comes with democracy, the large city, administrations, cybernetics. It is a flexible and continuous mass, woven tight like a fabric with neither rips nor darned patches, a multitude of quantified heroes who lose names and faces as they become the ciphered river of the streets, a mobile language of computations and rationalities that belong to no one.'[38] Digitisation, as a technological imperative, has been adopted by the Indian state without any public debate for employing biometrics, iris scan and fingerprints. 'Seeing' in modernity therefore has a distinct socio-technical character. It implies knowing what to see and what not to see, and absorbing the rules by which the prevailing threshold of visibility operates, that is socially prescribed and technically reproduced.[39]

Whatever little debate and deliberation around the UIDAI happen, it is restricted largely within academic and activist circles along with select media groups. The contentious scheme has, in the meanwhile, completed its first round. In the wake of this, it was felt that there exists a confusion, even among social scientists, about what the people's perceptions of the UID are. Through informal interviews and short narratives, it was apparent that migrant masses, across communities, had an opinion on UID; nevertheless, most of them had applied for and successfully obtained the Aadhaar card.

UID AND SUBALTERN EXPERIENCE

Three locations were chosen for the study, keeping in mind their marginality and hence, selective invisibility/visibility to the state. The first location was that of Rafiq Nagar, known as 'illegal settlement'. This is an area which borders the Deonar dumping ground in the M-East ward of Mumbai. The Deonar dumping ground is the oldest and the largest dumping ground in India. It is an area which reflects the underbelly of this mega-polis. The dumping ground relieves the city of tonnes of garbage and acts as a source of livelihood for many who work as rag pickers. The inhabitants of Rafiq Nagar have been sorting garbage for decades now. It is a dangerous and near fatal experience. Yet, the people who perform this service are one the most marginalised, vulnerable and voiceless of the communities we identified to capture subaltern experiences vis-à-vis the Aadhaar card. They are new and old migrants from within Maharashtra and other parts of the country; many of them are Bengali-speaking migrants from West Bengal and Bangladesh. The area is characterised by shanties, by single-room tenements, crowded lanes, overflowing drains and the overpowering stench from the dumping ground. The residents of Rafiq Nagar are sandwiched between the dumping ground on one side and a regularised locality on the other. They are accustomed to the fact that their homes will be bulldozed by the Municipal Corporation at least three times a year. The fear of the relocation of the ground, of the booming real-estate prices in the nearby eastern suburb of Chembur and of rag-picking increasingly becoming an unprofitable profession, stalk the life of the men, women and children as they sift through the garbage – they are uncertain of what the future holds. Excluded even in M-ward,[40] a ward that is infamous for its underdevelopment on most human development indicators in the city of Mumbai, Rafiq Nagar symbolises the poverty and vulnerability of the poor in the city. The area was chosen because of its existence on the fringes of the city; and the continuous endeavour of the people to become a part of the state's gaze so that they are counted as citizen.

Another site of study, Juhu line area, is a regularised area. It was regularised in 1988. People have photo-passes issued to them as proof of their legitimacy. The houses are permanent structures with two or three storeys. While the lanes are narrow and full of a plethora of hanging electricity wires and a mangled lot of cables, the drains are covered. Walking through the lanes lined with shops, one cannot help but notice the kind of goods sold. One observes everything ranging from meat to mobiles, from stationery to clothes and groceries. Young men on bikes whiz through these lanes and children in private-school uniforms walk by. Satellite dishes, LCD televisions and washing machines can be seen in some of the houses. The occupants of this area are employed in the formal and informal sectors. The community is dominated by a religious minority. Being a regularised colony in the western suburbs it does not face an existential risk. But because of its religious composition, it does face social exclusion and remains constantly on the surveillance radar of the state. Communities experience a high degree of suspicion owing to their social exclusion gave us an insight that was important to understand the ever-expanding gaze of the state.

The third area selected was that of migrants who have been in the city for so long that some of them are not even migrants in the real sense of the word. Jai Ambe Nagar is home to the Pardhi[41] community who are a de-notified tribe of Maharashtra. The community has its roots in the Marathwada region of the state. They were landless in Marathwada and are discriminated migrants in Mumbai. Yet, the desire to return is nonexistent. Memories of no land, no water, and poor wages are what remain of home. Their current settlement on the eastern express highway (which they helped in building) with a water body as a backdrop and a sewage pipe as a support wall is flanked by high-rise cooperative societies. The people work as labourers on construction sites, road-making, trench-digging and other odd jobs. Women work as labourers on these sites, being paid less than the men, but preferring this to domestic chores for others. They have been living in this site since 2003. Demolitions are routine for them and it is a regular fight for survival. The demolition squads come without prior notification and take away all that they have. People refrain from making better houses because of fear of demolition and eviction. Members of this community had even visited Delhi to give their memorandum to the central government about regularising their housing as part of the Ghar Bachao ghar banao andolan.[42] The Pardhi community faces exclusion – social, economic and political – despite being from within the state. In addition, their migrant character and the informal nature of their work along with the 'illegal' status accentuate their marginality and vulnerability. Their understandings of this new dimension of identity add to our understanding of the state.

As has been ascertained, while the state may want these communities to remain on the margins, there is an increasing desire for them to assert their citizenship rights. Proof of identity, and thereby belonging, is central to this assertion. So whether it is people who work as rag-pickers, construction workers, or belong to the Pardhi community; whether they are active members of the Left parties or members of civil society movements – the desire to belong to the city of Mumbai, and be recognised as such, is overarching.

THE NEED TO HAVE A 'VALID IDENTITY'

Our concern to capture the experiences of identity could be understood best from the point of view of one who does not seem to belong, the migrant. In all the three locations, people were migrants – be it recent or long-term ones. As our interviews revealed, almost everyone in these three communities, two of which are 'unrecognised' and hence illegal, possess ration cards (and BPL cards as the case may be), voter identity cards, photo-passes for the case of regularised colonies, PAN cards and now the Aadhaar card. One of the documents that migrant slum dwellers got issued was PAN card that is meant for filing income tax returns and for other economic transaction. The migrants have little or nothing to do with such transactions; however, they find it easy to procure the PAN card which is subsequently used for getting other documents. Though the migrant masses are not using PAN card for income tax purposes, not having a PAN card would mean the danger of being bereft of one more sign of identity. Similar was the rationale for obtaining the Aadhaar card. The information and propaganda for Aadhaar card were almost always circulated by word of mouth and hence the veracity of the information and its exactness remained rather ambiguous. Most of the people shared 'Humein toh kisi bhi sarkari officer ne jaankaari nahi di thi. Aas paas ke logon ne bataya ki aisa koi card ban raha hai toh hum bhi chale gaye.' (There was no official announcement which was made. We heard it from people in the neighbourhood and went where they said.)

A few official posters were seen only in the Andheri area where we interviewed a few people. The centres for application were usually never at a walking distance from where these communities were located. In all the three cases, the applicants had to obtain their turn almost two days in advance. People would queue up from daybreak. Fights and arguments would also be a common occurrence. When the turn arrived, the taking of photographs, fingerprinting and the iris scan, took a total of 10 minutes. However, the counters in all the three locations would remain open only for three hours in the whole day (from 9am-12pm in Rafiq Nagar and 10am-1pm in Andheri and Govandi).

Doubts had been kindled about the confidentiality of the date and maturity of the personnel involved in the process. The contract for data collection has been given to private vendors and there is absolutely no transparency of these procedures. People's fear and anxiety have been articulated and analysed in several writings. 'Hundreds of private agents acting as enrollers, data-collectors, data-transporters will have a potential to make a quick buck by selling UID data to market players. These enrollers could intentionally disclose, transmit copy or disseminate private biometric data in electronic form very easily.'[43] The personnel collecting the data were college students, though even the respondents themselves were not very sure about their exact identities. The personnel would have no identification cards on them. Hence, a very large and crucial amount of data was being given to people who had no apparent authority or means of identification; nor were these people given any receipt for having their data collected. The only check which was done was the striking-off of their names from the master list which the personnel would have.

The procedure brought about the question of the ease of application. In the case of Rafiq Nagar, the procedures were rather lenient. There was hardly any emphasis on the display of identity before the information would be gathered. In Andheri, any one of the family would have to have a proof of identity. In Govandi it was the most stringent. According to one narrative, 'Humein to ration card, PAN card, voter identity card sab dikhana para tha. Wo log unko check karte, phir list mein likhte. Mere to ration card mein bhi tick maar diya. Yeh baat to galat thi. Aage jaake mujhe dikkat bhi ho sakti hai.' (We had to show a ration card, a voter card and a PAN card. They would then write down the proof displayed. In my case they even put a tick on my ration card, which is not correct. I might have to face problem in the future.) Equally haphazard had been the delivery of the Aadhaar cards. In Andheri, day after day, the cards were dumped under an electricity pole unattended. Many school children picked up these cards and distributed them. But obviously, a large number of cards were left in the rain and hence, there are members within the same family who have not received the cards still. 'Jab humne post waalon se pucha to unhone kahaan ki hum kuch nahi kar sakte. Humne to baant diya. Aisa nahi tha. Woh toh phek ke chale gayein the. Jo bachchon ne uthaya, who mila, warna toh bahut log abhi bhi wait kar rahe hain. Kuch toh naale mein chale gayen. Unka kya hoga?' (When we asked the postal authorities, they pleaded their helplessness. They said we have already distributed them. But that is not the case. They dumped the cards under the electricity pole. Most of these cards were picked up by school children who distributed it. But there are many more which have found their way into the drains and people have been waiting for these to come. What about such cards?)

THREAT OF SURVEILLANCE

Through the interview with people in different localities, it is obvious that they realise that they live in an age of digital information and surveillance. The obsession of the state for surveillance of population has always been projected as a concern for national security and the idea to create a network of data through the UID for intelligence purposes is stated quite clearly. The increased probing and surrendering of information to the state or the voluntary disclosure on social networking sites, all involve large amounts of personal data. Data can be used by an increasingly digitised state to track down individuals or generally to stay abreast of their location. Tracking cell phones, hacking email accounts or accessing social networking accounts are common but limited to populations who use these. In order to keep a track of the population at large, far more skill is required. While all state-based identity documents require some mandatory information, what made Aadhaar unique was the extraordinary amount of biometric information it necessitated.

Interestingly enough, while the government has gone all out to promote this scheme, it is woefully unprepared for the magnitude of such a task. In the case of Govandi, people were given copies of one form bearing the same number since the office was short of forms. So many more than one person filled up the form with the same number. Nonetheless, the cards were all approved. One wonders if the process of collecting data can be so casual and ad-hoc, how is it guaranteed that the data thus collected is secure and tamper-proof. The concern or the lack of it for confidentiality of data and privacy of information figured in almost all narratives. In Rafiq Nagar, which is an unauthorised settlement and where almost the entire population is engaged in rag-picking at the Deonar dumping ground, the question of privacy of data does not mean much. The expectation that yet another proof of identity can in some way help them to regularise their living area is paramount. While they are fully aware that this card guarantees nothing, the hope remains. If they say no to the Aadhaar, they fear they may lose out on a scheme or may be a better housing opportunity. 'Humein kuch kaam nahin iss card ka. Par kya pata kal humein yahaan se jaana parein to shayad kahin aur ye card kaam aa jaaye.' (We have no use of this card as of today. But if ever we are evicted from here, maybe this card will help us either here or wherever else we go.) The fact that this is yet another identification document is not lost on them. But the fear of being left out is paramount.

In contrast, the situation in Andheri, a western suburb of Mumbai, could not be more different. Realising fully well, members of the community have written to the ministry about their knowledge of the UIDAI and the implications thereof. 'Humein pata hai ki aisi cheezen South Africa mein bhi hai jahaan poonji patiyon ko poori jaankari rahti hai ki kaun kahaan hai aur kis ke pas kya hai. Woh log aur raajneta iss desh ko lootne pe lage hain aur woh ye jaan lena chahta hai ki aise kaun log hain jinse unka paala padna hai. Woh yeh bhi poori jaankari rakhna chahte hain ki kisko kahaan se hatana hain aur woh kya kar sakte hain. Warna itna bada programme koi ek poonji pati ko kyun deta.' (This scheme was first implemented in South Africa. We know that in our country the corporate sector and the politicians are aiming to collect all this data so that if ever we have to be displaced for corporate interest, they would know the nature of the community very well and also about who will react in what manner when they are displaced. It is no coincidence that this programme is being run by a person from the corporate world (reference to Nandan Nilekani[44]).) The sangathan member of Medha Patkar led Ghar Bachao Ghar Banao Andolan in Jai Ambe Nagar said they knew that it was a method to map and track marginalised migrants. 'Iss se unko saari jaankari mil jayegi. Phir woh jo gareeb hain, unko pareshan kar sakenge. Humein terrorist ya chor bata sakenge. Unhe pata chal jayega ki hamaare paas paise ya power nahi hai. Toh woh humein aaram se bhaga sakte hain. Iss scheme ka udeshay humein kuch dilana nahin hai. Balki iss scheme ka toh matlab hi hai ki humein har cheez se baahar rakhi jaayein aur agar hum awaaz uthaye to humein aasani se pakda jaayein. Warna ration card jis se khana milta hai, use milne me itni pareshaani hui, par Aadhaar mein to aisi koi samasya nahi huin.' (We are aware that we are giving them all our information on a platter. This means that they can easily implicate us as rogues or terrorists if they wish to. The scheme is not inclusive at all. It is quite the opposite. It gives all the information about our lack of power and education. This means we can be removed very easily if we dare protest against our displacement and against other atrocities. Otherwise, why is it that procuring the ration card, which ensures delivery of food, proved so difficult, yet procuring the Aadhaar card was a relatively easy affair?)

AADHAAR AND LOGIC OF ACCESS TO SERVICES

People in Jai Ambe Nagar and Andheri denied any chance of being granted any citizenship rights based on the Aadhaar card. Based on their long interaction with and experiences of the state, they were not hopeful that the card would serve any purpose. If anything, it would only show them as helplessly dependent on the state for everything, and hence as easy targets for eviction. (This was so in the case of Jai Ambe Nagar.) Residents in both these areas said welfare was only meant for those who had something. As a resident of Andheri said: 'At first, a centre for the Aadhaar card had been set up in Juhu, near the beach. It is a posh area and there were very few people queuing up. We opposed it because it was far too inconvenient and expensive to go there. And anyway the rich do not require Aadhaar. It is only for people like us who can be branded miscreants anytime and anywhere.'

The response in Jai Ambe Nagar was equally blunt. People, who have to fight a lonely and expensive battle to secure a living, have no hopes from the state. 'Ration toh dhang se dete nahin. Ghar banaate hain toh tod dete hain. Ek baar nahin, kayi baar. Toh aisi sarkar se ummeed kya ki ja sakti hai? Ab humein sarkaar se kuch nahi chahiye. Na kambal na koi bheekh. Humara haq hai ki jis shahar ko hum Shanghai bana rahe hai usme humein bhi rahne ki jagah milein. Humaare bachche bhi school jaayein. Ye sarkaar humein nahi de sakti. Humein iske liye ladna hoga.' (The government denies us our share of ration despite having ration cards. We build houses and the government demolishes them – not once, but repeatedly. As such, what can one hope from this government? We do not need anything from this government; we do not seek alms from it. It is our right that we get a place to live in the city we are transforming into Shanghai. It is our right that our children go to schools as well. This, the government will not provide us. We will have to fight for this.) The Hope in Rafiq Nagar remains though. As Shefali and other women told us, they hope that the colony will be regularised like the others in the neighbourhood. They hope this card goes on to prove that they have been living in the area long enough and therefore are entitled to their share of a settlement which is legal. When it becomes legal, they hope the area will look different from how it looks today.

People have made varied sense of the UID based on experiential knowledge and prior understanding of dealing with the state. Yet, despite having doubt about the motive behind the UID, most of the residents in slum localities have applied and obtained the Aadhaar card. The reasons for this could be many. People, who have always been deprived by the state, may question the motive of the state but it remains the only institution to struggle against and negotiate with, in the process of striving for a better tomorrow. It is this paradoxical situation that necessitates engaging with the state and justifies the craving to be recognised as part of the state. In addition, all the people we met are migrants to the city. Some of them have been migrants for almost all their lives long enough to be understood as 'Mumbaikars'. The need for a decent livelihood and a legitimate roof over their head is perhaps the most felt in this city by all its residents. The achievement of owning one's own house is almost integral to existence in Mumbai. One can then only empathise with how acute this need must be for those who have only known systematic exclusion for all their existence. Any hope that promises legal residence in the city and a life free from the fear of demolition is therefore pounced upon. This can be one of the prime reasons why a new announcement always rekindles a yearning for better life and entitlements, no matter how many proofs of identification one may already possess. While members of Ghar bachao ghar banao andolan take on the state directly on several matters, it would seem unlikely that they would have the agency to sabotage the identity initiative of the state at any point since their demands are made on the state. As the community activist in Andheri told us, 'We realise the agenda of the state and the nexus with the corporate lobbies, but we hope to put up a fight.' Occasionally, people do organise themselves in networks to protest or to manipulate identity proof as counterstrategy to the state's strategies; however, success of such endeavours vis-à-vis the UID is insignificant. Only in minor matters like electricity supply have people in Rafiq Nagar and Jai Ambe Nagar managed to achieve certain goals despite living in 'illegal' areas. There is also the wish not to leave the land which they realise is not theirs to keep. The Aadhaar adds to the long list of documents which makes people hopeful of the state taking notice of a population which otherwise remains, metaphorically speaking, invisible.

CONCLUSION

The migrant masses in the city of Mumbai are increasingly becoming insecure and vulnerable and therefore susceptible to all kinds of threats and insecurities. The apathy, intolerance and hostility of dominant political players vis-à-vis the migrants become obvious when they are referred to as 'infiltrators'[45], required to possess 'permit'[46], made responsible for 'rising crime'[47] and 'responsible for crime against women'.[48] The political class, which demonstrates such an attitude, is either the custodian of the centralised database or is waiting to become the custodian in due course of time. It is this mindset of intolerance that makes migrant masses susceptible to the risk of breach of privacy and related mapping to identify them for the purpose of targeting and exclusion. Irrespective of the differing ideologies within the political class, they all seem to be using similar governmental language that is founded on suspicion, distrust, prejudice and intolerance towards the migrant. The logic that the data would be used to facilitate welfare and development for the dispossessed and the deprived is hard to believe, going by the mindset of the governing class. Although recording and documentation for tracking and surveillance of subaltern masses is not new, technological developments and heightened obsession for security concerns are making surveillance ubiquitous. Taking a cue from Foucault's reference to panoptic power over prisoners, one realises that a governmentalised/centralised database has the tendency to put unwanted migrants under the 'perpetual eye' which would in turn put them through processes of discipline whereby they would lose the opportunity, capacity and right to dissent. Anxiety to bring migrants under control is premised on the belief that 'Individuals who remain beyond the embrace of the state necessarily represent a limit on its penetration.'[49] Perceived to be a threat to culture, order, social fabric, civility and security, the 'unwanted migrants' would be identified and excluded with the help of the biometric database. Further, in contrast to earlier strategies of settlement of population in a territory for enhancing discipline, the digital database is equipped to map movement and ensure discipline anywhere anytime. Biometrics, a technology of measuring the living body, makes the body function as evidence and therefore makes it identifiable and verifiable anywhere. Besides, the perceived risk to personal privacy and freedom that these systems pose can become real due to the plan to develop a centralised or interrelated database.[50] Also, implementation of the biometric card runs a huge risk of deliberate or accidental mistaken identity.[51] The biometric data contained on a smartcard and on the national database is only as reliable as the original scanning – whether manual or automated – and only as secure as the trustworthiness of the officials charged with this task.[52] The experiences of data collection as shared by migrants from different slum settlements – which narrate a tale of the involvement of private and inexpert vendors and ambiguity in issuing contract – clearly underscore the possibility of the data being exposed. How would subaltern migrants deal with the issue of theft of data or mistaken identity? The data that is transported in memory sticks runs the huge risk of being copied, tampered with and destroyed. 'And finally the floating liquid biometric data can potentially act as a huge asset for communal forces in India in planning, profiling, detailing and executing pogroms and genocides or minor communal conflicts for immediate electoral, political or economic gain.'[53] Against this backdrop of concerns about UID vis-à-vis privacy, confidentiality, risks of theft of data and selective profiling, the sense of indeterminacy, insecurity and contingency in the life of subaltern migrants get further accentuated. Authoritative truth is being manufactured through a digital process that is claimed to be 'scientific, neutral, perfect and unbiased'[54] and, therefore, it leaves little room to complain about exclusion and discrimination. At this point in time, when the UID project has just started unfolding, apprehensions based on literature and field study might appear speculative and hypothetical. However, the history of similar processes in other parts of the globe provides enough evidence for such apprehension and scepticism.

NOTES

1. Dossal, Mariam, *Theatre of Conflict, City of Hope: Mumbai 1660 to Present Times.* Oxford University Press: New Delhi, 2010, p.xxx
2. Ibid, p.xxxii
3. Ibid, p.9
4. Ibid
5. Patel, Sujata, "Bombay and Mumbai," in Sujata Patel and Kushal Deb eds., *Urban Studies*, Oxford University Press: New Delhi, 2009, p.250.
6. Dossal, *Theatre of Conflict*, p.64
7. Burra, Sundar, "Towards a pro-poor framework for slum upgrading in Mumbai, India," Environment and Urbanisation, 17:1, April, 2005, p.69; http://eau.sagepub.com/content/17/1/67.full.pdf+html [last accessed 15 November 2012]
8. Dossal, *Theatre of Conflict*, p.34.

9. Unique Identification Authority of India, Planning Commission, Government of India;
http://uidai.gov.in/aadhaar.html accessed on 18-08-12 [last accessed 15 November 2012]
10. Ramanathan, Usha, "A Unique Identity Bill", *Economic and Political Weekly*, 45: 30, 24 July 2010, p.10
11. Das, P. K., "Manifesto of a Housing Activist" in Sujata Patel and Alice Thorner eds., *Bombay: Metaphor for Modern India*, Oxford University Press: Delhi, 1996, p.180
12. Dirks, Nicholas B., Castes of Mind: Colonialism and the Making of Modern India, Permanent Black: Delhi, 2002, p.44
13. Breckenridge, Keith, "The Biometric State: The Promise and Peril of Digital Government in the New South Africa," *Journal of Southern African Studies*, 31:2. June, 2005, p.271
14. Das, Veena and Deborah Poole, "Introduction: State and Its Margins: Comparative Ethnographies" in Veena Das and Deborah Poole eds., *Anthropology in the Margins of the State*, Santa Fe, NM: School of American Research Press, 2004, p.15
15. Scott, James C., *Seeing Like a State: How Certain Schemes to Improve the Human Condition Have Failed*, Yale University Press: New Haven, CT, 1998, p.78
16. Cited in Das and Poole, *Anthropology in the Margins*, p.16
17. Zuboff, Shoshana, *In the Age of the Smart Machine: The Future of Work and Power*, Basic Books: New York, 1988
18. Ibid, p.332
19. Scott, *Seeing Like a State*, p.311
20. Ibid
21. Singha, Radhika, "Settle, Mobilize, Verify: Identification Practices in Colonial India," *Studies in History*, 16:2, 2000.
22. Browne, Simone, "Digital Epidermalization: Race, Identity and Biometrics," *Critical Sociology*, 36:1, 2010, p.139
23. NCEUS (National Commission for Enterprise in the Unorganized Sector), "Report of the Condition of Work and Promotion of Livelihood in the Unorganized Sector" New Delhi, August 2007; http://www.prsindia.org/uploads/media/Unorganised%20Sector/bill150_20071123150_Condition_of_workers_sep_2007.pdf [last accessed 15 November 2012]
24. Monteiro, V., "Another India is Possible: Basic Needs, the Unorganized Sector and Science in India" in M. Malhotra ed., *India: The Next Decade*, Academic Publishers: New Delhi, 2006
25. Chawls are multi-storied one-room tenements created initially as residences of the working-class population in the city of Mumbai.
26. Jha, Manish K., P. K. Shajahan and Mouleshri Vyas, *Biopolitics and Urban Governmentality in the City of Mumbai*, in press

27. Rose, Nikolas, "Governing 'Advanced' Liberal Democracies" in Aradhana Sharma and Akhil Gupta eds., *The Anthropology of the State: A Reader*, Wiley-Blackwell: Malden, 2005, p.147
28. Burra, "Towards a pro-poor framework," p.69
29. Arputham, Jockin, "How community-based enumerations started and developed in India," *Environment & Urbanization*, 24: 1, April 2012, pp.27-28
30. Risbud, Neelima, "Urban Slum Reports: The Case of Mumbai, India," *Understanding Slums: Case Studies for the Global Report on Human Settlements*, UN-Habitat, 2003, p.6; http://www.ucl.ac.uk/dpu-projects/Global_Report/pdfs/Mumbai.pdf [last accessed 15 November 2012]
31. Kumar, Anu, "Mumbai's Expendable Poor," *Economic and Political Weekly*, 40: 6, 5-11 February 2005, p.506
32. Panwalkar, Pratima, "Upgradation of Slums: A World Bank Programme" in Sujata Patel and Alice Thorner eds., *Bombay: Metaphor for Modern India*, Oxford University Press: Delhi, 1996, p.122
33. Arputham, "How community-based enumerations started"
34. Kumar, "Mumbai's Expendable Poor" p.508
35. Neuwirth, Robert, *Shadow Cities: A Billion Squatters, A New Urban World*, Routledge: New York, 2005, p.115
36. Mumbai Metropolitan Region Development Authority (MMRDA) is an apex body for planning and coordination of development activities in the Mumbai region.
37. Robins, Steven, "At the Limits of Spatial Governmentality: A Message from the Tip of Africa," *Third World Quarterly*, 23:4, 2002, p.680
38. Harris, Jan Ll., and Paul A. Taylor, *Digital Matters: Theory and Culture of the Matrix*, Routledge: London and New York, 2005, pp.x-xi
39. Rajagopal, Arvind, "Notes on Postcolonial Visual Culture," *BioScope: South Asian Screen Studies*, 2:1, January 2011, p.15
40. Mumbai is divided into six zones, each consisting of three to five wards. These wards are named alphabetically.
41. The Pardhi community is one of the de-notified tribes, mostly residing in Maharashtra. Commonly perceived as thieves since colonial times, most members fled to Mumbai from their villages in Marathwada in the 1960s. They often face harassment from different government agencies.
42. The Ghar Bachao Ghar Banao Andolan is a part of the National Alliance for People's Movement. It works on housing-rights issue in the slum areas and fights against demolition and eviction
43. Mehmood, Taha, "UID/Aadhar: A Threat to Indian Democracy," Countercurrents.org, April 2012. http://www.countercurrents.org/mehmood010412.htm [last accessed 15 November 2012]
44. Nandan Nilekani is currently serving as the chairman of the Unique Identification Authority of India (UIDAI). He is also now heading the

Government of India's technology committee, TAGUP or Technology Advisory Group for Unique Projects.

45. Following protests from the Bihar government after an alleged Azad Maidan rioter was picked up from that state, Maharashtra Navnirman Sena chief Raj Thackeray has threatened to brand every migrant from Bihar an 'infiltrator'. "Raj threatens to dub Bihari migrants 'infiltrators'," *The Hindu*, 31 August 2012; http://www.thehindu.com/news/national/article3845043.ece [last accessed 15 November 2012]
46. "Uddhav [Thackeray] wants permit system for Biharis in Mumbai," *Hindustan Times*, 4 September 2012; http://www.hindustantimes.com/India-news/Mumbai/Uddhav-wants-permit-system-for-Biharis-in-Mumbai/Article1-924181.aspx [last accessed 15 November 2012]
47. P. Chidambaram, the then Home Minister, blamed migrants for rising crimes in Delhi. "P Chidambaram blames migrants for crimes in Delhi, triggers reaction," *DNA*, 13 December 2010, http://www.dnaindia.com/india/report_p-chidambaram-blames-migrants-for-crimes-in-delhi-triggers-reaction_1480629 [last accessed 15 November 2012]
48. Delhi Chief Minister Sheila Dikshit blamed migrants for increasing crime against women in Delhi. "Sheila Dikshit blames migrants, porous border for Delhi rapes," *India Today*, 12 April 2012. http://indiatoday.intoday.in/story/sheila-dikshit-rising-rape-in-delhi-migratory-population/1/184091.html [last accessed 15 November 2012]
49. Torpey, John, "Coming and Going: On the state monopolisation of the legitimate 'means of movement'," *Sociological Theory*, 16:3, 1998, p.244
50. Nisbet, Nancy, "Resisting Surveillance: Identity and Implantable Microchip," *Leonardo*, 37: 3, 204, pp.210-14. http://www.jstor.org/stable/1577723?origin=JSTOR-pdf [last accessed 15 November 2012]
51. The False Rejection Rate of NIST (National Institute of Standards and Technology, US) database was at 4 percent. The False Rejection Rate is a probability that a system will reject a fingerprint pattern as false even though it is true. The database, which NIST used to study, was derived from three sources, i.e. the US department of state (DoS) Mexican Border Crossing data and US-VISIT data from Ohio and Atlanta. The total data size of these tests was around 6 million. The population of India is 1.2 billion or 200 times the size of the sample data. The NIST report clearly states, 'The false accept rate (FAR) using index finger pairs is linearly increasing with database size.' C.L. Wilson, M.D. Garris and C.I. Watson, "Matching Performance for the US-VISIT IDENT System Using Flat Fingerprints," NISTIR 7110, May 2004, p.2; ftp://sequoyah.nist.gov/pub/nist_internal_reports/ir_7110.pdf [last accessed 15 November 2012]; The argument made here is taken from Mehmood, "UID/Aadhar"
52. Breckenridge, "The Biometric State" p.280

53. Mehmood, "UID/Aadhar"
54. There is the notion that these technologies are infallible and that they are objective technologies of mathematical precision, without error or bias on the part of the computer programmers who calibrate the search parameters of these machines or on the part of those who read these templates to make decisions, such as the decision in 2004 in which US citizen Brandon Mayfield was wrongfully determined to be involved in the Madrid train bombings based on a latent fingerprint. See Simon A. Cole, "Brandon Mayfield, Suspect" in John Knechtel ed., *Suspect* (*Alphabet City* Number 10), MIT Press: Cambridge, MA, 2005, pp.170–85

IX

Digitisation of Identity of Migrant Workers and Financial Inclusion

Byasdeb Dasgupta

This essay deals with the financial inclusion of migrant workers in the context of the digitisation of their identity through the Unique Identification Authority of India (UIDAI) project of the Government of India. As noted in the Economic Survey (2011-12), 'The UIDAI is on the verge of commencing Phase III of the scheme, which apart from enrolling residents and issuing Aadhaar numbers extends to providing updation services, a robust authentication process as a means of enhancing service delivery of various social schemes, and facilitating financial inclusion and development of Aadhaar-enabled applications to leverage Aadhaar.'[1] About 13 crore Aadhaar-s (or UID numbers) have already been generated. In fact, the UIDAI has started interactions with Ministries/ Departments for developing applications leveraging the Aadhaar number, Aadhaar-enabled transactions and infrastructure to improve the service delivery of various social-sector schemes.[2] The following steps or actions have already taken in this regard by the UIDAI:

a. The Ministry of Communications and Information has notified that Aadhaar shall be treated as a valid proof of identity (PoI) and proof of address (PoA) after confirming identity and address through Aadhaar authentication procedure.

b. The Department of Health and Family Welfare has decided to recognise UID numbers (Aadhaar) as PoI and PoA for extending financial assistance to BPL patients who are suffering from major life-threatening diseases and receiving medical treatment at any of the super-speciality hospitals/institutes or other government hospitals under the Rashtriya Arogya Nidhi (RAN).
c. The Ministry of Road Transport and Highways has issued necessary instructions for recognition of Aadhaar as PoI/PoA for evidence of age and address for issuing a driving licence and for registration of vehicles.
d. The Department of Expenditure has issued instructions for the revision of the format for submission of proposals for approval of the Expenditure Finance Committee wherein the linkage of the beneficiary identification mechanism with the Aadhaar number is to be indicated.
e. The Aadhaar number has been recognised as valid PoI/PoA for obtaining new LPG connections.
f. An Aadhaar Payments Bridge has been designed and is being tested on pilot basis for Mahatma Gandhi National Rural Employment Guarantee Scheme (MGNREGS) payments in Jharkhand. This payment bridge will enable the transfer of funds directly into the bank accounts of beneficiaries on the basis of Aadhaar number. It is claimed that this will considerably simplify the process of disbursement of welfare funds by government departments.

At the various state-governments level also there is an ongoing process of linking the welfare schemes at the state levels with the Aadhaar number:

a. The state governments of Sikkim, Tripura and Andhra Pradesh have declared the Aadhaar number valid PoI and PoA for their various schemes.
b. Karnataka has drawn up a plan for the implementation of the Aadhaar project and also for the Karnataka Resident Data Hub for integration of the Aadhaar number with various services.

Aadhaar, in a sense, is an additional number which is being generated as proof of identity (PoI) and proof of address (PoA). If we start with the PoI, the list includes the following: Ration Cards, Electoral Photo Identity Card (EPIC) or Voter Card, Permanent Account Number (PAN) Card, Passport, and Driving Licence. Similarly, the list of the proof of address (PoA) includes the following: Ration Card, EPIC or Voter Card, Passport, Electricity Bill, and Telephone Bill.

Apart from these, as one's proof of age, birth registration certificate issued by the concerned municipality/municipal corporation/panchayat and/or School Leaving Certificate is accepted. Is Aadhaar just an addition to these identity/address proofs? The answer is yes and no at the same time. Yes, because when there exists a plethora of recognised identity/address proofs Aadhaar as PoI and PoA will merely supplement them. It is in no way going to add extra information as PoI and PoA. The question then remains, when Aadhaar comes into operation in full swing will these other proofs of identity and address become null and void? Again, Aadhaar may not be looked upon as just another addition to the list of PoIs and PoAs mentioned above. If one has any one of the PoIs and/or PoAs it implies that he/she is a citizen of India. Prior to the Aadhaar project there has been no attempt by the Government of India to demarcate the line between a citizen and non-citizen through some authentication process. Note that having any of the above PoIs and/or PoAs implicitly or indirectly signifies one's citizenship. Our Population Census or for that matter any Census or Estimate (e.g. BPL Census, Poverty Estimate) is a process of estimating the number of people or stakeholders in the country but not a process of identification. Aadhaar in that sense is a direct process of identifying a citizen and therein lies its difference with the other PoIs and PoAs. This identification is on two counts – one, which is related to the personal information of the citizen, such as name, address, date of birth etc. and the other, which is related to the physical (body-related) identification of the individual in terms of certain biometric information (like the individual's finger prints, iris scan, etc).

The question is why now this direct identification of Indian citizenship is called for? The answer to this question rests with the nature of the state and mechanism of governance that the present age is witnessing.

The contemporary Indian state can best be described as the neoliberal state where neoliberalism stands for market-centricism as envisaged in terms of (a) free market-orientated state policies, (b) deregulation (which implies replacing older interventionist type of controls and regulations by newer market-friendly and market-sensitive regulations), (c) target-oriented approach (which implies replacing universalisation as an objective of social welfare by target-driven policies where targets are quantifiable and monitorable), (d) shrinking of the size of the government (evidenced in terms of lowering government expenditure especially through contraction in social sector related expenses and subsidies, and (e) withdrawal of the government from direct economic activities of production, paving the way for the private sector (as is evident from the disinvestments of public-sector enterprises).

The neoliberal agenda of the state envisages an individual not in the specifics of human beings in community or groups or organisation. In fact, it attempts to destroy the group-identity of the individual. For instance, through the labour market flexibility it tries to stall the collective bargaining process through labour organisations/trade unions and thereby, tries to abolish the voice representation of labour. It does not recognise an individual within his/her community. For example, tribal community and its customs and cultures and politics are not acceptable to neoliberal state as it wants to mainstream each and every community which is still outside the jurisdiction of the market and/or non-monetised economy. Neoliberalism cannot actually afford to recognise the existence of anything non-market and non-monetised. Hence, one of the major agenda of the neoliberal mission is to bring these groups and communities in the fold of market and monetise them, which is popularly known as mainstreaming, where the mainstream society includes those who are within the jurisdiction of market and that too, money-using market. In the neoliberal project an individual cannot remain community-bounded and group-bounded for four interrelated reasons which are discussed below.

First, neoliberalism only recognises market-based transactions. It does not recognise any community-based exchange or transaction as that violates its basic norm which is defined specifically in terms of the logic of the market viz. buying and selling of commodities and making profit. The latter is negated by any community-based transactions where community customs, conventions and norms prevail, not the norms of market.

Second, neoliberalism, being a market-centric economic mission of global capitalism, wants sustained and continuous expansion of market. It is also a continuous and never-ending process of accumulation by dispossession as is evident from the ongoing displacement and dislocation of people from their land for the sake of industrialisation. This is perhaps comparable to the process of primitive accumulation of capital as observed and analysed by Marx in the context of Industrial Revolution in Great Britain in the eighteenth and nineteenth century. But neoliberal primitive accumulation is somewhat distinct from what Marx described it as. Primitive accumulation of capital which is accumulation by dispossession à la Marx was characterised by proletarianisation of displaced and dislocated people. However, in the neoliberal era such is not the case most of the time. People who are displaced and dislocated either from the land used by them for their subsistence, or from the land where they used to reside, or both, join the ranks of the migrant/transit workforce mostly. Through dispossession, these people most of the time are routed out of their community and society. Now, neoliberalism desires continuous expansion of market and that is possible by bringing more and more people into the fold of the market. So, an individual is valuable to neoliberalism when he/she joins the market; otherwise not.

Third, neoliberalism posits an individual as a self-accomplished, self-motivated and capable person – as human resource – who can generate for himself/herself income from the market. To generate income he/she has to participate in the market. This is not possible on one's own when one is located within a community. Note that neoliberalism treats an individual as human resource and resource is something which is capable of producing return to the resource-holder. This return is generated only through market mechanism. Like any resource in the market space human resource too has its (exchange) value and therefore, it is like any other commodity in the market. So, neoliberalism does not recognise an individual in community as then his/her human resource-focused identity is lost and this neoliberalism finds hard to accommodate.

Fourth, neoliberalism works by destroying group-identity of individuals as certain groups (like trade unions) pose security threat to it. Such threat is minimal when an individual is an individual, concerned only with his/her well-being, when he/she is depoliticised, when he/she is just an optimising agent forgetful of his/her community or group-based locations. In fact, neoliberalism always wants to make sure that no security threat to its very existence is posed. It perceives existence of different groups as its threat since groups mean collectivity, sharing and above all conscious voice representation. Sharing and collectivism goes against the capitalist appropriation of surplus labour and hence, they are to be rejected. Now, when an individual is placed in the market he/she will remain concerned with, focused on his/her capability of generating income and taking part in market-based exchanges and nothing else. And, thereby, the security threat to neoliberalism is reduced as the individual, once he or she becomes human resource, remains preoccupied with himself/herself as a self-propelling economic agent leaving not much scope for any collectivism. In fact, neoliberalism tries to glorify every individual as an entrepreneur, an individual as self-enterprising one. This is evident in the much-hyped focus of the Indian state on self-employment. A person who is self-employed implies he/she is self-enterprising. A self-enterprising individual works for himself/herself in the market and for the market which strengthens market-centricism of the neoliberal state.

Given these four inter-related reasons neoliberalism finds community, groups and organisations of people to be anathema to its own project. It works through fragmenting people in new groups wherein individuals cannot shape any collective vision. For instance, transit and migrant labour groups actually remain isolated from each other and hence, cannot form a collective to produce resistance to the neoliberal agenda.

Does neoliberalism reject all groups? The answer is no. In fact, it goes on producing new groups (not community) which cater to the needs of the market. For example, the notion of self-help group is a neoliberal product which is intimately linked to the market. Note that a member of a self-help group is considered to be a self-enterprising individual. The collectivism of self-help groups does not pose any security threat to neoliberalism as it is meant for the market and guided by the logic of the market.

With the dismantling of the welfare state, does the neoliberal state negate welfare? The answer again is no. It rather produces a new concept of welfare in terms of its inclusive growth agenda. Inclusive growth is targeted for those who do not have the capability to participate in the market. So, the objective of inclusive growth is to include the left-out population in the purview of the market so that they are also automatically benefitted by the economic growth process. It is not to provide special welfare-based assistance to them to redress their economically and socially poor condition. Rather, it is to supplement their efforts so that they can participate in the market. Inclusive growth is target-oriented. First of all it divides the population between poor and non-poor in terms of certain fixed poverty lines and targets the below-poverty-line population. It opposes any universal welfare scheme as it presupposes that those who are not below the poverty line are market participants. So, we have instead of universal public distribution system (PDS) targeted public distribution system (TPDS). But what is noteworthy regarding this target-oriented inclusive growth agenda of the neoliberal state are the following.

The welfare measures most of the time aim at direct cash assistance to the beneficiaries. Cash assistance will help beneficiaries to purchase the product – be it any commodity (like food), education, and healthcare from the market. Hence, on the one hand, it relies more and more cash transfer to the beneficiaries and, on the other hand, it reduces the direct provision of goods and services by the state to the targeted population.

Given the above, inclusive growth project needs identification of beneficiaries. And this is made possible with information technology. It is not sufficient to merely estimate the number of beneficiaries; for direct online cash transfer to succeed, it is also important to identify beneficiaries as such. And in India, as we have mentioned above, estimation of target population does not necessarily produce their identity. So, a separate identification process is called for.

Furthermore, what we observe is that neoliberalism does not recognise any democratic rights, like community rights, over a common pool of resources; rather it only recognises civil rights – rights of citizens.

So, in the neoliberal agenda, subject cannot be community; subject is always an individual as citizen. The neoliberal state targets individual citizens for their welfare. This necessitates the identification of citizens, separating them out from those who are not citizens.

Financial inclusion is a programme of inclusive growth of the Indian state under neoliberalism. Hence, it is very much a neoliberal project which targets unbanked population. In India, so far the meaning of financial inclusion has been to convert those who are unbanked into banked ones. It is based on the presupposition that one of the reasons of marginalisation of some sections of the population is due to their incapacity to be within the purview of organised finance and in that respect they should have bank accounts first. Their condition cannot be improved if they continue to be in the grip of unorganised finance. Secondly, having bank accounts would also serve the purpose of the neoliberal welfare stance of direct cash transfer to the bank accounts of the beneficiaries. But opening bank accounts warrant that these groups of people must conform to the identity norms for opening such accounts. And if they do not have it, accounts cannot be opened. Hereby the need for proper and authentic identification procedure arises. Hence, the idea of Aadhaar seems to serve that purpose as it is claimed by the UIDAI that Aadhaar number can be used to open bank accounts.[3]

But what happens to those marginalised and vulnerable sections of the population, who are footloose labour and whose number is swelling from the very beginning of the adoption of economic liberalisation and globalisation programme by the Indian state? How can they be financially included and be targeted for any welfare scheme? Is it possible to target them? Will digitisation of identity facilitate the process of financial inclusion for them? And what is the probable implication of digitisation of identity for the footloose migrant and transit labour? Questions like these continue to crop up in the context of financial inclusion – especially for the migrant workers – vis-à-vis the Aadhaar programme.

In this essay, we have three inter-related issues to deal with, viz. financial inclusion, migrant workers and digitalisation of identity. Financial inclusion which is also termed as inclusive financing refers to the delivery of financial services at affordable costs to the disadvantaged and vulnerable sections of the population, who mainly belong to the low-income category. Financial services like banking services are like public goods, which are characterised by non-exclusion and non-rivalry. This means financial services provided to one cannot eliminate another and hence, these two beneficiaries are not rivals to each other. It is held that in modern money-using society every individual irrespective of his/her income or wealth, class or caste, nature of occupation, etc should have unrestrained access to the financial services. This implies unrestrained access to organised finance and less and less access to unorganised finance. This is because, it is argued, unorganised finance is usurious, more costly and above all extremely exploitative, whereas organised finance, that is banking services, is less costly, and not exploitative. Therefore, unrestrained access to the financial services is regarded as one of the parameters of betterment of one's economic life in a modern-money using society where finance, and hence financial system, plays a very pivotal role in intermediating financial resources between the finance-deficit units and finance-surplus units.

In India, the government's policy of financial inclusion basically implies the availability of banking and payment services to the entire population without discrimination. This, in other words, means provision of access to banks to those marginalised and vulnerable sections of the population who do not have any bank accounts. The term financial inclusion has gained importance since the early 2000s. Financial exclusion signifies exclusion from the organised financial services. It is held now by the international agencies like the World Bank that financial exclusion is directly correlated to poverty. That means financial exclusion and poverty go hand in hand. If people are poor then they will be financially excluded. Or, if they are financially excluded then they will be poor. This means both financial exclusion and poverty are the cause and effect of each other.

Given the basic drift of financial inclusion in India, the financially excluded population is that segment of the population which is unbanked. Who are they? These are the people engaged in farming activities as landless workers, marginal and small farmers, rural non-farm workers, urban poor and the migrant and transit labour all over the country. The avowed objective of financial inclusion in India is to provide banking services to the hitherto unbanked population at no costs, which is technically known in the parlance of the Reserve Bank of India as opening 'no frills' accounts. Now, a vast section of this unbanked population is migrant population. Migrant population may either be high-income earning class or be low-income earning class. It is expected that high-income earning migrant population is already banked. Hence, the migrant population in the context of financial inclusion project of the Government of India includes mainly those migrants who are low-income earning, who do not have much assets (physical or financial), and also, who suffer from great uncertainty in terms of job retention and earn a bare-minimum income. Moreover, this category of workers frequently change the places of their occupation. There are two questions with respect to the financial inclusion of the migrant workers. First, does financial inclusion ultimately help the migrant workers achieve a better quality of living? Secondly, how this financial inclusion is to be achieved for the migrant workers? In this paper we will not dedicate much space in seeking answer to the first question. Rather, we will focus our attention on the second question. This is particularly relevant in the context of the expected linkage between financial inclusion and the UIDAI's Aadhaar project, both of which are essentially neoliberal projects aimed at mainstreaming the poor and disadvantaged sections of the population in the domain of market mechanism. We will be concerned with the low-income-earning migrant workers mainly. However, we will touch upon the issues pertaining to the non-migrant poor workers and other vulnerable sections of the population too.

The paper is organised as follows. The first section deals with the issues related to financial inclusion in India, while the second section takes up the problems of financial inclusion of the migrant workers. How digitisation of identity of migrant workers will affect the financial inclusion programme of the Government of India is discussed in the following section. Finally the concluding section sums up the major arguments of the paper.

FINANCIAL INCLUSION IN INDIA

Early attempts at financial inclusion can be traced to those of the Reserve Bank of India (RBI) when it set up the Khan Commission in

2004 to look into it and the recommendations of the commission were incorporated into the mid-term review of the Bank's policy (2005–06). In the report, RBI exhorted the banks with a view of achieving greater financial inclusion to make available a basic 'no-frills' banking account. In India, financial inclusion first featured in 2005, when it was introduced by K.C. Chakraborty, the chairman of the Indian Bank. Mangalam Village became the first village in India where all households were provided banking facilities. Norms were relaxed for people intending to open accounts with annual deposits of less than Rs.50,000. General credit cards (GCCs) were issued to the poor and the disadvantaged with a view to help them access easy credit. In January 2006, the RBI permitted commercial banks to make use of the services of non-governmental organisations/self-help groups (NGOs/SHGs), micro-finance institutions, and other civil society organisations as intermediaries for providing financial and banking services. These intermediaries could be used as business facilitators or business correspondents by commercial banks. The RBI asked the commercial banks in different regions to start a 100 per cent financial inclusion campaign on a pilot basis. As a result of the campaign states or Union Territories like Pondicherry, Himachal Pradesh and Kerala announced 100 per cent financial inclusion in all their districts. The RBI's vision for 2020 is to open nearly 600 million new customers' accounts and service them through a variety of channels by leveraging on IT. However, illiteracy and the low income savings and lack of bank branches in rural areas continue to be a roadblock to financial inclusion in many states and there is inadequate legal and financial structure.

With a view to enhancing financial inclusion and understanding its contemporary significance and relevance to the economy, Government of India set up the Rangarajan Committee on Financial Inclusion. The Committee submitted its final report to the Union Finance Minister on 4 January 2008. The Committee defines financial inclusion as the 'process of ensuring access to financial services and timely and adequate credit where needed by vulnerable groups such as weaker sections and low income groups at an affordable cost.'[4]

The scope of financial inclusion can be expanded in two ways. It can be expanded through state-driven intervention by way of statutory enactments (for instance the US example, the Community Reinvestment Act and making it a statutory right to have bank account in France) and also through voluntary effort by the banking community itself for evolving various strategies to bring within the ambit of the banking sector a large strata of the society. In India, the second route has been adopted by the state to achieve financial inclusion of the vulnerable section of the society. The RBI has asked the commercial banks to focus upon opening no-frills accounts for the lower strata of the population.

The Rangarajan Committee felt that the task of financial inclusion must be taken up in a mission mode at the national level. The mission should be responsible for suggesting the overall policy changes required for achieving financial inclusion and for supporting a range of stakeholders. It made the following suggestions:

a. Launching of a National Rural Financial Inclusion Plan (NRFIP) in mission mode with a clear target to provide access to comprehensive financial services, including credit, to at least 50 per cent of the financially excluded rural households by 2012 through rural/semi-urban branches of commercial banks and RRBs. The remaining households have to be covered by 2015. For the purpose, a National Mission on Financial Inclusion is proposed to be constituted comprising representatives from all stakeholders to aim at achieving universal financial inclusion within a specific time frame.
b. Constitution of two funds with NABARD – the Financial Inclusion Promotion & Development Fund (FIPF) and the Financial Inclusion Technology Fund (FITF) with an initial corpus of Rs.50 billion each to be contributed by the government/RBI/ NABARD. The FIPF will focus on interventions like Farmer's Service Centres, Promoting Rural Entrepreneurship, Self-Help Groups and their Federations, Developing Human Resources of Banks, Promotion of Resource Centres and Capacity Building of Business Facilitators and Correspondents. Similarly, the FITF will focus on funding of low-cost technology solutions.
c. Deepening outreach of microfinance programme through financing of SHGs and Joint Liability Groups (JLGs) and setting

up of a risk mitigation mechanism for lending to small marginal farmers/ share croppers/ tenant farmers through JLGs.

d. Use of Poorest Areas Civil Societies (PACSes) as Business Facilitators and Correspondents
e. Micro-Finance-Non-Banking Finance Companies (MF-NBFCs) could be permitted to provide thrift credit, micro-insurance, remittances and other services up to a specified amount to the poor in rural, semi-urban and urban areas. Such MF-NBFCs may be recognised as Business Correspondents for providing savings and remittance services and also acting as micro-insurance agents.
f. Targets for rural/ semi-urban branches
g. Targeted Branch Expansion in identified districts
h. Business Facilitators and Business Correspondents (BF/BC)

Note that financial inclusion does not mean only bringing the unbanked population of the society into the ambit of banking services and payments. It should include, along with the provision of banking services and payments at no cost to the vulnerable groups, other financial services as well like easy access to formal and cheap credit, insurance and other services like investment opportunities for the lower strata of the population.[5] However, financial inclusion as it has evolved in India so far is focused mainly on the provision of banking and payments services to the poor and vulnerable sections of the population who are still unbanked.

It is not that financial inclusion as a strategy was not there prior to 2005. It was implicitly present in the state policy. For example, during 1960-1990 (especially after the nationalisation of some scheduled commercial banks in 1969), the focus was on channelling of credit to the neglected sectors of the economy. Special emphasis was also laid on weaker sections of the society. During 1990-2005, at a time when financial sector reform was initiated, implicit financial inclusion was encouraged mainly by the introduction of SHG-bank linkage programme in the early 1990s and Kisan Credit Cards for providing credit to farmers. The SHG-bank linkage programme was launched by the NABARD in 1992, with policy support from the RBI, to facilitate collective decision making by the poor and provide 'door step' banking. However, it was only in 2005 that financial inclusion was explicitly made a state-policy objective and thrust was on providing safe facility of savings deposits through 'no frills' accounts. However, the difference between the explicit and implicit financial inclusion as strategies is that during the implicit-phase financial inclusion took care of targeted lending so as to reduce the menace of informal lending (particularly by the money-lenders) to the vulnerable groups. With the inception of economic liberalisation as banking sector reforms got momentum, and as the public sector banks were told to be more profit-oriented than social-objective-oriented, priority-sector lending lost its importance. Lending to the vulnerable sections of the population got reoriented and restructured through the micro-finance-based programme. However, despite all these efforts since the 1960s, a large section of the population remained excluded from the ambit of banking services and easy access to cheap formal credit. So, reliance on informal-sector credit continued unabated. Hence, as part of state policy of inclusive growth and development during the Eleventh Plan, when the Indian state itself recognised the huge presence of socially and economically excluded population from the benefits of economic growth and development, financial inclusion was made an explicit state policy. In fact, the social and economic exclusion of the lower strata of the population is multi-dimensional and financial exclusion is identified as one among them. But as we have already stated, in India the focus of financial inclusion as avowed state policy since 2005 is confined to ensuring a bare-minimum access to a savings bank account without frills to all, especially to the vulnerable sections of the population. Vulnerability may be defined in terms of one's low income or earning capacity (economically poor), one's involvement in low-paid informal jobs/ occupations, or in terms of uncertainty regarding one's earning opportunities, continuing with the same job/occupation which may force one to move frequently from one geographical area to another in search of job. In fact, one can ascribe vulnerability of the lower strata of the population to various other parameters, some of which are economic, some political and some cultural. For example, people may remain vulnerable due to their caste positions in the society, or one may be vulnerable to the emerging market system as it has evolved over the years since the inception of economic reforms in this country.

According to the RBI, around 400 million people have bank accounts in India which is less than 40 per cent of the country's population. In 1993, only 51 per 100 had bank accounts. The number has marginally increased to 54 in 2007, which means over a period of 14 years average increase in the number of banked population is only three. That is to say during 1993-2007 less than one per cent increase in banked population has taken place. Out of every 100 adult population only 59 has bank accounts and there is a large gap between the rural and urban coverage of banking services. In rural India, the coverage among the adult population is 39 per cent as against 60 per cent in urban India. This, of course, does not necessarily mean that 60 out of every Indian adult in cities have bank accounts, as many people operate multiple accounts. The picture of other financial services is quite dismal. Only four per cent of the population which is around 45 million invest in mutual funds, and only 15 million Indians hold demat (electronic share) accounts that one needs to buy stocks. Nearly 80 per cent of the Indian population is without life, health and non-life insurance coverage. While life insurance penetration is a mere four per cent, non-life cover is even lower at 0.6 per cent. The per capita spending on life and non-life insurance is just about Rs.2,000 and Rs.300 respectively against the global average of around Rs.18,000 and Rs.13,000. Only 5.2 per cent of India's 650,000 villages have bank branches even though 39.7 per cent of the overall branch network of Indian banks, or 31,727, are in rural India. The population covered by each branch has come down from 63,000 in 1969 to 16,000 in 2007 and the total number of check-in accounts held at commercial banks, regional rural banks, primary agricultural credit societies, urban cooperatives banks and post offices during this period has increased from 454.6 million to 610.2 million. Still, very few people in the low-income bracket have access to formal banking channels. Only 34 per cent of people with annual earnings of less than Rs.50,000 in urban India had a bank account in 2007. The comparative figure in rural India is even lower – 26.8 per cent.

Depending on the nature and extent of services denied, it is held that financial exclusion may lead to the following social and economic pitfalls: (a) increased travel requirements, (b) higher incidence of crime, (c) general decline in investment, (d) difficulties in gaining access to credit or getting credit from informal sources at exorbitant rates, (e) increased unemployment, (f) loss of access by the small business to middle income and higher income customers, (g) higher cash handling costs, (h) delays in remittances of money, and (i) other social exclusion.

The financial inclusion process which has started since 2005 is based on the voluntary action of the public sector commercial banks only at the insistence of the RBI and the Government of India. These banks have been asked to go for financial inclusion in the following ways: (a) by offering no-frills savings bank accounts to the disadvantaged sections of the population who are still unbanked; and, (b) by opening new bank branches in areas hitherto uncovered by banking services. So, the success of the current financial inclusion project depends heavily on the willingness of the public-sector banks to open new branches in commercially unviable areas and also, on their willingness to offer no-frills savings bank accounts to the vulnerable groups. This remains a difficult proposition for the banks in the context of the present financial reform scene which asks the banks to be more profit-oriented than social-objective-oriented even though it is claimed by the proponents of financial inclusion that it is a win-win strategy for both the banks and the vulnerable sections of the population.

The current financial inclusion programme of the Indian state is necessarily part of its neoliberal inclusive growth agenda. Among many types of inclusion, the state has perceived financial inclusion as one. Note that being inclusive means one is included in the market mechanism, in the ambit of the market, since neoliberalism is essentially a process that seeks to relate every subject and object to the market. So, any type of social exclusion in this context basically signifies exclusion from the reach of the market. The question is how financial inclusion can be regarded as an attempt to link the vulnerable and the marginalised to the market? Markets are of different types – commodity markets, factor markets, financial markets etc. Financial inclusion is related to the financial market – the organised financial market. The presupposition is that one's exclusion from the organised financial market, if it is not voluntary, signifies that one is vulnerable. So, the vulnerable and marginalised people are unbanked. Being unbanked, they are deprived of various financial products, especially credit from the formal financial sector. So, if the state facilitates their link with the banks, their condition will improve. There will be net welfare gain for them. The logic runs like this: the vulnerable and the marginalised are so because they do not have access to the formal financial sector.

Neoliberal economic programme is essentially a process of capital accumulation by dispossession. And dispossession leads to greater vulnerability and marginalisation. It is a never-ending process as is evident from the land grabbing projects in the name of industrialisation and urbanisation. It is true that one of the basic needs of the poor people – particularly those who belong to the farming community of this country – is credit. Credit is a necessary input in agriculture and many non-farm activities in the rural India. However, a vast segment of the rural population is deprived of formal-sector credit as they barely satisfy the necessary conditions or standard norms for availing such credit. In most of the cases, the vulnerable and marginalised population is that population which do not possess any asset. Neoliberal economic development has further accentuated their asset-less position. So, they are left with no other alternative but to approach unorganised moneylenders and to accept the severe terms and conditions, including very high rate of interest, associated with such loans. Financial inclusion, as it is planned in India, will only provide them with bank accounts free of cost. But one wonders how that will help them avail of the bank credits as they still do not have anything to offer as collateral against loans. The neoliberal economic development is characterised by inherent contradiction. On the one hand, it produces exclusion and on the other, it seeks for inclusion. The very neoliberal economic growth process is exclusive. It is jobless growth. With more and more growth fewer and fewer jobs are created and existing jobs are lost. Exclusion is produced with dispossession of people from their land, jobs and assets. People are displaced and dislocated from their own spaces. At the same time, the neoliberal state wants a so-called democratic façade in the name of inclusion. It seeks to reach the benefits of growth to those who remain left out from them. Both the process of exclusion and inclusion proceed in terms of an economy which is geared to the market. And hence, both the processes of exclusion and inclusion are geared to the needs of the market. Neoliberalism wants continuous expansion of the market. And in this venture it warrants a state which is market-friendly. Viewed from this self-contradictory context, financial inclusion is an attempt to include the unbanked left-out population into the jurisdiction of market, i.e. (organised) financial market. It is nothing more than a façade which makes neoliberal growth look more democratic.

The project of financial inclusion targets those segments of the population which do not have bank accounts, the unbanked population. These include landless agricultural labourers, small and marginal farmers, rural non-farm workers, petty traders, urban informal workers, micro-entrepreneurs or self-employed persons and migrant and transit labourers. The latter group of workers include various categories of footloose workers engaged in construction activities, various urban services like courier services, urban unorganised/ informal wage labourers, street vendors, hawkers, rickshaw pullers and the like. It is claimed that the digitisation of identity will go a long way towards facilitating the financial inclusion of these migrant and transit labourers.

FINANCIAL INCLUSION AND MIGRANT WORKERS

One of the most vulnerable sections of the population includes the low-income earning migrant workers. It has been argued in several recent studies that the current high economic growth is a jobless one.[6] The joblessness of the current growth regime mainly pertains to the elimination of scope of new job creation in the formal sector of the economy. As a result, the unemployed workers are seeking their livelihood in the informal sector. Even within the formal sector there are evidences of what is known as the informalisation of the formal space, understood in terms of large-scale casualisation, contractualisation, etc. Neoliberalisation, which started around 1991, is constantly producing displacement and dislocation of people from their land and jobs. This has given rise to large-scale migration. People are forced to migrate for their sheer subsistence. For example, in a study in the district of Murshidabad, West Bengal, the author found that the male population of the remote rural areas of the district are forced to leave their farming jobs since with increase in the cost of production they find it difficult to somehow maintain their livelihood. Hence, they have no other alternative but to leave their villages (leaving in most of the cases their families behind) in order to seek some subsistence-level livelihood in the urban areas. They migrate to the urban areas within the state and to those of other states as construction workers mainly. Some take up jobs as street vendors or hawkers in the train. So, neoliberal exclusion is producing large-scale migration by displacing and dislocating people from their land and jobs in the name of development. Therefore, in this neoliberal era large sections of the vulnerable and marginalised population are migrant people.

There is no official data so far available on the magnitude of this migration. Mainstream economic theory describes migration as search for better wage, better living and upward social and economic mobility. Standard Lewisian transfer of labour is supposedly from the so-called 'backward' and 'traditional' and 'informal' agricultural activities to the so-called 'modern' and 'formal' industrial sector. In the Indian context, scope of such migration, even during the heydays of planning, remained quite limited. Rather, most of the rural-urban migration which took shape over the years is from the informal agricultural activities to the informal industrial and services activities. The informal sector remains the main absorber of the unemployed in the economy. A large chunk of informal workers – either in industrial activities, like construction, or in services activities, like transportation – is migrant. To use the term coined by Jan Breman, these are footloose labourers[7] and their numbers are swelling under the neoliberal economic policy regime. Rarely a very few of these low-paid or low-earning workers get a better wage, attain better living and become upwardly mobile socially and economically. Migration to them is a necessity for somehow remaining alive. Through frequent migration they eke out a bare-minimum livelihood. These footloose workers, in fact, can technically be classified as the working poor. And as poverty is a multi-dimensional social evil, they do not have access to many important resources and services which are necessary for a decent human living. One of such resources is financial. It is claimed that the lack of access to (formal) financial resources and services like banking services is one among the many reasons behind their vulnerability in the society vis-à-vis the affluent class. True, but the question is whether the problem of their financial exclusion can be resolved by a neoliberal market-focused stance of financial inclusion which in the Indian context refers to the mere access to banking services. We should not forget that financial inclusion in this country is set entirely against the backdrop of neoliberal inclusive growth strategy, as we have already analysed above.

Neoliberal inclusive growth talks of mainstreaming that segment of the population who are outside the domain of the different markets – the goods market, the factor market, the financial market, etc. In fact, as one can observe from the stated policy of financial inclusion in India the commercial banks are not compelled to open no-frills accounts for the vulnerable groups. It is not made mandatory by some state dictate. Whether the banks will allow the unbanked population to open accounts with no costs depends entirely on the voluntary willingness or choice of the banks. The project of financial inclusion is posed to them by both the RBI and the government as a win-win situation. That means financial inclusion will benefit both the banks and the targeted beneficiaries of the programme. So, the welfare of the financially excluded people is tagged with the expected profitability of the banks from the financial inclusion project. Theoretically, speaking in terms of simple supply-demand framework if banks supply no-frills accounts to the disadvantaged in the society, including the poor migrant workers, demand for such accounts will automatically be generated. It is a Say's-law-like proposition that production is the source of demand.[8] On the other hand, it appears that financial exclusion defined in terms of unbanked-ness is due to the unwillingness of the banks to offer the no-frills account to the poor and the disadvantaged. This proposition to us remains questionable as most of the lower strata households do not have enough financial resources to open and operate a bank account. Hence, it is a demand-sided problem – lack of effective demand (for bank accounts) in the Keynesian sense. Secondly, they do not have enough funds which can be held with the banks so that they can take advantage of modern banking technology to make even micro-payments. Thirdly, having a bank account does not necessarily facilitate one's access to other important financial products of the formal financial sector – the most important among them being formal sector credit. Availability of credit is conditioned by the creditworthiness of the borrower which in turn is largely dependent on the current and future income potential of the borrower and also his/her asset position.

One of the basic needs of the poor migrant workers may be to remit a part of their earnings back home. This can be effectively done by modern core-banking technology and also through ATMs. Once again there is a transaction cost for the banking operation. This cost may be low in recent times, thanks to modern technology. Still, many poor migrant workers may find even that low cost to be prohibitive, given their meagreness of income.

For demand for financial inclusion to be generated, it appears what requires to be ensured is a steady stream of cash flows to the poor migrant workers and other similar disadvantaged groups. Otherwise, even after opening accounts they may not operate their accounts. In fact, from a personal interview with some of the public-sector bank managers in Kolkata, it became clear that many of the no-frills-accounts are rarely operated.

So far, we have confined ourselves to a very narrow understanding of financial exclusion (that is the lack of access to formal bank savings deposit accounts). But financial inclusion can have a broader canvas. We can pose the issue of financial inclusion and exclusion by classifying the entire population of the country in two broad groups: users of formal financial services, on the one hand, and non-users of formal financial services, on the other. Again, the non-users of formal financial services may be distinguished into those having voluntary self-exclusion and those having involuntary exclusion. Properly speaking, financial exclusion refers to the second group, i.e. those who experience involuntary exclusion from the formal financial system. They have access to informal finance and there they are appropriated at exorbitant rates. Voluntary self-exclusion may be due to the fact that this category of people has no need of financial services and/or is debarred by certain cultural/ religious/political practices. On the contrary, involuntary exclusion implies there is willingness to avail of the formal financial services but the people belonging to this group lacks easy access. And this may be due to several reasons, such as insufficient income, risky and uncertain income, discrimination against this category of people by the formal financial institutions as giving access to them may not be viable and profitable for the institutions, lack of information or information asymmetry, contractual frame of the formal financial system, prices of financial products, and features of the financial products which may not suit them.

In India, the policy of financial inclusion hardly touches upon these issues. The reasons mentioned above for involuntary financial exclusion may be true for poor migrant workers. So, without a holistic approach towards the entire issue of involuntary financial exclusion, it is doubtful whether even the neoliberal goal of achieving 100 per cent financial inclusion in terms of converting unbanked population into banked population can be achieved.

Even if we presume that financial inclusion will better the life of the poor migrant workers the question is what then causes their financial exclusion from the banking system? Is it their lack of some permanent identity as a worker of a particular place and/or lack of proof of permanent residence? If yes, then the question is whether the UID/ Aadhaar project will be able to solve that problem? This issue we have taken up for discussion in the following section. But we should bear in mind that Aadhaar is necessarily a national security project. It poses the problem of identity (as it is being done through biometric identification) in the larger context of national security and surveillance. It is not primarily aimed at facilitating the delivery of services of the welfare scheme. Further, it has not been made mandatory to obtain Aadhaar. Even if it becomes mandatory, will it automatically ensure cost-effective financial inclusion of poor migrant workers? Further, as argued by Srinivasan, financial exclusion remains a major issue in the unorganised sector of the economy but expansion of services in this area by banks will not be very easy because of the special situation and needs of the unorganised sector.[9] And there is considerable amount of effective costs involved for the banks in their attempt to outreach the unorganised sector. At a time when banks are becoming more and more profit-oriented the question is whether they will want to incur this huge burden of costs.

DIGITISATION OF IDENTITY AND FINANCIAL INCLUSION

The key features of the Aadhaar-based micropayments as mentioned in the UIDAI website are the following: 'UIDAI Know Your Residence (KYR) sufficient for Know Your Customer (KYC): Banks in India are required to follow customer identification procedures while opening new accounts, to reduce the risk of fraud and money laundering. The strong authentication that the UIDAI will offer, combined with its KYR standards, can remove the need for such individual KYC by banks for basic, no-frills accounts. It will thus vastly reduce the documentation the poor are required to produce for a bank account, and significantly bring down KYC costs for banks.

'Ubiquitous BC network and BC choice: The UIDAI's clear authentication and verification processes will allow banks to network with village-based BCs such as self-help groups and kirana stores. Customers will be able to withdraw money and make deposits at the local BC. Multiple BCs at the local level will also give customers a choice of BCs. This will make customers, particularly in villages, less vulnerable to local power structures, and lower the risk of being exploited by BCs.

'A high-volume, low-cost revenue approach: The UIDAI will mitigate the high customer acquisition costs, high transaction costs and fixed IT costs that we now face in bringing bank accounts to the poor.

'Electronic transactions: The UIDAI's authentication processes will allow banks to verify poor residents both in person and remotely. Rural residents will be able to transact electronically with each other as well as with individuals and firms outside the village. This will reduce their dependence on cash, and lower costs for transactions. Once a general purpose Aadhaar-enabled micropayments system is in place, a variety of other financial instruments such as micro-credit, micro-insurance, micro-pensions, and micro-mutual funds can be implemented on top of this payments system.'[10]

It is claimed by the UIDAI that the Aadhaar scheme will achieve financial inclusion by providing identity to the poor and the homeless. The unique ID number or the Aadhaar is expected to act as a valid document for opening a bank account. Making the Aadhaar number an officially valid document to satisfy the KYC norms for opening bank accounts is likely to facilitate financial inclusion. UIDAI claims to have partnered with various banks that would facilitate the opening of bank accounts for the residents at the time of enrolment for Aadhaar.[11]

The pertinent questions at this juncture are the following: Will all the banks accept Aadhaar as the standardised identity of a person to satisfy their KYC norms? Is financial exclusion of the poor and vulnerable groups including the migrant workers due to lack of their proper identity? It is expected that not all types of banks in this country may not be interested in the financial inclusion project first and then adopting Aadhaar number to satisfy their KYC norms unless they find in it a win-win situation. This is doubtful, especially because banks are told to be more profit-oriented in the current neoliberal regime. Moreover, it is expected that private banks will not be interested to put the financial inclusion project in their priority list. Even for the public sector banks it is not absolutely mandatory to achieve financial inclusion and accept Aadhaar number to satisfy their KYC norms. So, the claim that Aadhaar will be ubiquitous is barely acceptable in practice.

One of the major requirements for opening bank account is residential proof. Despite having different cross-identification systems like voter card, PAN card and ration card most of the banks ask for separate residential proof like passport, electricity bill or telephone bill etc. This is because proof of permanent residence as well as temporary residence helps to trace the individual at times of need. Besides, these days most of the banking services (like sending of bank statements, letters and cheque books) are done through postal services, which of course require the address of the account holder. Residential proof is also necessary to minimise the incidence of fraud.

As far as the migrant workers are concerned, their major hindrance is this proof of residence as they change their place of residence quite often. Now, the question is whether biometric identification provided by

Aadhaar will satisfactorily fill this gap or not? Even if Aadhaar is made mandatory for the banks, say, will the biometric identification of a migrant worker satisfy the requirement of proof of residence? This will to a great extent depend on the technology of the Aadhaar. And we do not know how effectively fraudulent practices can be avoided or prevented using the Aadhaar technology? This question remains open.

In fact, there are ample reasons to believe that bank accounts may not be opened despite one having the Aadhaar card. To quote from the UIDAI website, the reasons for rejection of bank accounts are as follows:

a. Duplicate – The Aadhaar No. was found to be already existing in the receiving system (Bank) for processing and account generation
b. Address does not match
c. Name does not match
d. Gender does not match
e. Date of birth does not match
f. Photograph does not match
g. Minor whose guardian is not identifiable
h. Finds a place in SDN (Specially Designed Nationals) list
i. Finds a place in RBI negative list
j. Not contactable at address provided by UIDAI
k. Belongs to Financial Inclusion village of other bank
l. Aadhaar details entirely different from the actual details of the person

Of the above reasons, in case of migrant workers most are applicable. This is especially expected in the presence of the large incidence of illiteracy, and particularly financial illiteracy, among the migrant workers. These reasons may debar a non-migrant worker too from opening a new bank account. The chances are more in the case of migrant workers because clause (b), i.e. 'address does not match', will mostly deter them from opening a new bank account.

Also, Aadhaar is an identity system which is supposed to be universal. And an Aadhaar, apart from being a number, contains information regarding the number-holder. And some of this information may be absolutely private which the individual may not want to share. Now, what guarantees that privacy will be maintained? Or what guarantee is there that Aadhaar will ensure security of information of many migrant workers who in general lack privacy in their lives? Do we need separate privacy laws like the ones the United States has in connection with their social security provision schemes?

The nation has seen a series of initiatives from the Finance Ministry and the RBI towards achieving financial inclusion. However, even the provision of 'no-frills' account to the poor and linking of these accounts with schemes like the National Rural Employment Guarantee Act (NREGA) have not been able to achieve financial inclusion so far. Moreover, the objective of financial inclusion cannot be achieved by ensuring that people open an account in a bank. People who are given bank accounts under the financial inclusion scheme may have zero deposits in their accounts and they may never operate their bank accounts. This further raises doubts about the usefulness of such accounts and economic viability for banks in maintaining such accounts.

Extreme poverty, illiteracy, and lack of awareness and trust, corruption at various levels of the system and lack of willingness among the banks have adverse effects on the mission of financial inclusion. This may hold good for the financial inclusion of low-income earning migrant workers too. There are serious doubts whether providing the UID will actually facilitate financial inclusion or will it become an additional requirement for people to open and access a bank account?

Let us assume for a moment that Aadhaar will sufficiently trigger financial inclusion. But the UID authority does not have any measure by which they can estimate the impact of UID on financial inclusion. The question is whether this is the only alternative or there are other alternatives which may be more cost effective to achieve the same amount of impact. As of yet, we do not have answers to these questions.

Finally, the larger question remains whether financial exclusion persists because of a lack of proper identity? Or is it due to endemic poverty and also due to other social exclusions within the system? A low-income earning migrant worker may not find it cost-effective to operate a bank account given his/her meagre earnings. For him/her survival is of paramount significance most of the time. Availing a bank account facility may not necessarily solve the problem of his or her low and uncertain income.

One of the major uses of banking service by a migrant worker may be for the purpose of remitting part of his/her earnings to the family members at home. With the advent of core banking technology this can be cost-effectively done using the banking services. This is an aspect which may prompt a migrant worker to open a bank account and operate it regularly. But for this to happen, one must make sure that his application for new account does not get rejected for the reasons cited above.

CONCLUDING REMARKS

Summing up the major arguments in this paper, it can be asserted that achieving cent per cent financial inclusion for the poor migrant workers through digitisation of their identity may not be feasible in the present neoliberal scenario. Aadhaar is necessarily a national security project. The larger question of identity is posed in the context of national security. As a by-product, the scheme is tagged with the delivery of welfare schemes and services like the formal financial services. It is presumed that delivery of welfare schemes and services, which are public goods in nature (like financial services), have failed so far miserably owing to the lack of identity of the targeted population. So, Aadhaar project will fill that gap. However, the big question remains whether the lack of proper identification of the poor and migrant workers is the principal reason behind the benefits not accruing to them. In our understanding, both Aadhaar and financial inclusion are neoliberal projects. And like any neoliberal developmental agenda they lack any holistic approach and do not take into account the fact that exclusion, be it financial or otherwise, is systemic in nature.

NOTES

1. Economic Survey 2011-12, Chapter 13: *Human Development, Government of India*, p.319;
   http://indiabudget.nic.in/es2011-12/echap-13.pdf [last accessed 15 November 2012]

2. Ibid
3. Speaking at the annual Bankers' Conference (BANCON), Union Finance Minister P Chidambaram said banks would play an essential role in the direct cash transfer scheme, as every person with an Aadhaar card would be asked to open a bank account to enable such transfers. "Direct cash transfer of subsidies through Aadhaar from January 1" *The Hindu*, 24 November 2012; http://www.thehindu.com/news/national/direct-cash-transfer-of-subsidies-through-aadhaar-from-january-1/article4129971.ece [last accessed 28 November 2012]
4. See, "Financial Inclusion," National Bank for Agriculture and Rural Development (NABARD), http://nabard.org/financial_inclusion.asp [last accessed 15 November 2012]. 'The "inclusive growth" as a strategy of economic development received attention owing to a rising concern that the benefits of economic growth have not been equitably shared. Growth is inclusive when it creates economic opportunities along with ensuring equal access to them. Apart from addressing the issue of inequality, the inclusive growth may also make the poverty reduction efforts more effective by explicitly creating productive economic opportunities for the poor and vulnerable sections of the society. The inclusive growth by encompassing the hitherto excluded population can bring in several other benefits as well to the economy. The concept "Inclusion" should be seen as a process of including the excluded as agents whose participation is essential in the very design of the development process, and not simply as welfare targets of development programmes.' "Inclusive Growth – Role of Financial Sector," Address delivered by K. C. Chakrabarty, Deputy Governor, Reserve Bank of India, at the National Finance Conclave 2010 organised by KIIT University on 27 November 2010 at Bhubaneswar; http://rbi.org.in/scripts/BS_Speeches View.aspx?Id=538 [last accessed 15 November 2012]
5. Having a current account/savings account on its own, is not regarded as an accurate indicator of financial inclusion. There could be multiple levels of financial inclusion and exclusion. At one extreme, it is possible to identify the 'super-included', i.e. those customers who are actively and persistently courted by the financial services industry, and who have at their disposal a wide range of financial services and products. At the other extreme, we may have the financially excluded, who are denied access to even the most basic of financial products. In between are those who use the banking services only for deposits and withdrawals of money. But these persons may have only restricted access to the financial system, and may not enjoy the flexibility of access offered to more affluent customers.
6. Sen, Sunanda and Byasdeb Dasgupta, *Unfreedom and Waged Work: Labour in India's Manufacturing Industry*, Sage: New Delhi, 2009
7. Breman, Jan, *Footloose Labour: Working in India's Informal Economy* (Contemporary South Asia, 2.), Cambridge University Press: Cambridge, 1997

8. According to Say's Law, named after French classical liberal economist Jean-Baptiste Say, when an individual produces a product or service, he or she gets paid for that work, and is then able to use that pay to demand other goods and services. http://www.investopedia.com/terms/s/says-law.asp [last accessed 15 November 2012]
9. Srinivasan, N., "Policy Issues and Role of Banking System in Financial Inclusion," *Economic and Political Weekly*, 42:30, 28 July 2007, pp.3091-95.
10. UIDAI, Vision on Micropayments, Unique Identification Authority of India, Planning Commission, Government of India; http://www.uidai.gov.in/index.php?option=com_content&view=article&id=142&Itemid=135 [last accessed 15 November 2012]
11. Pandit, Ambika, "UID gives Identity, Bank Account to 27 Homeless," *The Times of India*, 29 November 2010; http://articles.timesofindia.indiatimes.com/2010-11-29/delhi/28263762_1_night-shelter-uid-card-homeless-persons [last accessed 15 November 2012]

X

The Political Economy of India's Unique Identification Project

Ritajyoti Bandyopadhyay

This paper is about the UID project and the future of the Indian state.[1] Much of the propositions made here are scattered speculations in the realm of the possible. An important historical question that may be asked is: to what extent have the central functions of the Indian state transformed in the post-liberalisation decades? This paper seeks to tease out some of the important reorientations of the functions of the Indian state using the debate surrounding the formation and operation of the Unique Identification Authority of India, or the UIDAI. I will largely view UIDAI as an important moment of the corporate capture of state power. It is well known that the dominance of the corporate elite in the running of the Indian state did not happen through the mechanism of electoral politics. This paper historicises the UID moment as a landmark in the history of Indian state and democracy. It argues that Nandan Nilekani's rise to prominence cannot be analysed in isolation from the changes in the dominant class coalitions within the Indian state in the post-liberalisation decades. The paper also garners evidence to support the proposition that the Aadhaar moment indicates a major alteration in the function of the state in the spheres of production, redistribution and consumption. It argues that the UID project is part of a series of processes that reify the individual as the unit of the economy and governance bridging the gap between finance capital and commercial capital.

WHAT DOES NANDAN NILEKANI'S RISE TO PROMINENCE SIGNIFY?

It is worth noting that UIDAI lacks a 'determinate legal status' being an executive authority formed by an Executive Decision. It does not have any constitutional or statutory status.[2]

It is not surprising that when Nandan Nilekani assumed the Chairmanship of the UIDAI he was given a cabinet rank without any direct or indirect commitment to the electorate. Nilekani after all represents a generation of Indian entrepreneurs who converted their intellectual and technical skills to usher in the IT boom in 1990s. In this, he represents the post-Rajiv-era upper-caste and middle-class dream of becoming billionaires by virtue of entrepreneurial and cultural capital exploiting competitive spaces opened by economic liberalisation. Therefore, Nilekani's rise to prominence indicates a new regime of 'dominant class coalition' in India which is traditionally constituted by the industrial big bourgeois with ability to influence policy-making at the Centre, the agrarian *kulak* with enormous capacity to mobilise the rural masses and influence policy at the state levels, and a permanent techno-managerial bureaucracy. They are tied to each other in a series of mutual collaborations and conflicts rendering the state autonomous being nursed by a political elite, an independent judiciary and the executive.[3] One needs to account for the state's changing role in mediating class coalitions in the post-liberalisation period. In the pre-liberalisation era, the state had monopoly control over heavy industry, mining, telecommunication and infrastructure development.[4] Further, the state used to control private industries by means of licensing. In such a context, domestic industries were allowed to flourish through a highly protectionist regime. The capitalist class was tiny but used to have oligopolistic control over sectors such as the automobile industry.

What are the changes that came about in the 'dominant class coalition' once the minority government of P.V. Narasimha Rao began a set of structural economic reforms? With the dismantling of the License Raj, the allowing of private capital in hitherto prohibited sectors such as telecommunications, mining, transport, banking and insurance, and the opening of the Indian market to the foreign players, there has been a phenomenal increase in the number of Indian capitalists in all sectors in the crucible of a few old monopoly houses leading to a change in the very composition of the capitalist class at all levels.[5] The Ambanis and the Sahara in the 1980s brought with them new corporate cultures and new entrepreneurial ethics. Further, in the 1990s, the old manufacturing sector decidedly took a back seat in the upsurge of the capital-intensive service sector and the booming IT industry. New relations of interdependence between nation-states were formulated. The English-educated pool of cheap labour in India attracted the foreign industries to outsource some of their service work to India. Thus, at the wake of the Y2K crisis, some of the Indian IT entrepreneurs offered the California computer firms a lucrative offer of resolving the problem at half the cost should they outsource the task to Indian firms. Michael Goldman records: 'India's premier firm, Infosys, offered to do the tedious job, promising it could pay its workers US$15 per hour and not the US$30 per hour which US firms were paying its local engineers; the fledgling Infosys instead paid Indian engineers US$2 and kept US$13, and made millions instantly.[6]

Goldman has shown how the domestic investment strategy of Bangalore's IT firms gradually shifted from the IT industry to land, 'converting cheap public and undervalued private or community land into real estate.' As is well-known, much of the rigour in India's Mission Mode Projects of e-governance (UID is a part of it) is designed to be spent on the regularisation of land titles[7] and to create infrastructure for the steady growth of the financial markets through financial inclusion. Thus, Nandan Nilekani's important presence in India's governing infrastructure reveals the capture of state power by a powerful oligarchy of the new capitalists that seeks to insulate the realm of policy-making from the world of mass democracy. While mass politics in Indian cities made a powerful transition in capturing elected bodies[8] and also in going beyond electoral calculations in forging extra-electoral linkages more intimately connected to the control of urban space, violence and local commercial capital,[9] the elite groups were seen taking recourse to some kinds of 'enlightened' institutions standing above the everyday world of mass politics. They, for example, started forming Resident Welfare Associations (RWAs) in middle-class neighbourhoods and engaged in civic activism influencing the function of the civic bodies most notably by earning an order from the Court. The enlightened reason of judiciary thus merged with middle-class civic activism. One may remember that Nilekani has been active in many such initiatives of enlightened politics. To cite an example, in 1999, the then Karnataka Chief Minister S.M. Krishna, known for his pro-reform administrative activism, set up the Bangalore Action Task Force (BATF) with Nilekani as the Chairman. The Government Order authorised the BATF to provide recommendation with a report to be submitted within three months; the members of the BATF, most of whom were connected to the IT giant Infosys, decided not to write any more reports.[10] They rather chose to concentrate on the implementation of projects. Nilekani declared with profound confidence, 'we are not here to make suggestions, but to explore possibilities of work and ensure that they are implemented.'[11] BATF declared itself to be a mediating agency between the government and the public, working for transparency, accountability and good governance by using the Public-Private Partnership (PPP) model. It identified seven stakeholders[12]: Bangalore Development Authority (BDA), Bangalore Water Supply and Sanitation Board (BWSSP), Bangalore Electricity Supply Company (BESCOM), Bharat Sanchar Nigam (BSNL), Bangalore Metropolitan Transport Corporation (BMTC), Bangalore City Police, and Bangalore Mahanagara Palike (BMP). Thus, the agencies selected represented concerns on the overall urban development agenda centred on land, development and infrastructure planning and excluded social welfare departments, so much so that, at the end of the BATF tenure, Nilekani had to concede that BATF did not actively undertake any pro-poor programmes.[13] In its heyday, BATF hired an army of 20 planners, architects and engineers. The BATF Office was financed by the Nilekani family's private trust, the "Adhaar Trust" to which the Nilekani family endowed Rs. 5 crore of their personal fortune (Ghosh 2005). A few years later, the nation's largest e-governance project would be named after the Nilekani family's private trust with Nilekani as the Chairman. If the first decade of economic reforms were carried out 'by stealth'[14] due to the lack of a critical public support for reform measures, the second decade of reforms witnessed the recruitment of non-political brand ambassadors of reform into the mainstream of governance as the emissaries of the 'New India's' aspirations to manufacture consent for reforms and to bridge the gap between the realm of reform and the arena of mass politics.[15] Clearly, these new faces at the heart of policymaking lacked the intellectual capital of the non-political policymakers of an earlier generation, although they superseded the preceding generation in terms of personal wealth. This new generation of policy elite brought with them a 'world class' corporate ethics of accountability, transparency and deliverability.[16] Indeed, N.R. Narayana Murthy, the co-founder of Infosys, said in a television interview that 'the biggest challenge all of us face is . . . we operate in a Third World environment. But our aspirations are all synergised with the First World.'[17] This new class of elite partially combines the attributes of both the financially powerful capitalist class and the culturally rich techno-managerial elite of the pre-liberalisation era.

The intellectual trajectory of the UIDAI may be understood as a part of a much larger history of the steady emergence of a tiny Bangalore-based IT elite in the policy market of New Delhi, marking the retreat of Calcutta and Bombay policy elites. Any discussion on the intellectual history of Aadhaar has to be understood in the context of Bangalore's intellectual tradition in the last few decades coinciding with the IT boom and the ever-growing appeal of technological utopia among the middle class. To cite an example, one of my senior colleagues, in the Institute that I served until recently (Indian Institute of Science, Bangalore, or IISc), has devoted his life to create a repository of data that he lovingly calls 'Qualiapedia' containing classified information of millions of years to be accessible through an ordinary cell phone enabling all essential everyday-to-obscure data to everyone. Again, another colleague from one of the engineering departments of IISc assures me that every human being will very soon have recorded health histories for the application of individual specific medicines. Such techno-Brahmanisms of the IT era reify information and technology as endowed with an inner sense of justice shifting the focus from the social contexts in which information is embedded.[18] I think that such optimism to the technological solution to all problems has to be provincialised to a certain intellectual world of Bangalore which had global connections long before being nationalised.[19] Like my engineering department colleague who seeks to find uniqueness in an individual's response to medicine, the UIDAI under Nandan Nilekani attempts to individualise poverty through a robust centralisation of poverty data of not just the 'citizens of India' but the entire resident population of the country. What implication does such a precision in the manufacturing of an 'individual' have on the classic mechanism of governmentality that relies on the arithmetic of 'aggregation' and 'average'? What does it tell us about the project of a largely corporate-driven state at the neo-liberal turn of capital? In the remaining sections of this paper, I will try to flag certain issues from my engagement with a very nebulous anti-UID movement on the IISc campus.

THE UID DEBATE

Commentators on the UID project are sharply divided in eulogy and denunciation. IT elite of India as well as a section of the urban middle class unequivocally supported the idea of an identifier that would enable the government to identify the deserving poor for welfare and check welfare fraud. Such a position is represented by various reports of the UIDAI and Nilekani's book *Imagining India*[20] that gives a clarion call to poverty crusaders to 'get rid of our phantoms' by instituting an infrastructure of information technology through which, as Ravi Shukla has pointed out, the notions of empowerment and inclusion invariably convert into a possible increase in purchasing power primarily through the enhancement of 'debt legibility'.[21] In the reports of the UIDAI, technology appears to be the only means to 'get things right'. Thus, the Task Force on India's Public Delivery System (PDS), headed by Nilekani, in its interim report clearly asserts: 'A subsidy, by its very nature, introduces two or more prices for the same good, and creates incentives for pilferage and diversion. As a result, the underprivileged suffer the most. Ensuring that goods move in the supply chain at market prices can minimise the incentives for diversion. . . . The transition to direct transfer of subsidies will lead to best practices in modern retail being incorporated in public provisioning, and also to increased competition and efficiency in the manufacturing, distribution, and retailing.'[22] They acknowledge the need for subsidy in a country like India, but concede that subsidy needs to be managed in such a way so that it becomes the new frontier for the accumulation of capital. As Usha Ramanathan has pointed out in a recent talk, in this account welfare fraud gets more importance than welfare itself.

The commentators who have largely denounced the UID project have three overlapping positions.

The first position for our discussion is concerned primarily with civil liberties issues, that UID creates a super-powerful apparatus of surveillance and as one of the protest posters of IISc student association CONCERN put it in a caption, on the occasion of Nandan Nilekani's talk, 'the big brother is looking at us'. Usha Ramanathan has commented extensively about the breach of privacy norms by UID in her numerous public lectures.

The second position reflects robustly on technical issues, that such a project without any precedence anywhere in the world is bound to fail to create a flawless database on a billion-plus population.[23] Scholars and activists also interrogated the projected infallibility of biometric mapping in determining the identity of an individual. The point at stake here is whether the numerical identity of a person changes over time. Since biometric information of a person is collected at one point of time and verified at another point of time, the question remains as to whether biometric information of a person remains the same over time. What is involved in the continued existence of a person over time? Can the identity of a person be determined if physical qualities of the same have changed over time? To solve this puzzle, we know that Locke relied on a distinction between personal identities that he called the 'personness of person' defined by a certain continuity of memory and the biological determinants of 'man'.[24] UID obscures the subjective foundations of 'personness of person' and sets the biological specificities as the supreme determinant of individual identity. The 'selfhood' component of identity is thus deliberately set aside to privilege 'sameness' over time in everyday transaction. Bestriding the stage of the National Institute of Advanced Studies' JRD Tata Auditorium (at IISc), Nilekani thus declared, 'UID pinpoints that x is x' based on the algorithmic techniques of pattern matching. The ethical question that scholars and activists have pointed out is, what if the criteria for sameness, much of which are indeed the reincarnation of eugenics and racial profiling for pre-literacy societies, are not infallible over a period of time?[25]

In addition to these two positions, I should make reference to a very interesting set of discussions which happened in the pages of the *Economic and Political Weekly* in which Anant Maringanti[26] and Ravi Shukla participated. Shukla observed that the UID scheme had the potentiality to augment the consumption patterns to an integrated database which was absolutely essential to promote India as a lucrative destination for banking and retail. In management and marketing circles in India, there has been a well-known concern about the lack of quantitative data on consumers. This is compounded by the diversity of Indian consumers compared to the existing US standards.[27]

The UIDAI informs us that the cash transferred to the UID-enabled accounts of individuals below the poverty line (as a part of PDS) will be managed online. The adjustments will be made according to their consumption behaviour. Going one step further, in an article, Arka Roy Chaudhuri and E. Somanathan model such a transaction as follows: 'The amount can be indexed to the price of food, and updated monthly. Of course, many people do not have bank accounts. But with weekly government transfers in place, shopkeepers will have a strong incentive to invest in a fingerprint scanner that can connect to the government network. After correct identification the transfer can be made to the shopkeeper electronically. The central database will ensure that there are no duplicates. This method will provide an assured transfer of money, equivalent to a fixed amount of food, to every adult every week, and will go a long way towards assuring food security for the poor.'[28]

As is evident from the above quote, the main purpose of direct cash transfer is to open up the grain procurement mechanism to the open market and gradually substitute redistribution by consumption. Such a move is justified in terms of the expansion of 'consumer choice'. Thus, the Interim Report asserts: 'In this context, the issue of the beneficiary's choice assumes significance. The direct transfer of subsidy to beneficiaries makes it possible for the beneficiary to access the product or service from more than one pre-defined channels and locations. Government distribution channels can coexist with private providers in this subsidy framework and the beneficiary could be provided a choice. Public provisioning can be greatly improved and made effective with the approach discussed in this report, while simultaneously deepening and widening the distribution network. This enhances the delivery of goods and services for the ultimate beneficiary.'[29]

The transition from the existing system of PDS to the proposed regime of direct cash transfer to targeted individuals[30] is sought to be accomplished through a calculated mobilisation of the discourses of 'rights' and 'security'. We may remember the 2007 ration riots in the 6 CPI(M)-dominated districts of West Bengal. Bhattacharyya and Rana in a contemporary commentary of the event aptly pointed out how the material background of what they called 'PDS anger' lay in the unchecked rise of prices of food grains due to the gradual dismantling of Food Corporation of India (FCI) and opening up the grain market to the corporate players.[31] The commentators opined that the price-rise affected the APL populations who started relying on ration shops creating a sudden rise in the demand for cheap rice and wheat that the ration shop dealers failed to provide.

The second significant point that Roy Chaudhuri and Somanathan make in the above quote is that the relation between the *kirana* shop-owner and the BPL customer mediated by UID information and cash transfer in bank account is also a mapping of the spending behaviour of the person. The relationship between the financial institutions, micro-credit organisations and UIDAI will also create credit histories of individuals. The spending behaviour and credit history together may be a valid document for the mapping of consumption that the person does.

In such a context, schemes like the Mahatma Gandhi National Rural Employment Guarantee Scheme (MGNREGS) attempt to nationalise a common minimum wage line based on which the poverty line could be determined. It is well-known that back in September 2011 the Planning Commission Deputy Chairman Montek Singh Ahluwalia filed an affidavit to the Supreme Court that individuals capable of spending

Rs.965 a month (Rs.32 per day) in urban areas and Rs.781 a month (Rs.26 per day) in rural areas would not be considered poor and thus, they should be barred from getting the benefits meant for the people below the poverty line.[32] In January 2011, the MGNREGS wage rates hiked between 17 per cent and 35 per cent depending on the Consumer Price Index for Agricultural Labour (CPIAL) in different states. Thus, the lowest minimum wage in MGNREGS in Meghalaya was Rs.117, while the highest wage was fixed in Andaman and Nicobar Islands at Rs.181.[33] Since the MGNREGS guarantees 100-day work for an individual, the daily wages varied between Rs.32.05 (i.e. (117×100)/365) and Rs.49.58 (i.e. (181×100)/365). Clearly, the Ahluwalia poverty line attempted to make parity between the lowest official wage and the official version of poverty and placed individuals attaining the officially declared lowest wage above the poverty line. The UIDAI claims to maintain coordination between many such operations ensuring transparency in determining the separation between the deserving and the undeserving poor. This means that by enabling the government to execute the poverty line in the strictest possible way, the UID will help shrink the spending on subsidy. Simultaneously, it attempts to restructure PDS to allow the entry of the private corporations in this sector. Together, the UID project makes an enabling environment for the corporate players to colonise the terrain of commercial capital which is still largely dominated and populated by small players along with the state-owned FCI that controls the prices of food grains and procures food grains.

THE PROSPECTS OF THE UID PROJECT

Let me now take the privilege to make a few propositions on the prospects of UID.

Proposition I: State subsidizes leading IT firms by bringing them into the arena of the governance of populations

The UID experience reveals a new era of state-corporate partnership in the market of policy and governance. To cite an example, the HCL Infosystems has recently signed a contract with the UIDAI whereby it has been awarded the contract for the Managed Service Provider (MSP) to implement and manage the Central ID Repository (CIDR) for UIDAI.[34] This contract is for seven years, which means the contract is valid whoever comes to power at the Centre in 2014. This is one of numerous instances of how the sector of governance becomes the new field for capital investment for the IT industry. In recession years, such initiatives will definitely help the IT industry to withstand the global shock. It would not be out of place to mention here that in February, 2012, the UIDAI 'reduced' the revenue requirement of the MSP contract by Rs.2,000 crore from the earlier limit of Rs.6,000 crore to enable the participation of 'mid-sized' companies in the project. However, it only short-listed the Tata Consultancy Services and the TCS Infosystems for the final bid. Incidentally, TCS had already been awarded two contracts by the UIDAI for the re-design, development, maintenance and support of the UIDAI web portal along with purchase of biometric devices. On the other hand, HCL Infosystems received no less than four prized contracts from the UIDAI for managing its intranet and knowledge-management portal, procurement of biometric devices, procurement of biometric authentication devices and hard disk drives.[35]

Proposition II: From populations to individual

In May 2010, it became widely known that the state of Andhra Pradesh, one of the pioneers in digital governance, had, over a period of five years, collected biometric information of about 6 crore people which was followed by an online database for digitised ration cards.[36] The Karnataka state government did not lag far behind. Based on a massive survey of citizens below the poverty line, in 2006, it started preparing biometric ration cards involving figure prints and photographs. However, what makes the UID project unique from many such already-initiated exercises is that it *does not* target households. Rather, it targets individuals on the basis of which an external agency, with an electronic access to the UID database, can verify the identity of a person. Thus, the unique feature of UID is that it manufactures the *individual* and defines poverty *individually*. Such a move has the potential to radically alter the discourses and methods of poverty management in India. The individual replaces old categories of community and household as units of poverty governance. The Interim Report writes: 'Aadhaar provides only authentication for individuals. Given that many subsidies are directed towards families, it is essential that the CSMS [Core Subsidy Management System] be designed to capture the Aadhaar numbers of all family members. The definition of beneficiaries and families could be laid down in the policies of the concerned Implementing Ministry.'[37]

Proposition III: The UID is a tool for the financialisation of society; finance capital requires the 'individual'

A lot has been said on the connection between the banking system and the UID. The leading commercial banks of India such as the State Bank of India, Bank of India, Central Bank, etc, were quick to ink a pact with the UIDAI to act as a registrar. Being a registrar, the bank would help the UIDAI in enrolling residents in the UID system. They would also utilise the database of their customers and enrol them in the UIDAI. In return, the banks would get several important benefits. First, the UID enables the banking institutions to 'build an accessible, low cost micropayments model.'[38] The poor can easily establish his/her identity as his/her UID is connected to the bank account.[39] Second, UID KYR (Know Your Resident) is considered to be sufficient for a bank's KYC (Know Your Customer). This reduces the cost that the banks otherwise had to incur to create a credible database for its customer base. This is how the UIDAI with taxpayers' money subsidises the banking system. Further, one UIDAI document adds that 'the UID will mitigate the high customer acquisition costs, high transaction costs and fixed IT costs that we now face in bringing bank accounts to the poor.'[40] Universalisation of electronic cash transaction also helps the financial institutions to reduce the costs associated with cash handling. Third, UID enables the poor even in remote areas to make electronic transactions of very small amounts that substantially reduce their erstwhile dependence on cash. The UIDAI notes: 'Since the UID enables remote authentication of identity, it empowers the poor in making electronic transactions in small, micro-amounts, remotely and at low-cost, through BC networks connected by mobile phones. The model would thus be accessible and affordable across the country. Such a UID-enabled micropayments approach can bring about universal financial access for the poor – they would be able to access their accounts on the move, wherever they are, through any mobile phone, from any BC or bank. The UID-enabled bank account can thus be a global address for residents, similar to an email id or a mobile phone number.'[41]

Apart from this, the UID also enables the poor to access microloans from the microcredit organisations and banks as these institutions can easily track and retrieve the sum from the beneficiary thanks to the UID.

If the central purpose of UID is to expand the reach of finance capital through formalised credit and banking, then manufacturing the individual at the level of the hitherto non-integrated groups is a compulsory situation. *Finance capital cannot operate without targets at the level of the individual.* Arguably, this is where finance capital is crucially different from other forms of capital that can prosper in collective social network. This is why the sway of finance capital is crucially linked to the formation of the liberal individual. Such a shift from collective to individual is associated with another equally important process. While the formalised and individualised and more centralised management of poverty leads to a fundamental change in the mechanisms of *redistribution*, the identity element of the PDS is kept intact and reinvigorated. The expectation is that with the growth of economy redistribution will be substituted by consumption, while the identity element of the PDS that even the members of the middle class widely use in their official identifications is strengthened, centralised, digitised and immortalised.

Proposition IV: Ascendance of resident and decline of citizen

The UIDAI mandates on the obverse of each Aadhaar card that 'Aadhaar is proof of identity, not of citizenship'. Thus, it creates a new governmental category of the empirical body of the 'resident' and jettisons the politically loaded notion of the 'citizen' while preserving 'rights' in the technological justice of the ruling elite. This is how it extends governance beyond citizenship, but curbs the radical potential of subject formation that any form of governmental identification brings with it. *UID thus simultaneously individualises poverty management and depoliticises rights.*

Proposition V: The UID marks a watershed in the neo-liberal commonsense of property regime

We know that one of the central tenets of liberal economic theory holds that right of private property is central for economic development. H. de Soto opined that simplifying the process of property registration would turn dead assets of the poor into live capital.[42] Such a model of financial inclusion of the poor through property-titling and mortgage-lending dominated policy discourses until the global recession. The UID was born in the context of recession. It seeks to accomplish financial inclusion just by minutely documenting the poor and acting as a mediator between the individual and the financial organisations.

Proposition VI: Rehabilitation of the state from governing production and redistribution to managing consumption

Being slowly estranged from managing production (as evident from the growing corporate involvement in contract farming) and re-distribution, the state is seeking rehabilitation in governing consumption. The very fact that the UIDAI is hosted in the state's central planning organ indicates that new governmental data will be produced on spending and consuming behaviours of the residents. New consumption categories will parallel the classic categories of governmentality in the spheres of production and redistribution. In short, the shift of the state from the spheres of production and redistribution renders a certain visibility of it in the governance of consumption. Usha Ramnathan's (2009) caution of data interface in the absence of a strong privacy law in India can only add substance to the point I am trying to make here. The recent global instances of the sheer physical violence associated with microfinance industry and the global proliferation of private militia of different corporate credit organisations and banks seems to give birth to corporate forms of feudalism in those sectors.

Proposition VII: Mobile technology for mobile bodies

The very reality of labour migration from one place to another necessitates the need for mobile identity of the labourer to harness the resources for the reproduction of his labour power.[43] Further, UID enables the state to track and manage the migrant labour force with more sophisticated mechanisms of surveillance and discipline. Such legibility, the critics have pointed out, can prove to be counterproductive to the migrants if a regime with an access to the UID database is vindictive towards ethnic and religious minorities.[44]

WHAT HAPPENS TO HARD-CASH?

My first direct encounter with the UID project happened in December, 2010 when National Institute of Advanced Studies (NIAS) at Bangalore invited Nandan Nilekani to deliver a lecture on the Aadhaar project. The NIAS talk of Nilekani was marked by protests by the IISc student body 'Concern'– known as an eclectic left organisation having horizontal links with several civil-liberties organisations. As a Concern member, I had the opportunity to see anti-UID protests by different civil-liberties organisations in Bangalore's iconic Town Hall. The anxiety for privacy seemed to envelop all other possible logics of protesting against the UID. Such associations with the anti-UID movement made me interrogate the strong middle-class content of participation. Why, for example, is the middle class particularly invested in such a protest? Are they not already adequately mapped by the apparatuses of biometric surveillance, thanks to their participation in trans-national white-collar labour networks? Can such participation be fully explained in terms of their concerns about the absurdity of the new poverty line? If so, then why was there so little attempt by these organisations to connect the movement with larger masses just above the poverty line who are supposed to bear the brunt of the poverty-line-related UID legibility? If the state has already entered a post-liberal phase of intervention, then can a liberal agenda of resistance based primarily on privacy concerns be effective in exposing the violence of the UID project? Clearly, in this case, middle-class resistance has failed to pre-empt 'power'. During my fieldwork in 2011-12, I rarely came across similar initiatives taken by political parties in West Bengal that, we all know, politically manage poverty and organise local capital in a paralegal sphere. Does it then mean that UID has acquired legitimacy at the grassroots level, even though it will inevitably politicise the marginal APL population across the country by identifying the *deserving poor* according to the official poverty line?

I found a very tentative answer to these questions while closely studying the UID enrolment form and the enrolment process in Bangitolla – a village in Malda district. Although, in the latest version of the UID enrolment form, the block on financial and bank information are made explicitly optional after a lot of complaint from activists that the earlier form had kept the optional element on that block vague causing confusion, we found that whoever came to the enrolment centre asked the opinion of the 'scribe-in-charge' and the latter would invariably insist that the client put a positive mark against the designated options. In effect, we found that all the clients, on that particular day, cutting across class demarcations, ended up providing their bank information to the UIDAI. This implies that the UIDAI will have a much larger database than it has officially set out to acquire from the population. Recent reports on the Mysore pilot survey on LPG clients cutting across class lines adequately show that surveillance on individual consumption is far from being just a BPL issue. The privacy fear of the concerned members of the middle class comes from such a sense of a breach of trust – of losing 'freedom' in the sphere of consumption. The UIDAI appears to them to be an illiberal institution curbing their anonymity as consumers. However, in actuality, as we have seen in preceding sections, UID seeks to organise the classic functions of the state according to the 'principles of market'.

As I have already mentioned, the UID manufactures the entrepreneurial individual in the sense that the individual is a man of consumption producing his own satisfaction. As Foucault has taught us, one of the central concerns of liberalism was 'to cut out or contrive a free space of the market within an already given political society.'[45] On the contrary, Foucault holds that the central problem of neoliberalism is 'how the overall exercise of political power can be modelled on the principles of a market economy.'[46] Here, the problem is that Foucault treats liberalism 'in theory' while showing the insularity of the market from the intervention of the state, and treats neoliberalism as a set of practices where the boundary between the two is blurred and the rules of market dictates the state. I would say that in semi-socialist economies such as India, the state historically controls the bulk of finance capital through nationalised banks. Therefore, the UID project aspires to serve both the state and the financial market by minimising the circulation of hard cash in the market.[47] As we have seen in the preceding sections, this has been a persistent official claim of the UIDAI as well. Now, the issue is that in India quite a substantial section of the economy exists outside the reach of finance capital. The move to formalise PDS through the sieve of the poverty line and the spending history of the poor may incentivise the marginal APL population to manipulate the situation by hiding their real income. Our food-supply-chain ethnography in West Bengal[48] suggests two tentative ways in which economic transactions can happen outside the hard cash exchange. First, we saw how actors in different stages of commodity metamorphosis crucially rely on instalment payment which is nothing but a promissory system enabling the players in the existing network to depend on each other and to carry forth the network to a new cycle. Since one commodity cycle inevitably overlaps with another, in many instances financial calculations happen in a virtual space. This helps the small players withstand periodic shocks. Second, we have noticed the existence of a service-based system of exchange network in parts of Malda district where labour time is being exchanged instead of cash. I am of the opinion that such pre-existing networks of economic activities are perfectly in tune with the basic architecture of finance capital in so far as their respective positions to hard cash is concerned. Therefore, I have a suspicion that the combination of finance capital and commercial capital controlled by big corporates will comfortably emulate the principles of the existing social networks of provisioning. Far from being in tussle with the pre-capitalist institutions, capital today is more adept and agile to come to terms with them. The spectacular insertion of household labour (especially women's labour) in capitalist production through microfinance is one such instance of how capital comes to inhabit vernacular spaces.

Here, it would not be out of place to cite two more examples from our supply-chain ethnography. First, we noticed that the R&D units of corporate retail entities had invested on research teams to study how different rural-urban commodity chains operated in the immediate vicinities of the areas where they were active. Second, microfinance agencies and banks have similar investment in R&D to understand why institutionalised credit systems had largely failed in many regions of India where informal caste- and ethnicity-based credit systems had operated with considerable success despite their predatory character and coercive manifestations. In such a context, the UID project creates the crucial infrastructure in which finance capital and corporate-driven commercial capital converge. Such a convergence is crucial as it completes an important circuit of the dialectical relation between use value and exchange value. If finance capital is the moment of liberation of exchange value from use value, commercial capital is the moment of a dialectical renegotiation between use value and exchange value.

CONCLUDING REMARKS

This chapter has tried to establish that the anti-UID resistance has largely failed to formulate powerful counter-strategies. This failure can be located in a naïve general understanding of the nature of capital and the project of the state in the second decade of liberalisation. The protesting middle class has to come to terms with the populations that would be hit first by the UID project's move to 'transparent' governance. My initial encounters with the grassroots political managers in West Bengal clearly show that the populations marginally above the poverty line will bear the brunt of the UID-led policy reforms. The first move to resist UID should come from this group. The initial subversive step from them will be to hide formal monetary transactions backed by a technologically superior counterfeit establishment. The protesting middle-class groups have to take an active role in connecting different pockets of subterranean protests through a combination of theory and practice. The first step to challenge the industry and the establishment of the ruling elite is to form an understanding of the political economy of the era.

NOTES

1. I am thankful to Atig Ghosh, Iman Mitra, Bodhisattva Kar, Partha Chatterjee, Anwesha Sengupta and Priyankar De for positive suggestions at different stages of the paper's metamorphosis.
2. Krishnaswamy, Sudhir, "Unique Identity Numbers: The Enabler of Policy Reform?" *India in Transition*, Centre for the Advanced Study of India (CASI), University of Pennsylvania, 2010; http://casi.ssc.upenn.edu/iit/krishnaswamy [last accessed 15 November 2012]; Usha Ramanathan, "A Unique Identity Bill," *Economic & Political Weekly*, 45:30, 24 July 2010, pp.10-14.
3. Bardhan, Pranab K., *The Political Economy of Development in India*, Oxford University Press: New Delhi, 1984; Achin Vanaik, *The Painful Transition: Bourgeois Democracy in India*, Verso: London, 1990; Francine R. Frankel and M.S.A. Rao eds., *Dominance and State Power in India: Decline of a Social Order*, Oxford University Press: New Delhi, 1990; Sudipta Kaviraj, "A Critique of Passive Revolution," *Economic & Political Weekly*, 23:45/47, November 1988, pp.2429-44; Partha Chatterjee, *Nationalist Thought and the Colonial World: A Derivative Discourse?* Zed Books: London, 1986; Partha Chatterjee, "Democracy and Economic Transformation in India," *Economic & Political Weekly*, 43:16, 19 April 2008, pp.53-62
4. Chatterjee, "Democracy and Economic Transformation"
5. Ibid
6. Goldman, Michael, "Speculative Urbanism and the Making of the Next World City," *International Journal of Urban and Regional Research*, 35:3, May 2011, p.572.
7. Benjamin, Solomon, R. Bhuvaneswari, P. Rajan and Manjunatha, "Bhoomi: E-Governance or an anti-politics necessary to globalize Bangalore," A CASUM-m Working Paper, 2007; http://casumm.files.wordpress.com/2008/09/bhoomi-e-governance.pdf [last accessed 15 November 2012]
8. Chatterjee, Partha, *Politics of the Governed: Reflections on Popular Politics in Most of the World*, Permanent Black: Ranikhet, 2004
9. Bandyopadhyay, Ritajyoti, "Politics of Archiving: Hawkers and Pavement Dwellers in Calcutta," *Dialectical Anthropology*, 35:3, 2011, pp. 295-316; Ritajyoti Bandyopadhyay, "A Historian among Anthropologists: Comments on 'Politics of Archiving'," *Dialectical Anthropology* 35:3, 2011, pp.331-39
10. Ghosh, Asha, "Public-Private or a Private-Public: Promised Partnership of the Bangalore Agenda Task Force," *Economic & Political Weekly*, 40:47, 19-25 November 2005, pp.4914-22
11. Pani, Narendar, "Icons and Reform Politics in India: The Case of S.M. Krishna," *Asian Survey*, 46:2, March/April 2006, p.248
12. Ghosh, "Public-Private or a Private-Public"
13. Ibid

14. Jenkins, Rob, *Democratic Politics and Economic Reforms in India*, Cambridge University Press: Cambridge, 2000
15. Pani, "Icons and Reform Politics in India"
16. Ibid
17. Ibid, quoted in p.249
18. Srinivasan, Janaki, "The Political Life of Information and the Practice of Governance in India," Unpublished PhD Thesis, Department of Information Management and Systems, University of California, Berkeley, 2011
19. Janaki Srinivasan has recently shown that the meaning(s) and usage of the term 'information' shifted in 1980s in the market-oriented developmental discourses of the World Bank. The 'World Development Reports (WDR)' in 1980s started using the word information in both particularistic (of, about something) and abstract (of what?) senses. The emphasis shifted to justify market based transaction and the receding role of the state from many of its erstwhile activities. Thus, the WDR in 1988 writes: 'The central government's roles would shift from those of primary decision maker, investor, maintainer, and overseer to those of regulator, technical adviser, and dispenser of information.' (World Bank 1988, 153, quoted in Srinivasan, "The Political Life of Information," p.31)
20. Nilekani, Nandan, *Imagining India: The Idea of a Renewed Nation*, Penguin: Bangalore, 2009
21. Shukla, Ravi, "Reimagining citizenship: Debating India's Unique Identification Scheme," *Economic & Political Weekly*, 45:2, 9 January 2010, pp.31–36
22. "Interim Report of the Task Force on Direct Transfer of Subsidies on Kerosene, LPG and Fertiliser," Ministry of Finance, Government t of India, June 2011, pp.1-2; http://finmin.nic.in/reports/Interim_report_Task_Force_DTS.pdf [last accessed 15 November 2012]
23. Ramkumar, R., "What the UID Conceals," *The Hindu*, 21 October 1949; http://www.thehindu.com/opinion/lead/article839590.ece [last accessed 15 November 2012]; Jean Drèze and Reetika Khera, "The BPL Census and a Possible Alternative," *Economic & Political Weekly*, 45:9, 27 February 2010
24. Chatterjee, Partha, *A Princely Impostor? The Strange and Universal History of the Kumar of Bhawal*, Permanent Black: Ranikhet, 2002
25. Sarkar, Swagato, "The Unique Identity (UID) Project and the New 'Bureaucratic Moment' in India," Working Paper 194, Queen Elizabeth House, University of Oxford, 2011
26. Maringanti, Anant, "Sovereign States and Mobile Subjects: Politics of UIDAI," *Economic & Political Weekly*, 44:46, 14 November 2012, pp.35-40
27. Shukla, "Reimagining citizenship"
28. Roy Chaudhuri, Arka and E. Somanathan, "Impact of Biometric-Identification-Based Transfers," *Economic & Political Weekly*, 46:21, 21 May 2011, p.78
29. "Interim Report of the Task Force," p.11

30. Very little justification can be gathered whatsoever for the endorsement of cash transfers as a proper substitution to subsidy-in-kind. This is starkly true if we consider food, nutrition and education sectors where state provision of commodities and services historically has more positive outcomes. Sudha Narayanan, in a very useful survey of global literature on different systems of subsidy, has shown that (a) in order for cash subsidy to work according to a well-planned way it requires massive investment on tracking infrastructure (read UID) which increases the cost of subsidy; (b) Marginal Propensity to Consume (MPC) from food grain transfers tend to be much higher than the MPC out of cash transfers; (c) even in developed economies like the US, food stamp programmes make available around two to 10 per cent extra nutrient per household than the rate of an equal value of cash income; (d) under inflationary conditions, in particular, in-kind-transfers, or 'inflation indexed stamps' are observed to have worked better than that of a mere cash transfer; (e) if in the condition of a weak market cash transfers are designed to protect particular populations against inflation, the very cost of transfers tend to increase downplaying any 'cost advantage' that cash transfers bring with them; (f) transfers in kind received by female members of the household results in higher levels of calorie consumption than that of cash transfers that have more chance to be appropriated by dominant male members of the household. Sudha Narayanan, "A Case for Reframing the Cash Transfer Debate in India," *Economic & Political Weekly*, 46:21, 21 May 2011, 41-48
31. Bhattacharyya, Dwaipayan, and Kumar Rana, "Politics of PDS Anger in West Bengal," *Economic and Political Weekly*, 43:5, 2 February 2008, pp.63-69
32. Rahman, A. Faizur, "Which World do Economists Live in?" *The Asian Age*, 23 September 2012; http://www.asianage.com/columnists/which-world-do-economists-live-754 [last accessed 15 November 2012]
33. Balchand, K., "Wage Hike for MGNREGA Workers," *The Hindu*, 7 January 2011, http://www.hindu.com/2011/01/07/stories/2011010759880100.htm [last accessed 15 November 2012
34. "UIDAI Inks Contract with HCL Infosystems," *The Indian Express*, 10 August 2012; http://www.hclinfosystems.in/news252.htm [last accessed 15 November 2012]
35. Suneja, Kirtika, "UIDAI Shortlists TCS, HCL Infosystems for R2,000-cr Service Provider Contract," *The Financial Express*, 7 February 2012; http://www.financial express.com/news/uidai-shortlists-tcs-hcl-infosystems-for-r2000cr-service-provider-contract/908638/1 [last accessed 15 November 2012
36. "Ration Cards: 1.1 Crore Biometric Samples Found to be Duplicate," *Business Line*, 13 May 2010, www.thehindubusinessline.com/2010/05/13/stories/2010051351831900.htm [last accessed 15 November 2012]

37. "Interim Report of the Task Force," p.16
38. UIDAI, "UIDAI Strategy Overview: Creating a Unique Identity Number for Every Resident in India", Unique Identification Authority of India, Planning Commission, Government of India, April, 2010, p.40; http://uidai.gov.in/UID_PDF/Front_Page_Articles/Documents/Strategy_Overveiw-001.pdf_[Accessed on 15 November 2012]
39. Ibid
40. Ibid, p.41
41. Ibid, p.40
42. de Soto, Hernando, *The Mystery of Capital: Why Capitalism Triumphs in the West and Fails Everywhere*, Basic Books: New York, 2000
43. Samaddar, Ranabir, "What is Postcolonial Predicament?" *Economic and Political Weekly*, 47:9, 3 March 2012, pp.41-50
44. Ramkumar, "What the UID Conceals"
45. Foucault, Michel, *The Birth of Biopolitics: Lectures at the Collège de France, 1978-79*, edited by Michel Senellart: translated by Graham Burchell. Palgrave Macmillan: New York, 2008, p.131
46. Ibid
47. I am thankful to Iman Mitra for a discussion on this point.
48. In the context of the current debate on FDI in retail in India, the project explored the possible impacts of FDI on urban provisioning mechanisms. It tried to answer the following questions: Will FDI in wholesale-retail directly take control over food production and distribution, completely replacing the older structures of surplus extraction? Or, will FDI take over the existing processes of production by small producers and distribution by small players, without leading to any technical or organisational transformations? What are the possible ways in which different class interests would react to the corporatisation of retail? The project has attempted to answer these questions by delineating the existing mechanisms of the metamorphosis of food commodities from the green field to the kitchen of a consumer in Calcutta. A multi-sited ethnographic survey was conducted along with archival-historical research to unravel the existing mechanisms of food provisioning in Calcutta. We have sought to understand the social and financial networks that mobilise the systems of urban provisioning

Bibliography

BOOKS AND ARTICLES

Aas, Katja Franko, "'Crimmigrant' Bodies and Bona Fide Travellers: Surveillance, Citizenship and Global Governance," *Theoretical Criminology*, 15:3, 2011, pp.331-46.

Aas, Katja Franko, "'The Body Does Not Lie': Identity, Risk and Trust in Technoculture," *Crime, Media, Culture*, 2:2, 2006, pp.143-58

Ahmed, Kamaluddin, *Assam's 'Doubtful Citizens': Fact or Fiction?* Pharos Media & Publishing Pvt Ltd: New Delhi, 2011

Anderson, Claire, *Legible Bodies: Race, Criminality and Colonialism in South Asia*, Berg: Oxford, New York, 2004

Arnold, David, "The Colonial Prison: Power, Knowledge and Penology in Nineteenth-Century India," in David Arnold and David Hardiman eds., *Subaltern Studies VIII: Essays in Honour of Ranajit Guha*, Oxford University Press: New Delhi, 1994

Arputham, Jockin, "How community-based enumerations started and developed in India," *Environment & Urbanization*, 24:1, April 2012, pp.27-30

Bandyopadhyay, Ritajyoti, "A Historian among Anthropologists: Comments on 'Politics of Archiving'," *Dialectical Anthropology* 35:3, 2011, pp.331-39

Bandyopadhyay, Ritajyoti, "Politics of Archiving: Hawkers and Pavement Dwellers in Calcutta," *Dialectical Anthropology*, 35:3, 2011, pp.295-316

Bardhan, Pranab K., *The Political Economy of Development in India*, Oxford University Press: New Delhi, 1984

Baruah, Sanjib, *India Against Itself: Assam and the Politics of Nationality*, University of Pennsylvania Press: Philadelphia, 1999

Bates, Crispin, "Race, Caste and Tribe in Central India: The Early Origins of Indian Anthropometry," in Peter Robb ed., *The Concept of Race in South Asia*, Oxford University Press: New Delhi, 1997

Bayly, Christopher A., *Indian Society and the Making of the British Empire* (the New Cambridge History of India series, Vol. 2.1), Cambridge University Press, Cambridge, 1988

Beck, Ulrich, "Subpolitics: Ecology and the Disintegration of Institutional Power," in *World Risk Society*, Polity: Cambridge, 1999, pp.91-108

Bhattacharyya, Dwaipayan, and Kumar Rana, "Politics of PDS Anger in West Bengal," *Economic & Political Weekly*, 43:5, 2 February 2008, pp.63-69

Bhaumik, Subir, *Troubled Periphery: The Crisis of India's North East*, Sage Publications: New Delhi, 2010

Breckenridge, Keith, "The Biometric State: The Promise and Peril of Digital Government in the New South Africa," *Journal of Southern African Studies*, 31:2, June, 2005, pp.267-82

Breman, Jan, *Footloose Labour: Working in India's Informal Economy* (Contemporary South Asia, 2.), Cambridge University Press: Cambridge, 1997

Broeders, Dennis, and Godfried Engbersen, "'The Fight against Illegal Migration': Identification Policies and Immigrants' Counterstrategies," *American Behavioural Scientist*, 50:12, 2007, pp.1592-609.

Broeders, Dennis, "The New Digital Borders of Europe: EU Databases and the Surveillance of Irregular Migrants", *International Sociology*, 22:1, January 2007

Browne, Simone, "Digital Epidermalization: Race, Identity and Biometrics," *Critical Sociology*, 36:1, 2010, pp.131-50

Burra, Sundar, "Towards a pro-poor framework for slum upgrading in Mumbai, India," *Environment and Urbanisation*, 17:1, April, 2005, pp.67-88

Burton, Antoinette, "Introduction: The Unfinished Business of Colonial Modernities," in Antoinette Burton ed., *Gender, Sexuality and Colonial Modernities*, Routledge: London, 1999

Caplan, Jane, and John Torpey, "Introduction," in Jane Caplan and John Torpey eds., *Documenting Individual Identity: The Development of State Practices in the Modern World*, Princeton University Press: Princeton, NJ, 2001

Chandra, Satish, *Medieval India: From the Sultanat to the Mughals, Part II: Mughal Empire (1526-1748)*, Har-Anand Publications: Delhi, 2006 (Second Reprint)

Chatterjee, Partha, "Democracy and Economic Transformation in India," *Economic & Political Weekly*, 43:16, 19 April 2008, pp.53-62

Chatterjee, Partha, *A Princely Impostor? The Strange and Universal History of the Kumar of Bhawal*, Permanent Black: Ranikhet, 2002

Chatterjee, Partha, *Nationalist Thought and the Colonial World: A Derivative Discourse?* Zed Books: London, 1986

Chatterjee, Partha, *Politics of the Governed: Reflections on Popular Politics in Most of the World*, Permanent Black: Ranikhet, 2004

Cohn, Bernard, *Colonialism and Its Forms of Knowledge: The British in India*, Princeton University Press: Princeton NJ, 1996

Cole, Simon A., "Brandon Mayfield, Suspect," in John Knechtel ed., *Suspect* (*Alphabet City* Number 10), MIT Press: Cambridge, MA, 2005

Cole, Simon A., *Suspect Identities: A History of Fingerprinting and Criminal Identification*, Harvard University Press: London, 2001.

Cooper, Frederick, "Identity" (with Roger Brubaker) in Frederick Cooper, *Colonialism in Question: Theory, Knowledge, History*, University of California Press: Berkeley, Los Angeles, London, 2005

Crystal, David, *The Cambridge Encyclopaedia of Language*, Cambridge University Press: Cambridge, 2007 (second edition)

Curry, J. C., *The Indian Police*, Faber and Faber: London, 1932

Das, P. K., "Manifesto of a Housing Activist," in Sujata Patel and Alice Thorner eds., *Bombay: Metaphor for Modern India*, Oxford University Press: Delhi, 1996

Das, Veena and Deborah Poole, "Introduction: State and Its Margins: Comparative Ethnographies," in Veena Das and Deborah Poole eds., *Anthropology in the Margins of the State*, School of American Research Press: Santa Fe, NM, 2004

de Soto, Hernando, *The Mystery of Capital: Why Capitalism Triumphs in the West and Fails Everywhere*, Basic Books: New York, 2000

Deleuze, Gilles, "Postscript on the Societies of Control," *October* 59, 1991, pp.3-7

Dirks, Nicholas B., *Castes of Mind: Colonialism and the Making of Modern India*, Permanent Black: Delhi, 2002

Dossal, Mariam, *Theatre of Conflict, City of Hope: Mumbai 1660 to Present Times*, Oxford University Press: New Delhi, 2010

Douglas, Mary, *Purity and Danger: An Analysis of Concepts of Pollution and Taboo*, Routledge & Kegan Paul: London, 1996

Draculic, Slavenka, *The Balkan Express: Fragments from the Other Side of the War*, translated by Maja Šoljan, W.W. Norton: New York, 1993

Drèze, Jean and Reetika Khera, "The BPL Census and a Possible Alternative," *Economic & Political Weekly*, 45:9, 27 February 2010, pp.54-63

Edwards, Elizabeth, *Raw Histories. Photographs, Anthropology and Museums*, Berg: Oxford/New York, 2001

Ellermann, Antje, "Undocumented Migrants and Resistance in the Liberal State," *Politics & Society*, 38:3, September 2010, pp.408-29

Foucault, Michel, "Governmentality," in Burchell, Graham, Colin Gordon and Peter Miller eds., *The Foucault Effect: Studies in Governmentality, with two lectures by and an interview with Michel Foucault*, Harvester, Wheatsheaf: Hemel Hempstead, Hertfordshire, 1991

Foucault, Michel, "The Birth of Biopolitics," in Michel Foucault, *Ethics, Subjectivity and Truth*, edited by Paul Rabinow, The New Press, New York, 1997

Foucault, Michel, *Discipline and Punish: The Birth of the Prison*, Penguin: India, 1991 (1977)

Foucault, Michel, *The Birth of Biopolitics: Lectures at the Collège de France, 1978-79*, edited by Michel Senellart: translated by Graham Burchell. Palgrave Macmillan: New York, 2008

Frankel, Francine R., and M.S.A. Rao eds., *Dominance and State Power in India: Decline of a Social Order*, Oxford University Press: New Delhi, 1990

Ghosh, Asha, "Public-Private or a Private-Public: Promised Partnership of the Bangalore Agenda Task Force," *Economic & Political Weekly*, 40:47, 19-25 November 2005, pp.4914-22

Giddens, Anthony, *The Nation-State and Violence*, University of California Press: Berkeley, 1987

Goffman, Erving, *Stigma: Notes on the Management of Spoiled Identity*, Simon & Schuster: New York, 1963

Goldman, Michael, "Speculative Urbanism and the Making of the Next World City," *International Journal of Urban and Regional Research*, 35:3, May 2011, pp.555-81

Guha, Amalendu, *Planter Raj to Swaraj: Freedom Struggle and Electoral Politics in Assam, 1826-1947*, Tulika Books: New Delhi, 2006 (revised edition)

Habermas, Jürgen, *The Theory of Communicative Action* vol. 2: *Lifeworld and System: A Critique of Functionalist Reason*, translated by Thomas McCarthy, Beacon Press: Boston, 1987

Hardt, Michael, "The Withering of Civil Society," *Social Text*, 45, 1995, pp.27-44

Hardt, Michael, and Antonio Negri, *Empire*, Harvard University Press: 2001 (New Edition)

Harris, Jan Ll., and Paul A. Taylor, *Digital Matters: Theory and Culture of the Matrix*, Routledge: London and New York, 2005

Hazarika, Sanjoy, *Rites of Passage: Border Crossings, Imagined Homelands, India's East and Bangladesh*, Penguin Books: India, 2000

Heidegger, Martin, "The Question Concerning Technology," in Martin Heidegger, *Philosophical and Political Writings*, edited by Manfred Stassen, Continuum (German Library series): London, 2003

Henry, E.R., *Classification and Uses of Finger Prints*, George Routledge and Sons: London, 1900

Herschel, William J., *The Origin of Finger-Printing*, Oxford University Press: London, 1916

Hirschman, A.O., *Exit, Voice, and Loyalty: Responses to Decline in Firms, Organizations, and States*, Harvard University Press: Cambridge, Mass., 1970

Jenkins, Rob, *Democratic Politics and Economic Reforms in India*, Cambridge University Press: Cambridge, 2000

Jha, Manish K., P.K. Shajahan and Mouleshri Vyas, *Biopolitics and Urban Governmentality in the City of Mumbai*, in press

Kahe Gaile Bides, why did you go overseas? On Bhojpuri migration since the 1870s and contemporary culture in Uttar pradesh and Bihar, Suriname and the Netherlands, compiled & edited by Mousumi Majumdar, Mango Books/Spot Creative Services, 2010

Kaviraj, Sudipta, "A Critique of Passive Revolution," *Economic & Political Weekly*, 23:45/47, November 1988, pp.2429-44

Klerk, Cornelis Johannes Maria de, *Boek-I: Cultus en Ritueel van het Orthodoxe Hindoeïsme in Suriname*, Amsterdam 1951, and *Boek-II: Immigratie der Hindostanen in Suriname*, Amsterdam; Amrit: Den Haag, 1998 reprint

Kumar, Anu, "Mumbai's Expendable Poor," *Economic and Political Weekly*, 40: 6, 5-11 February 2005, p.506-10

Legêne, Susan, *From India to Suriname: A journey into the future narrated by two photograph albums (1913-1930)* (Bidesia Occasional Papers Series no. 2), Manav Vikas

Sangrahalaya-GB Pant Institute: Allahabad, 2007

Mann, Michael, *The Sources of Social Power,* vol. 2: *The Rise of Classes and Nation-States, 1760-1914*, Cambridge University Press: New York, 1993

Maringanti, Anant, "Sovereign States and Mobile Subjects: Politics of UIDAI," *Economic & Political Weekly*, 44:46, 14 November 2012, pp35-40

Meyer, Thomas, and Lew Hinchman, *Media Democracy: How the Media Colonize Politics*, Polity Press: Cambridge, 2002

Monteiro, V., "Another India is Possible: Basic Needs, the Unorganized Sector and Science in India" in M. Malhotra ed., *India: The Next Decade*, Academic Publishers: New Delhi, 2006

Mouat, F.J., "Notes on M. Bertillon's Discourse on the anthropometric Measurement of Criminals," *Journal of the Royal Anthropological Institute of Great Britain and Ireland*, 20, 1891

Nandy, Ashis, *The Intimate Enemy: Loss and Recovery of Self under Colonialism*, Oxford University Press: Delhi, 1983

Narayanan, Sudha, "A Case for Reframing the Cash Transfer Debate in India," *Economic & Political Weekly*, 46:21, 21 May 2011, 41-48

Neuwirth, Robert, *Shadow Cities: A Billion Squatters, A New Urban World*, Routledge: New York, 2005

Nigam, Sanjay, "Disciplining and Policing the 'Criminals by Birth', Part 2: The Development of a Disciplinary System, 1871-1900," *Indian Economic and Social History Review*, 27:3, September 1990, pp.257-87

Nilekani, Nandan, *Imagining India: The Idea of a Renewed Nation*, Penguin: Bangalore, 2009

Nisbet, Nancy, "Resisting Surveillance: Identity and Implantable Microchip," *Leonardo*, 37: 3, pp 210-14

Noiriel, Gérard, *The French Melting Pot: Immigration, Citizenship, and National Identity*, translated by Geoffrey de Laforcade, University of Minnesota Press: Minneapolis, 1996 [1988]

Pani, Narendar, "Icons and Reform Politics in India: The Case of S.M. Krishna," *Asian Survey*, 46:2, March/April 2006, pp.238-56

Panwalkar, Pratima, "Upgradation of Slums: A World Bank Programme," in Sujata Patel and Alice Thorner eds., *Bombay: Metaphor for Modern India*, Oxford University Press: Delhi, 1996

Patel, Sujata, "Bombay and Mumbai," in Sujata Patel and Kushal Deb eds., *Urban Studies*, Oxford University Press: New Delhi, 2009

Philipose, Pamela, "Writing Displacement Creativity and Objectivity," in Nilanjan Dutta ed., *Forced Migration in North East India: A Media Reader*, Frontpage: Kolkata, 2012

Phukon, Girin, *Assam, Attitude to Federalism*, Sterling Publishing Private Limited: New Delhi, 1984

Pinney, Christopher, *Camera Indica: The Social Life of Indian Photographs*, Reaktion: London, 1997

Rabinow, Paul, ed., *The Foucault Reader*, Pantheon Books: New York, 1984

Rajagopal, Arvind, "Notes on Postcolonial Visual Culture," *BioScope: South Asian Screen Studies*, 2:1, January 2011, pp.11-22

Ramanathan, Usha, "A Unique Identity Bill," *Economic and Political Weekly*, 45:30, 24 July 2010, pp.10-14.

Robins, Steven, "At the Limits of Spatial Governmentality: A Message from the Tip of Africa," *Third World Quarterly*, 23:4, 2002, pp.665-89

Rose, Nikolas, "Governing 'Advanced' Liberal Democracies," in Aradhana Sharma and Akhil Gupta eds., *The Anthropology of the State: A Reader*, Wiley-Blackwell: Malden, 2005

Roy Chaudhuri, Arka and E. Somanathan, "Impact of Biometric-Identification-Based Transfers," *Economic & Political Weekly*, 46:21, 21 May 2011, pp.77-80

Ruppert, Evelyn, "Population Objects: Interpassive Subjects," *Sociology*, 45:2, April 2011, pp.218-33

Ryan, James R., *Picturing Empire: Photography and the Visualization of the British Empire*, Reakton: London, 1997

Samaddar, Ranabir, "What is Postcolonial Predicament?" *Economic and Political Weekly*, 47:9, 3 March 2012, pp.41-50

Samaddar, Ranabir, ed., *Refugees and the State: Practices of Asylum and Care in India, 1947-2000*, Sage: Delhi, 2003

Samaddar, Ranabir, *The Materiality of Politics, Vol I: Technologies of Rule*, Anthem: Delhi, 2007

Sarkar, Swagato, "The Unique Identity (UID) Project and the New 'Bureaucratic Moment' in India," Working Paper 194, Queen Elizabeth House, University of Oxford, 2011

Scott, James C., John Tehranian and Jeremy Mathias, "The Production of Legal Identities Proper to States: The Case of the Permanent Family Surname," *Comparative Studies in Society and History*, 44:1, January 2002, pp.4-44

Scott, James C., *Seeing Like a State: How Certain Schemes to Improve the Human Condition Have Failed*, Yale University Press: New Haven, CT, 1998.

Seal, Anil, *The Emergence of Indian Nationalism: Competition and Collaboration in the Later Nineteenth Century*, Cambridge University Press: Cambridge, 1971

Sekula, Allan, "The Body and the Archive," *October* 39, 1986, pp.3-64

Sen, Sunanda and Byasdeb Dasgupta, *Unfreedom and Waged Work: Labour in India's Manufacturing Industry*, Sage: New Delhi, 2009

Sengoopta, Chandak, *Imprint of the Raj: How Fingerprinting was Born in Colonial India*, Macmillan: London, 2000

Shreenivas and Saradindu Narayan Sinha, "Personal Identification by the Dermatoglyphic and the E-V Methods," *Patna Journal of Medicine*, 31:3, 1957

Shukla, Ravi, "Reimagining citizenship: Debating India's Unique Identification Scheme," *Economic & Political Weekly*, 45:2, 9 January 2010, pp.31–36

Simmel, Georg, "The Stranger," in Kurt H. Wolf ed. and trans., *The Sociology of Georg Simmel*, Free Press: New York, 1950.

Singha, Radhika, "Settle, Mobilize, Verify: Identification Practices in Colonial India," *Studies in History*, 16:2, August 2000, 151-98

Sinha, Dipankar, "On Forgetting History: Information and Communication Technology and the Colonization of Politics in Post-Colonial India," in Amiya K. Bagchi, Dipankar Sinha and Barnita Bagchi eds., *Webs of History: Information, Communication and Technology from the Early to Post-Colonial India*, Manohar: Delhi, 2005

Sinha-Kerkhoff, Kathinka, Ellen Bal and Alok Deo Singh (Traslators), *Autobiography of An Indian Indentured Labourer: Munshi Rahman Khan (1874-1972): Jeevan Prakash*, Shipra Publications: Delhi, 2005

Skocpol, Theda, *States and Social Revolutions: A Comparative Analysis of France, Russia and China*, Cambridge University Press: New York, 1978

Srinivasan, Janaki, "The Political Life of Information and the Practice of Governance in India," Unpublished PhD Thesis, Department of Information Management and Systems, University of California, Berkeley, 2011

Srinivasan, N., "Policy Issues and Role of Banking System in Financial Inclusion," *Economic and Political Weekly*, 42:30, 28 July 2007, pp.3091-95

Tilly, Charles, *Coercion, Capital and European States, AD 990-1992*, Blackwell: Cambridge Mass., 1990

Tilly, Charles, *Durable Inequality*, University of California Press: Berkeley CA, 1998

Tolen, Rachel J., "Colonizing and Transforming the Criminal Tribesmen: The Salvation Army in British India," *American Ethnologist*, 18:1, February 1991, pp.106-25

Torpey, John, "Coming and Going: On the State Monopolisation of the Legitimate 'Means of Movement'," *Sociological Theory*, 16:3, November 1998, pp.239-59

Vanaik, Achin, *The Painful Transition: Bourgeois Democracy in India*, Verso: London, 1990

Wajcman, Judy, "Addressing Technological Change: The Challenge to Social Theory," *Current Sociology*, 50:3, May 2002, pp.347-63

Weiner, Myron, *Sons of the Soil: Migration and Ethnic Conflict in India*, Princeton University Press: Princeton NJ, 1978

Wynne, Martin ed., *On Honourable Terms: The Memoirs of Some Indian Police Officers, 1915-1948*, British Association for Cemeteries in South Asia: London, 1985

Zuboff, Shoshana, *In the Age of the Smart Machine: The Future of Work and Power*, Basic Books: New York, 1988

Zureik, Elia (with contribution from Karen Hindle), "Governance, Security and Technology: The Case of Biometrics," *Studies in Political Economy*, 73, Spring/ Summer, 2004, pp.113-37

WEBLINKS

"12 lakh Bangladeshis missing after entering India: BSF," *The Indian Express*, 11 September 2008; http://www.indianexpress.com/news/12-lakh-bangladeshis-missing-after-entering-india-bsf/355978 [last accessed 15 November 2012]

"60 undocumented migrants pushed back while trying to enter Manipur," *The Hindu,* 2 September 2012; http://www.thehindu.com/news/national/article3850239.ece?homepage=true&css=print [last accessed 15 November 2012

"Annual Report, 2011-2012," Ministry of Home Affairs, Government of India; http://www.mha.nic.in/pdfs/AR%28E%291112.pdf [last accessed 7 September 2012]

"Chidambaram calls Direct Cash Transfer a magical step," *The Hindu*, 1 December 2012; http://www.thehindu.com/news/national/chidambaram-calls-direct-cash-transfer-a-magical-step/article4154155.ece [last accessed 4 December 2012]

"Conditions in Sri Lankan Tamil refugee camps," Tamil Nadu & Pondicherry People's Union for Civil Liberties (PUCL) Report, *PUCL Bulletin*, 18 June 2006; http://www.pucl.org/Topics/International/2006/refugees-srilanka-report.html [last accessed 27 June 2012]

"Court extends stay on J&K Resettlement Act," *The Hindu*, 21 February 2008; http://www.hindu.com/2008/02/21/stories/2008022151381300.htm [last accessed 15 November 2012]

"Direct cash transfer of subsidies through Aadhaar from 1 January," *The Hindu*, 24 November 2012;
http://www.thehindu.com/news/national/direct-cash-transfer-of-subsidies-through-aadhaar-from-january-1/article4129971.ece
[last accessed 28 November 2012]

"Entitlement Reform for Empowering the Poor: The Integrated Smart Card Report (ISC)," Planning Commission of India, http://planningcommission.nic.in/aboutus/committee/wrkgrp11/wg11_ smtcard.pdf [last accessed 8 September 2012]

"Financial Inclusion," National Bank for Agriculture and Rural Development (NABARD);
http://nabard.org/financial_inclusion.asp [last accessed 15 November 2012]

"Four student activists killed in police firing in Assam," *The Times of India*, 21 July 2010; http://articles.timesofindia.indiatimes.com/2010-07-21/india/28292131_1_student-activists-nrc-assam-assembly [last accessed 15 November 2012]

"From surprise to reckoning," Kargil Review Committee, Executive Summary, 25 February, http://nuclearweaponarchive.org/India/KARGILRCA.html [last accessed 6 September 2012]

"Hindu and Sikh refugees from Pakistan: Majority Kashmiris have a case of extreme discrimination to answer!" *Human Rights Report Quarterly*, Asian Centre for Human Rights, issue 2, Oct-Dec 2010; http://www.achrweb.org/ihrrq/issue2/

hindu_and_sikh_refugees.html [last accessed 15 November 2012]

"Home Minister P. Chidambaram wants cabinet panel meet on UID," *The Economic Times*, 19 November 2011; http://articles.economictimes.indiatimes.com/2011-11-19/news/30419509_1_uid-data-uidai-npr-project [last accessed 15 November 2012]

"HRCP's outrage at minorities' flight," Human Rights Commission of Pakistan (HRCP), 10 August 2012; http://www.hrcp-web.org/showprel.asp?id=292 [last accessed 15 November 2012]

"Inclusive Growth – Role of Financial Sector," Address delivered by K. C. Chakrabarty, Deputy Governor, Reserve Bank of India, at the National Finance Conclave 2010 organised by KIIT University on 27 November 2010 at Bhubaneswar; http://rbi.org.in/scripts/BS_SpeechesView.aspx?Id=538 [last accessed 15 November 2012]

"Information pertaining to Tibetan nationals," Bureau of Immigration, Ministry of Home Affairs, Government of India; http://www.immigrationindia.nic.in/Instr_Tibetans2.htm [last accessed 7 September 2012]

"Information Society in Brazil: Green Book," coordinated by Tadao Takahashi, Ministry of Science and Technology, Programa Sociedade da Informação (SocInfo): Brasilia, September 2000; http://www.ehealthstrategies.com/files/cap00.pdf [last accessed 15 November 2012]

"Interim Report of the Task Force on Direct Transfer of Subsidies on Kerosene, LPG and Fertiliser," Ministry of Finance, Government t of India, June 2011, pp. 1-2; http://finmin.nic.in/reports/Interim_report_Task_Force_DTS.pdf [last accessed 15 November 2012]

"National Citizen Database," Department of Electronics & Information Technology, Ministry of Communications & Information Technology, Government of India; http://deity.gov.in/content/national-citizen-database [last accessed 15 November 2012]

"National e-Governance Plan," Department of Electronics & Information Technology, Ministry of Communications & Information Technology, Government of India; http://deity.gov.in/content/national-e-governance-plan [last accessed 15 November 2012]

"Over 7,500 Pakistanis overstayed in India: RTI," *Jagran Post*, 14 November 2011; http://post.jagran.com/Over-7500-Pakistanis-overstayed-in-India-RTI-1321253851 [last accessed 15 November 2012]

"P Chidambaram blames migrants for crimes in Delhi, triggers reaction," *DNA*, 13 December 2010; http://www.dnaindia.com/india/report_p-chidambaram-blames-migrants-for-crimes-in-delhi-triggers-reaction_1480629 [last accessed 15 November 2012]

"Permanent settlement of Pak refugees: Hurriyat (G) sees red," *KashmirWatch*, 24 August 2012 http://kashmirwatch.com/index.php/2012/08/24/permanent-settlement-8217-of-pak-refugees-hurriyat-g-sees-red.html [last accessed 15 November 2012]

"Raj threatens to dub Bihari migrants 'infiltrators'," *The Hindu*, 31 August 2012; http://www.thehindu.com/news/national/article3845043.ece [last accessed 15 November 2012]

"Ration Cards: 1.1 Crore Biometric Samples Found to be Duplicate," *Business Line*, 13 May 2010; www.thehindubusinessline.com/2010/05/13/stories/2010051351831900.htm [last accessed 15 November 2012]

"Report of Refugee Populations in India, November 2007," Human Rights Law Network, New Delhi; http://www.hrln.org/admin/issue/subpdf/Refugee_populations_in_India.pdf [last accessed 15 November 2012]

"Report of the Condition of Work and Promotion of Livelihood in the Unorganized Sector," National Commission for Enterprise in the Unorganised Sector (NCEUS), Government of India, New Delhi, August 2007; http://www.prsindia.org/uploads/media/Unorganised%20Sector/bill150_20071123150_Condition_of_workers_sep_2007.pdf__ [last accessed 15 November 2012]

"Sheila Dikshit blames migrants, porous border for Delhi rapes," *India Today*, 12 April 2012; http://indiatoday.intoday.in/story/sheila-dikshit-rising-rape-in-delhi-migratory-population/1/184091.html [last accessed 15 November 2012]

"Survival, Dignity, and democracy: Burmese refugees in India," South Asia Human Rights Documentation Centre, 1997; http://www.hrdc.net/sahrdc/resources/survival_dignity.htm [last accessed 8 August 2012]

"Tibet's stateless nationals II: Tibetan refugees in India, A Report," Tibet Justice Centre, September, 2011; http://www.tibetjustice.org/reports/stateless-nationals-ii/stateless-nationals-ii.pdf [last accessed 8 August 2012]

"Uddhav wants permit system for Biharis in Mumbai," *Hindustan Times*, 4 September 2012; http://www.hindustantimes.com/India-news/Mumbai/Uddhav-wants-permit-system-for-Biharis-in-Mumbai/Article1-924181.aspx [last accessed 15 November 2012]

"UID poses national security threat: BJP," *Times of India*, 22 January 2012; http://articles.timesofindia.indiatimes.com/2012-01-22/india/30652633_1_uid-bill-national-population-register-bjp-demands [last accessed 15 November 2012]

"UID work to start in Assam," *The Sentinel*, 13 January 2011; http://followuidai.wordpress.com/2012/01/24/uid-and-bangladeshi-migrants-worries-from-an-assam-newspaper/ [last accessed 15 November 2012]

"UID AI Inks Contract with HCL Infosystems," *The Indian Express*, 10 August 2012; http://www.hclinfosystems.in/news252.htm [last accessed 15 November 2012]

"UIDAI's mandate expanded," *The Hindu*, 27 January 2012; http://www.thehindu.com/news/national/article2837329.ece [last accessed 15 November 2012]

"We are like forgotten people: unsafe in Burma, unprotected in India," Human Rights Watch, 2009; http://www.hrw.org/reports/2009/01/27/we-are-forgotten-people [last accessed 10 August 2012]

Abraham, Sunil, "Do we need the Aadhaar Scheme?" *Business Standard*, 1 February 2012, emphasis added; http://www.business-standard.com/india/news/do-we-needaadhar-scheme/463324/ [last accessed 15 November 2012]

Baabar, Mariana, "Sindh's stolen brides," *Outlook*, 23 January 2006; http://www.outlookindia.com/article.aspx?229886 [last accessed 15 November 2012]

Balchand, K., "Wage Hike for MGNREGA Workers," *The Hindu*, 7 January 2011; http://www.hindu.com/2011/01/07/stories/2011010759880100.htm [last accessed 15 November 2012]

Bali Process, Ad Hoc Group Workshop on Biometrics for Identity Integrity in Immigration, New Delhi, India, April 23-26, 2012; http://www.baliprocess.net/files/Final-Co-chairs%20Statement%20 Biometrics%20Workshop%202012.pdf [last accessed 8 September 2012]

Bali Process, Final co-chairs statement, Ad Hoc Group Workshop on Biometrics for Identity Integrity in Immigration, New Delhi, India, 23-26 April 2012; http://www.baliprocess.net/files/Final-Co-chairs%20Statement% 20Biometrics%20Workshop%202012.pdf [last accessed 8 September 2012]

Bali Process, UNHCR's Statement, Ad Hoc Group Workshop on Biometrics for Identity Integrity in Immigration, New Delhi, India, 23-26 April 2012; http://www.baliprocess.net/files/UNHCR%20-%20Biometrics.pdf [last accessed 8 September 2012]

Benjamin, Solomon, R. Bhuvaneswari, P. Rajan and Manjunatha, "Bhoomi: E-Governance or an anti-politics necessary to globalize Bangalore," A CASUM-m Working Paper, 2007; http://casumm.files.wordpress.com/2008/09/bhoomi-e-governance.pdf [last accessed 15 November 2012]

Bhattacharya, Gaurishankar, "Assam's problem of foreign infiltration," Headlines, *North East News Agency*, 2:7-8, 22 June to 6 July 1999; http://www.nenanews.com/OT%20June22-%20July6%20,99/oh3.htm [last accessed 15 November 2012]

Bhattacharya, Suryatapa, "India's Myanmar refugees get visas after month of protests in Delhi," *The National,* 17 May 2012; http://www.thenational.ae/news/world/south-asia/indias-myanmar-refugees-get-visas-after-month-of-protests-in-delhi [last accessed 12 August 2012]

Bowe, Rebecca, "Israel's Biometric Database Deemed 'Harmful' by High Court Justices," *Electronic Frontier Foundation*, 27 July 2012 www.eff.org/deeplinks/2012/07/israels-biometric-database-deemed-harmful-high-court-justices [Accessed on 15 November 2012]

Cabinet Committee on Economic Affairs, Implementation of mission mode project on "Immigration, visa and foreigners' registration & tracking (IVFRT)," Press Information Bureau, 13 May 2010; http://pib.nic.in/newsite/erelease.aspx?relid=61800 [last accessed 12 August 2012]

Deol, Rajesh, "Pakistani Hindus in India unwilling to return," *Deccan Herald*, 5 September 2012; http://www.deccanherald.com/content/86879/pakistani-hindus-india-unwilling-return.html [last accessed 15 November 2012]

Dey, Ishita, and Sucharita Sengupta, "An Interview with Ved Bhasin on Forced Migration in Jammu & Kashmir," *Refugee Watch 36*, December 2010; http://www.mcrg.ac.in/rw%20files/RW36/9.Interview.pdf [last accessed 15 November 2012]

Ebrahim, Zofeen, "Why are Hindus from Pakistan Crossing Over to India?" *Inter Press Service*, 24 August 2012; http://www.ipsnews.net/2012/08/why-are-hindus-from-pakistan-crossing-over-to-india [last accessed 15 November 2012]

Economic Survey 2011-12, Chapter 13: Human Development, Government of India; http://indiabudget.nic.in/es2011-12/echap-13.pdf [last accessed 15 November 2012]

Forty-Second Report, "The National Identification Authority of India Bill, 2010," Standing Committee on Finance (2011-2012), Ministry of Planning, Fifteenth Lok Sabha, Lok Sabha Secretariat, New Delhi, December, 2011; http://www.prsindia.org/uploads/media/UID/uid%20report.pdf [last accessed 15 November 2012]

Gupta, Smita, "Cash Transfer Scheme is a game-changer: Chidambaram," *The Hindu*, 27 November 2012; http://www.thehindu.com/news/national/cash-transfer-to-cover-29-schemes-in-first-phase/article4140318.ece [last accessed 4 December 2012]

Hussain, Kashif, "A Tale of Migrating Hindus," *The Daily Times*, 20 August 2012, http://www.dailytimes.com.pk/default.asp?page=2012%5C08%5C20%5Cstory_20-8-2012_pg7_10 [last accessed 15 November 2012]

Jaiswal, Umanand, "Move to empower NRC directorate," *The Telegraph*, 12 September 2012; http://www.telegraphindia.com/1120912/jsp/northeast/story_15966703.jsp#.ULSXZWcbFA8 [last accessed 15 November 2012]

Joshua, Anita, "'Forcibly converted' Hindu women choose to stay with husbands," *The Hindu*, 18 April 2012; http://www.thehindu.com/news/international/article3328893.ece [last accessed 15 November 2012]

Krishnaswamy, Sudhir, "Unique Identity Numbers: The Enabler of Policy Reform?" *India in Transition*, Centre for the Advanced Study of India (CASI), University of Pennsylvania, 2010; http://casi.ssc.upenn.edu/iit/krishnaswamy [last accessed 15 November 2012]

Kroker, Arthur, "The New Biometric State," in *Born Again Ideology: Religion, Technology, and Terrorism*, 2006; http://www.ctheory.net/articles.aspx?id=549 [Accessed on 15 November 2012].

Kumar, Ajay, "Impact of Internal Displacement in Jammu & Kashmir: Study of Pakistan occupied Kashmir Refugees," *Indian Streams Research Journal*, 2: 3 April 2012, pp. 1-4; http://www.isrj.net/PublishArticles/695.pdf [last accessed 15 November 2012]

Mani, Jyoti Thapa, "In-Depth Citizenship issues plague Nepali-speaking Indians too," *Business World*, 14 March 2008; http://www.businessworld.in/index.php/Miscellaneous/Identity-Crisis.html [last accessed 10 August 2012]

Masood, Bashaarat, "Will oppose settlement of Pak refugees, says Geelani," *The Indian Express*, 24 August 2012; http://www.indianexpress.com/news/will-oppose-settlement-of-pak-refugees-says-geelani/992342/ [last accessed 15 November 2012]

Mehmood, Taha, "Notes from a contested history of National Identity Card in India: 1999-2007," *South Asia Citizens Wire*, 9 December 2008; http://www.sacw.net/article391.html [last accessed 5 August 2010]

Mehmood, Taha, "UID/Aadhar: A Threat to Indian Democracy," *Countercurrents.org*, April 2012; http://www.countercurrents.org/mehmood010412.htm [last accessed 15 November 2012]

Mishra, Sudhanshu, "Pakistanis in India with expired visas under security scanner," *Mail Today*, 26 August 2012; http://indiatoday.intoday.in/story/security-on-alert-for-pakistanis-in-india-with-expired-visas/1/214759.html [last accessed 15 November 2012]

Pandey, Shailendra (text and photographs), "An uncertain refuge — three lakh refugees left their homes behind only to find they have restricted rights in J&K," *Tehelka*, 5 May 2012; http://www.tehelka.com/story_main52.asp?filename=hub050512UNCERTAIN.asp [last accessed 15 November 2012]

Pandit, Ambika, "UID gives Identity, Bank Account to 27 Homeless," *The Times of India*, 29 November 2010; http://articles.timesofindia.indiatimes.com/2010-11-29/delhi/28263762_1_night-shelter-uid-card-homeless-persons [last accessed 15 November 2012]

Puri, Balraj, "Refugee problem in Jammu & Kashmir," *Kashmir Newz*, http://www.kashmirnewz.com/a0002.html [last accessed 15 November 2012]

Rahman, A. Faizur, "Which World do Economists Live in?" *The Asian Age*, 23 September 2012; http://www.asianage.com/columnists/which-world-do-economists-live-754 [last accessed 15 November 2012]

Raina, Pamposh, "Thousands of Myanmar Rohingyas struggle for refugee status in India," *The New York Times*, India Edition, 18 May 2012; http://india.blogs.nytimes.com/2012/05/18/thousands-of-myanmar-rohingyas-struggle-for-refugee-status-in-india/ [last accessed 7 September 2012]

Rajshekhar, M., "Reasons why the Standing Committee on Finance rejected the UIDAI Bill," *The Economic Times*, 16 December 2011; http://articles.economictimes.indiatimes.com/2011-12-16/news/30525319_1_aadhaar-uid-scheme-data-protection [last accessed 15 November 2012]

Ramachandran, R., "How reliable is UID?" *Frontline*, 28:24, November 19 December - 02 December 2011; http://www.frontlineonnet.com/fl2824/stories/20111202282402500.htm [last accessed 15 November 2012]

Ramanathan, Usha, "Foreword," to Jijeesh P.B., "AADHAAR; How a Nation is Deceived," *Greenpeople*, 2011; http://aadhararticles.blogspot.in/2011/11/1770-aadhaar-how-n-t-i-o-n-i-s-deceived.html [Accessed on 15 November 2012]

Ramkumar, R., "What the UID Conceals," *The Hindu*, 21 October 1949; http://

www.thehindu.com/opinion/lead/article839590.ece [last accessed 15 November 2012]

Rehman, Ibn Abdur, "Perils of intolerance," *Dawn*, 16 August 2012; http://dawn.com/2012/08/16/perils-of-intolerance/ [last accessed 15 November 2012]

Risbud, Neelima, "Urban Slum Reports: The Case of Mumbai, India," *Understanding Slums: Case Studies for the Global Report on Human Settlements*, UN-Habitat, 2003; http://www.ucl.ac.uk/dpu-projects/Global_Report/pdfs/Mumbai.pdf [last accessed 15 November 2012]

Roy Choudhury, Shreya, "Pak Hindus narrate 'citizenship' woes," *The Times of India*, 28 December 2010; http://articles.timesofindia.indiatimes.com/2010-12-28/pakistan/28255011_1_tourist-visa-long-term-visas-refugee-status [last accessed 15 November 2012]

Sikand, Yoginder, "Pakistani Hindu migrants to India: Demanding to be heard," *Pakistan Hindu Post*, 30 December 2009; http://pakistanhindupost.blogspot.in/2009/12/pakistani-hindu-migrants-to-india.html [last accessed 15 November 2012]

Sinha, Dipankar, "(De)Politicizing Information Technology: Towards an Inclusionary Framework," Working Paper 19, Department of Media and Communications, London School of Economics, 2010, www2.lse.ac.uk/media@lse/research/mediaWorkingPapers/pdf/EWP19.pdf [Accessed on 15 November 2012]

Sinha, Lieutenant General (Retd.) Srinivas Kumar, "'Stateless' remedy to illegal problem," *The Asian Age*, 15 August 2012; http://www.asianage.com/print/180829 [last accessed 15 November 2012]

Sinha, Lieutenant General (Retd.) Srinivas Kumar, "Report on Illegal Migration into Assam" submitted to the President of India by the Governor of Assam, 8 November 1998; http://www.asomganaparishad.in/article/SK%20Sinha%27s%20REPORT.pdf [last accessed 15 November 2012]

Sirmed, Marvi, "Rinkle Kumari: A Test Case for Jinnah's Pakistan," *The Friday Times*, 25-31 May 2012; http://www.thefridaytimes.com/beta3/tft/article.php?issue=20120525&page=6 [last accessed 15 November 2012]

Suba Chandran, D., "The forgotten people of Jammu & Kashmir — 'Refugees' from PoK," Institute of Peace and Conflict Studies, 8 January 2007; http://www.ipcs.org/article/india/the-forgotten-people-of-jammu-and-kashmir-refugees-from-pok-2182.html [last accessed 15 November 2012]

Suneja, Kirtika, "UIDAI Shortlists TCS, HCL Infosystems for R2,000-cr Service Provider Contract," *The Financial Express*, 7 February 2012; http://www.financialexpress.com/news/uidai-shortlists-tcs-hcl-infosystems-for-r2000cr-service-provider-contract/908638/1 [last accessed 15 November 2012]

Thomas, Mathew *et al*, *UID is Not Yours: Your ID under Government/ Political/ Bureaucratic/ Private Company Control!* November, 2012;

http://kractivist.files.wordpress.com/2012/12/uid-is-not-yours.pdf [last accessed 3 December 9, 2012]

Tun, Salai, "Border fence unnecessary, Mizoram authorities say," *Mizzima News*, 9 September 2010; http://www.mizzima.com/news/regional/4339-border-fence-unnecessary-mizoram-authorities-say.html [last accessed 15 November 2012]

UIDAI, "Background," Unique Identification Authority of India, Planning Commission, Government of India; http://uidai.gov.in/index.php?option=com_content&view=article&id=141&Itemid=164_[last accessed 4 December 2012]

UIDAI, "Creating a unique identity number for every resident in India," Working Paper-version 1.1, Unique Identification Authority of India, Government of India, WikiLeaks Document Release: 13 November 2009; http://wlstorage.net/file/creating-a-unique-id-for-every-resident-in-india-2009.pdf [last accessed 8 September 2012]

UIDAI, "From Exclusion to Inclusion with Micropayments," Unique Identification Authority of India, Planning Commission, Government of India, April 2010; http://uidai.gov.in/UID_PDF/Front_Page_Articles/Strategy/Exclusion_to_Inclusion_with_Micropayments.pdf [last accessed 15 November 2012]

UIDAI, "UIDAI Strategy Overview: Creating a Unique Identity Number for Every Resident in India," Unique Identification Authority of India, Planning Commission, Government of India, April, 2010; http://uidai.gov.in/ UID_PDF /Front_Page_Articles/Documents/Strategy_Overveiw-001.pdf [Accessed on 15 November 2012]

UIDAI, "Vision on Micropayments," Unique Identification Authority of India, Planning Commission, Government of India; http://www.uidai.gov.in/index.php?option=com_content&view= article&id=142&Itemid=135 [last accessed 15 November 2012]

UIDAI, "What is Aadhaar?" Unique Identification Authority of India, Planning Commission, Government of India; http://uidai.gov.in/index.php?option=com_content&view=article&id=57&Itemid=105 [last accessed 15 November 2012]

UNHCR distributes pioneering smart ID cards to refugees in India, 1 August 2011; http://www.unhcr.org/4e4bd1506.html [last accessed 12 August 2012]

UNHCR handbook for registration: Procedures and standards for registration, population data management and documentation, September, 2003; http://www.unhcr.org/3f8e9ce14.html [last accessed 10 August 2012]

UNHCR Policy on Refugee Protection and Solutions in Urban Areas, September, 2009; http://www.unhcr.org/refworld/docid/4ab8e7f72.html [last accessed 12 August 2012]

UNHCR, Guidelines on Applicable Criteria and Standards relating to the Detention

S4/078/E

of Asylum-Seekers, February, 1999; www.unhcr.org/refworld/pdfid/3c2b3f844.pdf [last accessed 29 October 1949]

UNHCR, Procedural standards for refugee status determination under UNHCR's mandate, September, 2005, Geneva; http://www.unhcr.org/publPUBL/4316f0c02.html [last accessed 27 June 2012]

UNHCR, Q&A: Refugee registration takes UNHCR official across southern Africa, 30 March 2007; http://www.unhcr.org/460d08e34.html [last accessed 12 August 2012]

UNHCR, Summary conclusions of meeting with representatives of asylum-seekers from northern Rakhine State, Myanmar; http://www.unhcr.org.in/pages/showmainstory/10 [last accessed 11 August 2012]

Vij-Aurora, Bhavna, "No Country for Pakistani Hindus," *India Today*, 27 April 2012; http://indiatoday.intoday.in/story/pakistani-hindu-refugees-feel-betrayed-by-india/1/186304.html [last accessed 15 November 2012]

Wilson, C.L., M.D. Garris and C.I. Watson, "Matching Performance for the US-VISIT IDENT System Using Flat Fingerprints," NISTIR 7110, May 2004; ftp://sequoyah.nist.gov/pub/nist_internal_reports/ir_7110.pdf [last accessed 15 November 2012]

CASE LAWS

Mr. Bogyi v Union fo India, CR 1847 of 1989 (Guwahati High Court),

Dr. Malavika Karlekar v Union of India, WP 583 of 1992 (Supreme Court of India)

Digvijay Mote v Union of India, WA 354 of 1994 (Karnataka High Court)

P. Nedumaran v Union of Indiam WP 12298 and 12313 of 1992 (Madras High court)